ADVANCED CALCULUS

FOR ENGINEERING AND SCIENCE STUDENTS

ADVANCED CALCULUS
FOR ENGINEERING AND SCIENCE STUDENTS

IAN S. MURPHY

Department of Mathematics
University of Glasgow

ARKLAY PUBLISHERS

© Ian S. Murphy 2008.

ISBN: 978-0-9507126-8-0

First Edition 1984.
Second Edition (with corrections) 1986.
Third Edition (with three new chapters and
                    other minor alterations) 1989.
Fourth Edition (with a few corrections) 1993.
Reprinted 1999.

Reprinted again 2008.

Published by
Arklay Publishers,
6 Viewfield Place,
Stirling,
United Kingdom.   FK8 1NQ

Printed and bound in Scotland by Bell and Bain Ltd., Glasgow.

PREFACE

This book is intended for students who are attending courses on Advanced Calculus in universities, polytechnics and technical colleges. It seems to me that students tackling Advanced Calculus for the first time are primarily interested in (a) clear insight into the concepts, and (b) the ability to solve problems. They seem less interested in (c) formal proofs, and (d) pathological cases. Accordingly, in this book I have tried to give an uncluttered but incisive account of the subject, concentrating on (a) and (b). I have also included a good number of examples together with hints and answers.

The book is based on experience over recent years with students of Engineering and Science at the University of Glasgow.

There are many people who have given me help of one kind or another with this project. Firstly, there are three colleagues, Dr. Ian Anderson, Dr. Neil K. Dickson and Dr. Richard J. Steiner, who together looked at the completed text in detail. Their valuable efforts have ensured the elimination of many errors and inaccuracies. They also suggested a number of improvements, many of which I have gladly adopted. Secondly, there are my parents and my brothers who have given me all sorts of support and good advice. Finally, there are several other friends, some here in Glasgow, some elsewhere, who have spurred me on with timely words of encouragement at various points along the way.

University of Glasgow   Ian S. Murphy
June 1984

The main change made for the third edition has been the addition of three new chapters numbered 13, 14 and 15: these deal with extra topics. In the existing part of the book (apart from the correction of a small number of remaining errors) there are really only two alterations to notice. Firstly, §119 and §120 together with Examples 8.9 and 8.10 have been altered to improve the treatment of exact equations. Secondly, some extra examples on the solution of partial differential equations have been included as Examples 16 to supplement those already in Examples 7.

I am indebted to Dr. Neil Dickson for examining the new material carefully: I have accepted his judgment on several points. I am also grateful to all those who have made comments about the book to me (in person or by letter) over the past five years.

July 1989   I.S.M.

CONTENTS

I. DOUBLE INTEGRATION

1. THE INADEQUACY OF SINGLE INTEGRATION

The single integral $\int_a^b f(x)\,dx$ calculates the area of the region under the curve $y = f(x)$ between $x = a$ and $x = b$. Such integration is adequate for finding certain areas but it is <u>not</u> adequate for finding, for example, the volume left when the top is cut off a right circular cylinder by a plane inclined at an acute angle to its axis. Double integration can solve problems of this type (e.g. Ex.1.9).

2. THE ANALOGY BETWEEN SINGLE AND DOUBLE INTEGRATION

In single integration we integrate a function of one variable throughout an interval and so calculate the area under a curve; in double integration we integrate a function of two variables over a two dimensional region and so calculate the volume under a surface. How this operates is shown in the diagrams.

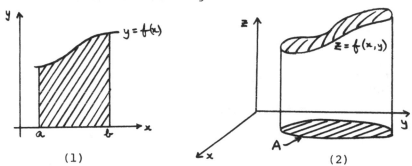

(1)   (2)

In (1), $\int_a^b f(x)\,dx$ measures the area bounded by the curve $y = f(x)$, the x-axis and the lines $x = a$ and $x = b$.

In (2), $\iint_A f(x,y)\,dxdy$ measures the volume enclosed by the surface $z = f(x,y)$, the xy-plane and the cylinder with sides parallel to the z-axis and whose base is the region A in the xy-plane. (A is called the <u>region of integration</u> or <u>field of integration</u>.)

<u>Notice</u>: (i) An example of a surface is $z = 6 - 3x - 2y$, which represents a plane in three dimensional space.

(ii) In effect, the cylinder can be thought of as a scone cutter which cuts out a volume down through the surface $z = f(x,y)$. The base of this cylinder (and consequently the shape of its cross section) is determined by the boundary curve of the region A. There is of course no need for this boundary curve to be a circle: it could be an ellipse, a triangle or any other well behaved closed curve.

Notice further that $\int_a^b f(x)\, dx$ arises as a limit as $\delta x \to 0$ of a sum $\Sigma\, f(x)\, \delta x$. In this sum each term is the area of a small rectangle of width δx and height $f(x)$ as shown. In a corresponding way,

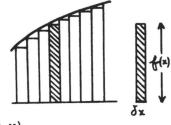

$\iint_A f(x,y)\, dxdy$ arises as a limit of a sum $\Sigma\, f(x,y)\, \delta x \delta y$ as δx and $\delta y \to 0$. In this sum each term is the volume of a cuboid with base of sides δx and δy and of height $f(x,y)$.

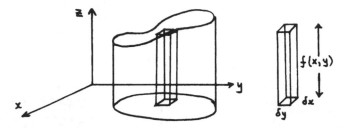

3. THE THINKING BEHIND THE EVALUATION OF A DOUBLE INTEGRAL BY REPEATED INTEGRATION

To calculate the volume under the surface $z = f(x,y)$ mentioned in §2, we cut the volume into slices by planes perpendicular to the x-axis - a typical slice of width δx is shown.

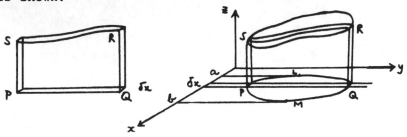

The contribution to the total volume from this slice is approximately (the area of face PQRS) × (the width δx),

i.e. $\left[\int_{y=y_P}^{y=y_Q} f(x,y)\, dy \right] \delta x$,

where x is treated as constant in the integration. The points P and Q are determined by the curves LPM and LQM, which have equations $y = \phi_1(x)$ and $y = \phi_2(x)$, say, respectively. So the volume of the slice is given approximately by the expression

$$\left\{\int_{\phi_1(x)}^{\phi_2(x)} f(x,y)\ dy\right\} \delta x \ .$$

Summation of all such slices corresponds (in the limit) to integrating from $x = a$ to $x = b$. So the volume is found as

$$\int_a^b \left\{\int_{\phi_1(x)}^{\phi_2(x)} f(x,y)\ dy\right\} dx \ ,$$

which we write as

$$\int_a^b dx \int_{\phi_1(x)}^{\phi_2(x)} f(x,y)\ dy. \qquad \ldots (\ast)$$

Here we integrate $f(x,y)$ first with respect to y (treating x as a constant) and then we integrate the result with respect to x.

4. FINDING THE LIMITS IN A DOUBLE INTEGRAL

In doing this be guided by the general rule that the outer limits (i.e. $x = a$, $x = b$ in $(\ast)$ in §3) are constants, while the inner limits (i.e. $y = \phi_1(x)$, $y = \phi_2(x)$ in $(\ast)$ in §3) are curves. We illustrate with an example.

EXAMPLE. Evaluate $\iint_A (2xy + 1)\ dxdy$, where A is the finite region in the first quadrant enclosed by the parabola $y = x^2$ and the line $y = 2x$.

Solution. First draw the region of integration as the shaded region shown. To find the limits in the form

$$\int dx \int (2xy + 1)\ dy$$

proceed in two stages.

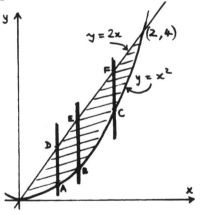

Firstly the x-limits are the constants given by the least and greatest values of x anywhere in the region – i.e. $x = 0$ [at $(0,0)$] and $x = 2$ [at $(2,4)$]. So the x-limits are 0 and 2.

Secondly, to find the y-limits, draw lines parallel to the y-axis and in the same direction across the region as shown. Coming from $-\infty$ these lines cut into the region

at points like A, B, C (i.e. along the <u>curve</u> $y = x^2$)
and they cut out of the region at points like D, E, F
(i.e. along the <u>curve</u> $y = 2x$).   So the lower y-limit
is $y = x^2$ and the upper y-limit is $y = 2x$.

  The double integral is therefore

$$I = \int_0^2 dx \int_{x^2}^{2x} (2xy + 1)\, dy = \int_0^2 [xy^2 + y]_{x^2}^{2x}\, dx$$

$$= \int_0^2 4x^3 + 2x - x^5 - x^2\, dx = [x^4 + x^2 - x^6/6 - x^3/3]_0^2$$

$$= 20/3.$$

<u>Notice</u>:   In the first integration, i.e. the integration
with respect to y, the variable x is treated as a
constant.

<u>EXAMPLES TO DO</u>:   Page 17: Exs. 1, 2.

5.   THE POSSIBILITY OF CHANGE OF ORDER OF INTEGRATION IN A DOUBLE INTEGRAL

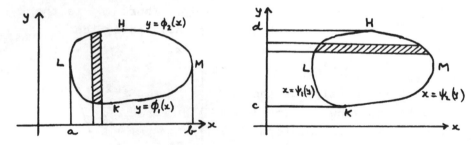

  In §3 we considered slices of the volume perpendicular
to the x-axis (first diagram) giving the integral

$$\int_a^b dx \int_{\phi_1(x)}^{\phi_2(x)} f(x,y)\, dy. \qquad \ldots (1)$$

However, clearly we may also cut the volume into slices by
planes perpendicular to the y-axis (second diagram above)
and the integral then becomes

$$\int_c^d dy \int_{\psi_1(y)}^{\psi_2(y)} f(x,y)\, dx, \qquad \ldots (2)$$

where the curve KLH is $x = \psi_1(y)$ and KMH is
$x = \psi_2(y)$.

  The values of (1) and (2) are equal - both measuring
the volume described in §3.   In some cases it turns out

that (2) is easier to work out than (1). Working out (2) means first integrating with respect to x (treating y as a constant) and then integrating the result with respect to y.

Notice that the <u>lower</u> limit $x = \psi_1(y)$ is the curve on which a line cutting across the region and moving in the positive x-direction <u>enters</u> the region; the <u>upper</u> limit is given by the curve on which such a line <u>leaves</u> the region.

6. CHANGING THE ORDER OF INTEGRATION IN A DOUBLE INTEGRAL

<u>EXAMPLE</u>.   Evaluate

$$I = \int_0^4 dx \int_{\sqrt{x}}^2 \frac{x}{1+y^5} \, dy.$$

<u>Solution</u>.   As there is no easy way of integrating $1/(1+y^5)$ with respect to y, direct evaluation is ruled out. We therefore change the order of integration. To do this start by drawing the region. Changing the order then gives

$$I = \int_0^2 dy \int_0^{y^2} \frac{x}{1+y^5} \, dx$$

$$= \int_0^2 \frac{1}{1+y^5} \, [\tfrac{1}{2}x^2]_0^{y^2} \, dy$$

$$= \int_0^2 \frac{y^4}{2(1+y^5)} \, dy$$

$$= \frac{1}{2} \left[\frac{1}{5} \log(1+y^5) \right]_0^2 \qquad \text{(on substituting } u = 1+y^5\text{)}$$

$$= \frac{1}{10} \log 33.$$

<u>Notice</u>:   There are two stages in the change of order, namely

1.   From the limits in the <u>given</u> order make a sketch of the region of integration.

2.   From the sketch read off the limits in the new order.

To do (1) notice that the x-limits (0 and 4) restrict attention to the band between the lines $x = 0$ and $x = 4$. The y-limits ($y = \sqrt{x}$, $y = 2$) then further restrict attention to the part of this band lying between the curves $y = \sqrt{x}$ (lower curve) and $y = 2$ (upper curve). This settles the region.

To do (2) keep in mind that the outer limits in the new order (here the y-limits) are to be constants while the inner limits (here the x-limits) are to be curves. The <u>constants</u> are the least and greatest values of y in the region [i.e. y = 0 at (0,0) and y = 2 at (4,2)]. The x-limits (<u>curves</u>) are found by drawing lines across the region parallel to the x-axis. These enter the region along the line x = 0 and leave on the curve y = √x, i.e. x = y². So the x-limits are 0 and y².

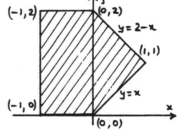

<u>EXAMPLES TO DO:</u>   Page 17: Ex. 3.

7. SPLITTING THE FIELD OF INTEGRATION

<u>EXAMPLE.</u>   Evaluate

$$I = \iint_A 2y \; dxdy,$$

where A is the pentagon with vertices at (0,0), (1,1), (0,2), (-1,2), (-1,0).

<u>Solution.</u>   Here we find that the integral cannot be written as a single repeated integral. Splitting it into the rectangle on the left and the triangle on the right gives

$$I = \int_{-1}^{0} dx \int_{0}^{2} 2y \; dy + \int_{0}^{1} dx \int_{x}^{2-x} 2y \; dy$$

[1st $\iint$ - rectangle, 2nd $\iint$ - triangle.]

$$= \int_{-1}^{0} [y^2]_0^2 \; dx + \int_0^1 [y^2]_x^{2-x} \; dx$$

$$= \int_{-1}^{0} 4 \; dx + \int_0^1 (2-x)^2 - x^2 \; dx$$

$$= [4x]_{-1}^{0} + [4x - 2x^2]_0^1 = 4 + 2 = 6.$$

<u>Notice:</u> In this example even if the order of integration is changed we still need to split the region giving

$$I = \int_0^1 dy \int_{-1}^{y} 2y \; dx + \int_1^2 dy \int_{-1}^{2-y} 2y \; dx.$$

In some examples (e.g. Ex.1.4(a)) the region may have to
be split for one order but not for the other.

<u>EXAMPLES TO DO</u>:   Page 18:   Ex. 4.

8.   THE INTERPRETATION OF A DOUBLE INTEGRAL:
      CALCULATION OF VOLUMES

The examples in §4, §6 and §7 focus on the technical-
ities of the integration process and not on the interpretation of the double integral as a volume as mentioned
in §2.   The following example focuses on the interpretation.

<u>EXAMPLE</u>.   Find the volume of a prism whose base is a
triangle with vertices at (0,0,0), (1,0,0) and (1,1,0),
with sides parallel to the z-axis and whose top is the
plane $6x + 4y + z = 12$.

<u>Solution</u>.

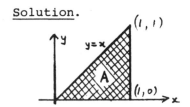

From §2 the volume is given as

$$\iint_A (12 - 6x - 4y)\, dxdy$$

$$= \int_0^1 dx \int_0^x (12 - 6x - 4y)\, dy$$

$$= \int_0^1 [12y - 6xy - 2y^2]_0^x\, dx = \int_0^1 (12x - 8x^2)\, dx$$

$$= \left[6x^2 - \frac{8x^3}{3}\right]_0^1 = 10/3.$$

<u>EXAMPLES TO DO</u>:   Page 18:   Ex. 5.

9.   CALCULATING AN AREA BY DOUBLE INTEGRATION

Notice that according to §2 the value of the integral

$$\iint_A 1\, dxdy,$$

where   A   is a region in the xy-plane, is the volume of a
cylinder whose base is the region   A   and with height
1 unit.   <u>Numerically</u> this value is therefore equal to the
area of the region   A.   So we have the following

result which is occasionally useful:

$$\iint_A 1 \, dxdy \; = \; \text{area of the region } A.$$

10. CHANGING THE VARIABLES IN A DOUBLE INTEGRAL TO POLAR COORDINATES

Just as in a single integral we can change the variable (i.e. integration by substitution) so in a double integral we can change the variables. There is a general rule for this given in §16. Here however we look at a useful particular case - the change from xy-coordinates to polar coordinates r and θ. In this connection recall that

$$x = r \cos \theta, \quad y = r \sin \theta, \quad r^2 = x^2 + y^2, \quad \tan \theta = y/x.$$

The rule, for suitably well behaved functions f, is:

<u>RULE</u>. $\quad \iint_A f(x,y) \, dxdy \; = \; \iint_A f(r \cos \theta, r \sin \theta) \, r \, drd\theta.$

To see why this rule is reasonable, recall that in the xy-form of the integral in §2 we considered a typical cuboid whose base is a small rectangle with area $\delta x \delta y$ as shown. For the $r\theta$-form, the natural base to choose is the area derived from small increases δr in r and $\delta \theta$ in θ, i.e. the area shown which lies between the circles centred at O, of radii r and $(r + \delta r)$ and in a sector of angle $\delta \theta$. The <u>area of this shaded region is given as</u>

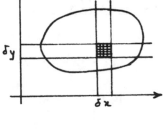

$\dfrac{\delta \theta}{2\pi} \times$ (the area between the two circles)

$\qquad = \dfrac{\delta \theta}{2\pi} \times (\pi(r + \delta r)^2 - \pi r^2)$

$\qquad = \tfrac{1}{2} \delta\theta (2r \, \delta r + (\delta r)^2)$

$\qquad = r \, \delta\theta\delta r + \tfrac{1}{2}\delta\theta(\delta r)^2$

$\qquad = r \, \delta\theta\delta r \;$ approximately, for small values of $\delta\theta$ & δr.

This is evidence of why the factor r appears on the right hand side in the above rule.

11. **EXAMPLE.** Using polar coordinates evaluate

$$I = \iint_R \frac{x^2}{\sqrt{(x^2 + y^2)}} \, dxdy,$$

where R is the region which lies between the circles $x^2 + y^2 = 1$ and $x^2 + y^2 = 4$ and above the x-axis.

Solution. Using the rule in §10 to change to polars gives

$$I = \iint \frac{(r \cos \theta)^2}{r} \, r \, d\theta dr = \int_0^\pi d\theta \int_1^2 r^2 \cos^2\theta \, dr$$

$$= \int_0^\pi \cos^2\theta \, d\theta \int_1^2 r^2 \, dr = \int_0^\pi \tfrac{1}{2}(1 + \cos 2\theta) d\theta \int_1^2 r^2 \, dr$$

$$= \left[\tfrac{1}{2}(\theta + \tfrac{1}{2}\sin 2\theta) \right]_0^\pi \cdot \left[r^3/3 \right]_1^2$$

$$= 7\pi/6.$$

Notice: (i) It is usually good policy to take such integrals in the order

$$\int d\theta \int \ldots dr \, .$$

The θ-limits are then <u>constants</u>, while the r-limits are <u>curves</u>.

        To find the limits draw radius vectors like OA, OB, OC <u>from the origin</u> out across the region of integration. The θ-limits are then the least and greatest values of θ on such radius vectors.   Here θ runs from 0° to 180°, i.e. from 0 to π.   The r-limits are given by the curves on which the radius vectors enter and leave the region, i.e. the circle $x^2 + y^2 = 1$ (entry) and the circle $x^2 + y^2 = 4$ (leaving);   in polar coordinates these are $r^2 = 1$ and $r^2 = 4$, i.e. $r = 1$ and $r = 2$.

        (ii) Tackling the above example in xy-coordinates would be much harder: the field would have to be split. In general in a double integral in which <u>either</u> the region of integration involves a circle or part of a circle, <u>and/or</u> the integrand contains a function of $(x^2 + y^2)$, it may be worth trying polar coordinates.   Both these features are present in the above example.

<u>EXAMPLES TO DO</u>: (See also §12.)   Page 18:   Exs. 6(a)-(d).

12. **EXAMPLE.**   Evaluate $\iint xy \, dxdy$, where the region of integration is

        (a) the region in the first quadrant that lies inside the circle $x^2 + y^2 = 4x$,

(b) the region in the first quadrant that lies inside the circle $x^2 + y^2 = 4x$ but outside $x^2 + y^2 = 4$.

Solution.　　(a)　　Notice that $x^2 + y^2 = 4x$ can be written as $x^2 - 4x + 4 + y^2 = 4$, i.e. $(x - 2)^2 + y^2 = 4$, and this is a circle with centre at $(2,0)$ and of radius 2. So

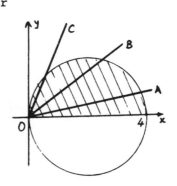

$$I = \int_0^{\frac{1}{2}\pi} d\theta \int_0^{4 \cos \theta} r^2 \cos \theta \sin \theta \, . \, r \, dr$$

$$= \int_0^{\frac{1}{2}\pi} \cos \theta \sin \theta \, d\theta \int_0^{4 \cos \theta} r^3 \, dr$$

$$= \int_0^{\frac{1}{2}\pi} \cos \theta \sin \theta \, [r^4/4]_0^{4 \cos \theta} \, d\theta$$

$$= 64 \int_0^{\frac{1}{2}\pi} \cos^5 \theta \sin \theta \, d\theta$$

$$= 64 \, [- \cos^6 \theta / 6]_0^{\frac{1}{2}\pi} = 32/3.$$

(b)　Here the two circles meet where $x^2 + y^2 = 4$ and $x^2 + y^2 = 4x$, i.e. where $x = 1$, $y = \sqrt{3}$. So the upper limit for θ is $\pi/3$. So, in this case,

$$I = \int_0^{\pi/3} d\theta \int_2^{4 \cos \theta} r^3 \cos \theta \sin \theta \, dr$$

$$= \int_0^{\pi/3} \cos \theta \sin \theta \, (\, 64 \cos^4 \theta - 4) \, d\theta$$

$$= \int_0^{\pi/3} 64 \cos^5 \theta \sin \theta - 4 \cos \theta \sin \theta \, d\theta$$

$$= [-64 \cos^6 \theta / 6 + 2 \cos^2 \theta]_0^{\pi/3} = 9, \text{ on evaluation.}$$

Notice: In each case the limits for r are found from the curves on which the radius vectors OA, OB, OC enter and leave the relevant region. In (a), these lines enter at $r = 0$ and leave on the circle $x^2 + y^2 = 4x$, which is $r^2 = 4r \cos \theta$, i.e. $r = 4 \cos \theta$ in polar coordinates.

EXAMPLES TO DO:　　Pages 18-19: Exs. 6(e)-(h), 7.

13. <u>EXAMPLE</u>. A solid hemisphere is given by $z \geq 0$ and $x^2 + y^2 + z^2 \leq 9$. Find the volume cut out of this hemisphere by

        (a) the cylinder $x^2 + y^2 = 1$,

        (b) the cylinder $x^2 + y^2 = 3y$.

<u>Solution</u>. Following the ideas of §2 we integrate the function $z = \sqrt{(9 - x^2 - y^2)}$ over the regions of the xy-plane which are the cross sections of the respective cylinders.

(a)

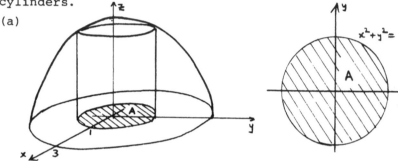

The volume cut out $= \displaystyle\iint_{x^2 + y^2 \leq 1} \sqrt{(9 - x^2 - y^2)}\, dxdy$

$$= \int_0^{2\pi} d\theta \int_0^1 r\,\sqrt{(9 - r^2)}\, dr \qquad \text{(in polars)}$$

$$= 2\pi \left[-\frac{1}{3}(9 - r^2)^{3/2} \right]_0^1 \qquad \begin{array}{l}\text{(either directly or by}\\ \text{setting } u = 9 - r^2.)\end{array}$$

$$= \frac{2\pi}{3}(27 - 16\sqrt{2}).$$

(b)

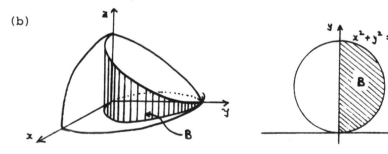

Here we calculate the volume in the first octant (i.e. where $x, y, z \geq 0$) and double it. So the volume is

$$2\iint_B \sqrt{(9 - x^2 - y^2)}\, dxdy = 2\int_0^{\frac{1}{2}\pi} d\theta \int_0^{3\sin\theta} r\,\sqrt{(9 - r^2)}\, dr$$

$$= 2\int_0^{\frac{1}{2}\pi} \left[-\frac{1}{3}(9-r^2)^{\frac{3}{2}}\right]_0^3 \sin\theta \ d\theta \ = 18\int_0^{\frac{1}{2}\pi}(1-\cos^3\theta)\ d\theta$$

$$= 9\pi - 12 \quad \text{(using the result of §39).}$$

Notice: (i) Both the features which militate for a change to polar coordinates mentioned in §11(ii) are present here.

(ii) In two dimensional space the equation $x^2 + y^2 = 1$ represents a circle, but in three dimensional space it represents an infinite cylinder with circular cross section. See §138 for some details of this.

EXAMPLES TO DO: Page 19: Exs. 8 - 10.

14. MAKING A GENERAL CHANGE OF VARIABLES IN A DOUBLE INTEGRAL

Suppose that we are to change the variables in a double integral

$$\iint_R f(x,y)\ dxdy$$

from x, y to u, v, where u and v are functions of x and y. (The change to polar coordinates (§10) is one such example.) In the change of variables we assume that u and v are independent functions of x and y in the sense of §108. With this assumption and for suitably well behaved functions f, the rule is:

RULE. $\iint_R f(x,y)\ dxdy = \iint_S F(u,v)\left|\frac{\partial(x,y)}{\partial(u,v)}\right|dudv,$

where $F(u,v)$ is derived from $f(x,y)$ by substituting for x, y in terms of u, v and S is the region in the uv-plane corresponding to R in the xy-plane, and where $\frac{\partial(x,y)}{\partial(u,v)}$ is a factor called the Jacobian. The vertical bars in the rule denote that the modulus (absolute value) of the Jacobian is to be taken.

Notice: (i) For the definition and properties of Jacobians see §107.

(ii) It is the modulus of the Jacobian that appears on the right hand side.

EXAMPLE. Show how the above rule applies to the change to polar coordinates r and θ.

Solution.   Here $x = r \cos \theta$, $y = r \sin \theta$.   So

$$\frac{\partial (x,y)}{\partial (r,\theta)} = \begin{vmatrix} \dfrac{\partial x}{\partial r} & \dfrac{\partial x}{\partial \theta} \\ \dfrac{\partial y}{\partial r} & \dfrac{\partial y}{\partial \theta} \end{vmatrix} = \begin{vmatrix} \cos \theta & -r \sin \theta \\ \sin \theta & r \cos \theta \end{vmatrix} = r.$$

So the rule above gives

$$\iint_R f(x,y) \, dxdy = \iint_S f(r \cos \theta, r \sin \theta) \, r \, d\theta dr,$$

which confirms the rule given in §10.

15.   **EXAMPLE.**   By making a suitable change of variables evaluate

$$I = \iint (1 + y^6) \, dxdy$$

where the region of integration is the region in the first quadrant bounded by the curves $y^2 = x$, $y^2 = 3x$, $xy = 1$, $xy = 2$.

Solution.   (A glance at the region of integration shows that integrating in xy-coordinates would require an elaborate splitting operation.)   So we let $u = y^2/x$ and $v = xy$. Then at every point of the region we have $1 \leq u \leq 3$ and $1 \leq v \leq 2$.   Also

$$\frac{\partial (x,y)}{\partial (u,v)} = \frac{1}{\dfrac{\partial (u,v)}{\partial (x,y)}} \qquad \text{(by §107)}.$$

Now $\dfrac{\partial (u,v)}{\partial (x,y)} = \det \begin{bmatrix} -y^2/x^2 & 2y/x \\ y & x \end{bmatrix} = -\dfrac{3y^2}{x}$.   So, using

the rule from §14, we have that

$$I = \int_1^3 du \int_1^2 (1 + y^6) \, \frac{x}{3y^2} \, dv = \int_1^3 du \int_1^2 (1 + u^2 v^2) \frac{1}{3u} \, dv$$

$$= \frac{1}{3} \int_1^3 du \int_1^2 \left(\frac{1}{u} + uv^2 \right) dv = \frac{1}{3} \int_1^3 \left[\frac{v}{u} + \frac{uv^3}{3} \right]_1^2 du$$

$$= \frac{1}{3} \int_1^3 \left(\frac{1}{u} + \frac{7u}{3} \right) du = (28 + 3 \log 3)/9.$$

Notice: (i) The choice $u = y^2/x$ and $v = xy$ reduces the new limits to constants: this is a common trick where the region of integration is bounded by <u>four</u> curves <u>two</u> of which have equations of one type (i.e. $y^2 = ax$) and <u>two</u> of another type (i.e. $xy = b$).

(ii) Since the change of variables arises in the form $u = \ldots$, $v = \ldots$ (rather than as $x = \ldots, y = \ldots$) it is much easier to calculate $\frac{\partial(u,v)}{\partial(x,y)}$ and then invert it,

rather than calculate $\frac{\partial(x,y)}{\partial(u,v)}$ directly. This uses the property of Jacobians given in §107.

(iii) The integrand $(1 + y^6)$ has to be changed to a function of u and v. In some examples (though not in the example above) it can be good policy to try to simplify the product of the integrand and the Jacobian <u>before</u> changing either to a function of u and v - e.g. it might be possible to remove some factor by cancelling.

<u>EXAMPLES TO DO</u>: Pages 19-20: Exs. 11 - 13.

16. <u>EXAMPLE</u>. Let R denote the interior of the ellipse $\frac{x^2}{a^2} + \frac{y^2}{b^2} = 1$. Find

(i) the area of the region R by double integration,

(ii) $\iint_R (x^2 + y^2)\, dxdy$.

<u>Solution</u>. (i) Make the change of variables $x = au, y = bv$. Then $\frac{\partial(x,y)}{\partial(u,v)} = \det \begin{bmatrix} a & 0 \\ 0 & b \end{bmatrix} = ab$. Also, under the change the change of variables the region R converts from

$$\frac{x^2}{a^2} + \frac{y^2}{b^2} \leq 1 \quad \text{to} \quad u^2 + v^2 \leq 1,$$

so that the integration is over the unit disc D in the uv-plane. So the area of the ellipse is, by §9,

$$\iint_R 1\, dxdy = \iint_{u^2+v^2 \leq 1} 1 \cdot ab\, dudv$$

$$= ab \times (\text{area of the disc } D) = \pi ab.$$

(i) Using the same change of variables as in (i), we have

$$\iint_R (x^2 + y^2)\, dxdy = \iint_D (a^2u^2 + b^2v^2)ab\, dudv$$

$$= ab \iint_D (a^2u^2 + b^2v^2) \; dudv$$

$$= ab(a^2 + b^2) \iint_D u^2 \; dudv \qquad \text{(by symmetry as in Ex.1.7)}$$

$$= ab(a^2 + b^2) \int_0^{2\pi} d\theta \int_0^1 r^3\cos^2\theta \; dr$$

$$= ab(a^2 + b^2) \int_0^{2\pi} \cos^2\theta \; d\theta \int_0^1 r^3 \; dr = \pi ab(a^2 + b^2)/4 .$$

EXAMPLES TO DO: Page 20:   Exs. 14 - 15.

17. THE MEAN VALUE OF A FUNCTION OVER A TWO DIMENSIONAL REGION

Definition.   The mean value of a function f of two variables over a two dimensional region R is

$$\frac{1}{\text{area of } R} \times \iint_R f(x,y) \; dxdy .$$

EXAMPLE.   A copper mining region R is in the form of a triangle with vertices at (0,0), (5,0) and (0,15), the distances being measured in kilometres.   The quality of the ore varies across the region so that the value per square kilometre of the land at   (x,y)   is represented by the function f where $f(x,y) = 35 - 3x - 2y$.   Find the average value of a square kilometre in the region.

Solution.   The definition of the mean value effectively tells us to find the value of the whole region and then divide by its area.   We have

$$\iint_R f(x,y) \; dxdy = \int_0^5 dx \int_0^{15-3x} (35 - 3x - 2y) \; dy$$

$$= \int_0^5 \left[(35 - 3x)y - y^2 \right]_0^{15-3x} dx$$

$$= \int_0^5 20(15 - 3x) \; dx = 750 .$$

So the average value per sq. km. $= \dfrac{750}{\text{area of } R}$

$$= \frac{750}{\frac{1}{2}.5.15} = 20 \text{ units.}$$

EXAMPLES TO DO: Pages 20-21:   Exs. 16, 20.

18. FINDING THE CENTRE OF GRAVITY OF A LAMINA

Elementary methods of doing this are given in books on Statics, but double integration can be useful too.

EXAMPLE.   A semi-circular plate is of uniform density
and of radius   a.   Find the position of its centre of
gravity.

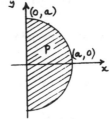

Solution.   Take the plate   P   as
the part of the disc $x^2 + y^2 \leq a^2$
for which $x \geq 0$.   Let the
centre of gravity   G   have the
coordinates $(\bar{x}, \bar{y})$.   Then by
symmetry $\bar{y} = 0$.   To find $\bar{x}$
let   M   be the mass of the lamina, let ρ denote the mass
per unit of area and consider a small piece of the lamina
of mass δm round the point (x, y).   Then, from the
definition of   G   (see books on Statics),

$$\bar{x} = \frac{1}{M} \sum x \, \delta m ,$$

where the summation is done over all such small pieces.

So $\bar{x} = \frac{1}{M} \sum x \, \rho dxdy = \frac{1}{M} \iint_P x\rho \, dxdy = \frac{1}{M} \int_{-\frac{1}{2}\pi}^{\frac{1}{2}\pi} d\theta \int_0^a \rho r^2 \cos \theta \, dr$

$\qquad = \frac{1}{M} \int_{-\frac{1}{2}\pi}^{\frac{1}{2}\pi} \cos \theta \, d\theta \int_0^a \rho r^2 \, dr = \frac{1}{M} \cdot \frac{2}{3} \rho a^3$

$\qquad = \frac{1}{\frac{1}{2}\pi a^2 \rho} \cdot \frac{2}{3} \rho a^3 = \frac{4a}{3\pi} .$ So   G   is $(4a/(3\pi), 0)$.

EXAMPLES TO DO: Page 20:   Ex. 17.

19.   FINDING THE MOMENT OF INERTIA OF A LAMINA

Elementary methods are given in books on Dynamics
but double integration can be used in some cases.

EXAMPLE.   Find the moment of inertia of a disc   D   of
mass   M   of radius   a   and whose mass per unit area is ρ,
when the axis of rotation is (i) a diameter, (ii) a tangent.

Solution.   The moment of inertia is calculated as the sum
$\sum b^2 \, \delta m$, where δm is the mass of a small rectangular
piece of the lamina with sides δx and δy and   b   is the
distance of this piece from the axis of rotation.   In this
problem we take the disc   D   as $x^2 + y^2 \leq a^2$.

For (i) take the axis of rotation as the   y-axis.   So
the moment of inertia $= \sum x^2 \, \delta m = \sum x^2 \rho \delta x \delta y$

$$= \iint_D x^2\rho \; dxdy = \rho \int_0^{2\pi} \cos^2\theta \; d\theta \int_0^a r^3 \; dr$$

$$= \pi\rho a^4/4 = (\pi a^2\rho)(a^2/4) = Ma^2/4 .$$

<u>For (ii)</u> take the axis of rotation as the line x = -a. So the moment of inertia (M.I.) is given by

$$M.I. = \sum (x+a)^2 \delta m = \iint_D \rho(x+a)^2 \; dxdy = \iint_D \rho(x^2+a^2) \; dxdy$$

$$[\text{by Ex.1.7}]$$

$$= \tfrac{1}{4}Ma^2 + \iint_D \rho a^2 \; dxdy \quad [\text{on using (i)}]$$

$$= \tfrac{1}{4}Ma^2 + Ma^2 = \frac{5Ma^2}{4} .$$

<u>Notice</u>: This method also applies to laminas of non-uniform density, e.g. Ex.1.19.

<u>EXAMPLES TO DO</u>: Pages 20-21: Exs. 18, 19.

EXAMPLES 1

1. Show that $\displaystyle\int_0^1 dx \int_x^1 30x^2y \; dy = 2.$

2. Evaluate each of the following for the given region R:

(a) $\iint (x^2 + 2y) \; dxdy$; R is the rectangle with vertices at the points (0,0), (2,0), (2,3), (0,3).

(b) $\iint y^2 \; dxdy$; R is the triangle enclosed by the x-axis, the line x = 1 and the line y = x.

(c) $\iint xy \; dxdy$; R is the triangle enclosed by the lines y = 2x, y = 4 and the y-axis.

3. By changing the order of integration in each case, evaluate the following:

(a) $\displaystyle\int_0^1 dx \int_x^1 \frac{x}{1+y^3} \; dy,$ (b) $\displaystyle\int_0^2 dx \int_{x^2}^4 \frac{x^3}{\sqrt{(1+y^3)}} \; dy,$

(c) $\displaystyle\int_0^1 dx \int_x^{\sqrt{x}} \frac{x}{\sqrt{(x^2+y^2)}} \; dy,$ (d) $\displaystyle\int_1^\infty dx \int_{1/x}^1 y^6 e^{-xy} \; dy,$

(e)[†] $\displaystyle\int_0^1 dy \int_y^1 3y^2 e^{-x^2} \; dx,$ (f) $\displaystyle\int_1^2 dx \int_2^{2x} \frac{x}{(16-y^2)^{3/2}} \; dy.$

† [Note in (e) that $\int e^{-x^2} \; dx$ is <u>not</u> possible in terms of elementary functions.]

4.   In each of the following cases, evaluate the double integral over the region   R   specified:

(a) $\iint (x + y)$ dxdy ;   R   is the triangle with vertices at   (1,0), (0,1), (-1,0) .

(b) $\iint x^2$ dxdy ;   R   is the interior of the square with vertices at   (-1,0), (0,-1), (1,0), (0,1).

(c) $\iint$ x dxdy ;   R   is the trapezium with vertices at   (0,0), (4,0), (3,1) and (1,1).

(d) $\iint e^{-(x + y)}$ dxdy ;   R   is the region given by the conditions $0 \le y \le 1$ and $y \le x$.

(e) $\iint$ xy dxdy   over the parallelogram with vertices at   (0,0), (1,0), (2,1) and (1,1).

(f) $\iint \dfrac{1}{y(x + y)^3}$ dxdy ;   R   is the finite region enclosed by the line   y = 1,   the hyperbola   xy = 1   and the line   4y = x.

5.   Find the volume of the prism whose base is the triangle with vertices at   (0,0,0), (1,0,0) and (0,2,0), which has sides parallel to the z-axis and the top of which is the plane   3x + 2y + z = 10.

6.   In each of the following cases, use polar coordinates to evaluate the double integral over the given region   R :

(a) $\iint xy^2$ dxdy ;   R   is the region in the first quadrant enclosed between the circles $x^2 + y^2 = 1$ and $x^2 + y^2 = 16$.

(b) $\iint \dfrac{y}{x^2 + y^2}$ dxdy ;   R   is the part of the disc $x^2 + y^2 \le a^2$ in the first quadrant.   (Here   a > 0.)

(c) $\iint x \sqrt{(x^2 + y^2)}$ dxdy ;   R   is the finite region in the first quadrant enclosed by the line $y = \sqrt{3}\, x$, the x-axis and the circle $x^2 + y^2 = a^2$.   (a > 0)

(d) $\iint (x^2 + y^2)\, e^{-(x^2 + y^2)}$ dxdy ;   R   is the region in the first quadrant but outside the circle $x^2 + y^2 = 1$.

(e) $\iint y(x^2 + y^2)$ dxdy ;   R   is the part of the interior of the circle $x^2 + y^2 = 2x$ in the first quadrant.

(f) $\iint xy \, dxdy$; R is the region in the first quadrant inside $x^2 + y^2 = 2x$ but outside $x^2 + y^2 = 1$.

(g) $\iint x \, dxdy$; R is the region in the first quadrant which lies inside the circle $x^2 + y^2 = 4ax$ but outside the circle $x^2 + y^2 = 2ax$. (Here $a > 0$.)

(h) $\iint \dfrac{x^3}{x^2 + y^2} \, dxdy$; R is the triangle with vertices at $(0,0)$, $(1,0)$ and $(1,1)$.

7. Let D denote the disc $x^2 + y^2 \leq 1$ and let Q denote the part of D in the first quadrant. Show that

$$\iint_D x^2 \, dxdy = 4\iint_Q x^2 \, dxdy = \frac{\pi}{4} ,$$

and

$$\iint_D x^2 \, dxdy = \iint_D y^2 \, dxdy .$$

Show also from symmetry considerations that

$$\iint_D x \, dxdy = \iint_D x^3 \, dxdy = \iint_D x^2 y \, dxdy = 0 .$$

8. Integrate $\sqrt{(a^2 - x^2 - y^2)}$ over the part of the disc $x^2 + y^2 \leq a^2$ in the first quadrant. Hence verify that the volume of a sphere of radius a is $4\pi a^3/3$.

9. A dummy funnel on a passenger steamer is to be used as a water tank. The tank is to have vertical sides, horizontal base and a slanting plane top. Find the volume of the tank if the base is the plane $z = 0$, the top is the plane $x + 3z = 24$ and the sides are determined by the circular cylinder $x^2 + y^2 = 9$. [N.B. It helps to notice that $\iint x \, dxdy$ over the disc in Ex.7 has the value 0.]

10. An inflatable rubber tent takes the form of the paraboloid $z = 1 - x^2 - y^2$ for $z \geq 0$. Find the volume of air which it encloses.

11. In each of the following cases make a suitable change of variables in the double integral to evaluate it over the region R given :

(a) $\iint xy \, dxdy$; R is the region enclosed by the hyperbolas $xy = 1$, $xy = 7$ and the parabolas $y = 2x^2$, $y = 4x^2$.

(b) $\iint x^2 \, dxdy$; R is the square region enclosed by the lines $x + y = -1$, $x + y = 1$, $y - x = -1$, y − x = 1.   (Compare Ex. 4(b) above.)

(c) $\iint (y^3 + 1)\, dxdy$;   R is the region in the first quadrant enclosed by the four parabolas $y^2 = x$, $y^2 = 2x$, $y = x^2$, $y = 4x^2$.

(d) $\iint (y + 2x)^3\, dxdy$;   R is the region in the first quadrant enclosed by the hyperbolas $xy = 3$, $xy = 6$ and the lines $y = 2x + 1$, $y = 2x + 2$.

12. Use double integration to find the area of the parallelogram enclosed by the lines $y = x + 1$, $y = x + 2$, $y = 5 − 3x$, $y = 9 − 3x$.

13. Show that the area of the region in the first quadrant enclosed by the hyperbolas $xy = a$, $xy = b$ ($b > a > 0$) and the lines $y = cx$, $y = dx$ ($d > c > 0$) is $\tfrac{1}{2}(b − a)\log(d/c)$.

14. Evaluate $\iint (x^4 + y^4)\, dxdy$ over the interior of the ellipse $\dfrac{x^2}{a^2} + \dfrac{y^2}{b^2} = 1$.

15. Repeat Ex. 9 replacing the circular cylinder (for the section of the tank) by the elliptic cylinder $x^2 + 4y^2 = 16$.

16. Find the mean value of

(a) x^2 over the disc $x^2 + y^2 \le a^2$,

(b) $(x^2 + y^2)$ over the square with vertices at the points $(1,1)$, $(1,-1)$, $(-1,-1)$, $(-1,1)$.

17. In each of the following cases find the centre of gravity of a lamina of uniform density and of the given shape:

(a) the triangle with vertices at $(0,0)$, $(1,0)$ and $(0,1)$,

(b) the part of the disc $x^2 + y^2 \le a^2$ which lies in the first and fourth quadrants and which lies below the line $y = x$ and above the line $y = -x$.

18. A uniform lamina is in the shape of a triangle with vertices at $(0,0)$, $(a,0)$ and $(a,2a)$, where $a > 0$. Its mass per unit of area is k, so that its total mass M is given by $M = ka^2$.   Show that its moment of inertia about the x-axis is $2Ma^2/3$.

19.   A lamina of non-uniform density is in the form
of a square with vertices at   (0,0), (a,0), (a,a), (0,a),
where   a > 0.   Its mass per unit of area at the point
(x,y)   is given by $k(x + 2y)$,   where   k   is a constant.
Find the mass of the lamina, the coordinates of its
centre of gravity and its moment of inertia about the
x-axis.

20.   The region covered by a rescue helicopter is
a disc of radius   a.   Find the average flying distance
to a randomly chosen point within the disc from the
helicopter base when the base is located at   (a) the
centre of the disc,   (b) a point on the circumference of
the disc.   [Considerations of this type may also arise
in choosing the location of a standby rescue ship in an
offshore drilling area or the depot for a breakdown crane
in a railway network.   Numerical integration or the
concentration of contributions at particular points may
help in such general problems.]

21.   The yearly outputs of two mines   A   and   B   can
be regarded as independent random variables   X   and   Y
with respective probability density functions

$$f(x) = \begin{cases} e^{-x} & (x > 0), \\ 0 & \text{otherwise,} \end{cases} \qquad g(y) = \begin{cases} 4e^{-4y} & (y > 0), \\ 0 & \text{otherwise.} \end{cases}$$

Find the probability that in a given year

(a)   the output of mine A   exceeds the output of
mine B,

(b)   the sum of the outputs of the two mines is
greater than   1 unit.

II.   TRIPLE INTEGRATION

---

20.   As mentioned in §2, the double integral

$$\iint_A f(x,y) \, dxdy$$

arises as the limit of sums of the form $\Sigma f(x,y) \, \delta x \delta y$ as δx and $\delta y \to 0$ and the summation is taken over all small rectangles of sides δx and δy within the two dimensional region A in the xy-plane.

In a similar way, the triple integral

$$\iiint_V f(x,y,z) \, dxdydz$$

arises as the limit of sums of the form $\Sigma f(x,y,z) \, \delta x \delta y \delta z$ as δx, δy and $\delta z \to 0$ and the summation is taken over all small cuboids of sides δx, δy and δz within the three dimensional region V in xyz-space.

The value of a triple integral can be calculated as a repeated integral of the form

$$\int_a^b dx \int_{\phi_1(x)}^{\phi_2(x)} dy \int_{\psi_1(x,y)}^{\psi_2(x,y)} f(x,y,z) \, dz \, .$$

In this repeated integral, notice that the x, y and z-limits represent <u>constants</u>, <u>curves</u> and <u>surfaces</u> respectively, as explained in the example of §21.   For a double integral there are two possible orders of integration; for a triple integral there are six.

For an interpretation of triple integrals see §25.

21.   <u>EXAMPLE.</u>   Evaluate $\iiint x \, dxdydz$, where the region of integration is the tetrahedron given by $x \geq 0$, $y \geq 0$, $z \geq 0$ and $2x + 2y + z \leq 6$.

<u>Solution.</u>   It's a good idea to sketch the region first, i.e. the tetrahedron OABC.   Notice that the plane $2x + 2y + z = 6$ meets the axes at $(3,0,0)$, $(0,3,0)$ and $(0,0,6)$.   So

$$I = \int_0^3 dx \int_0^{3-x} dy \int_0^{6-2x-2y} x \, dz$$

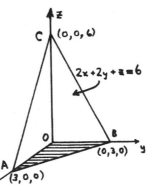

$$= \int_0^3 x \, dx \int_0^{3-x} [z]_0^{6-2x-2y} \, dy$$

$$= \int_0^3 x \, dx \int_0^{3-x} (6 - 2x - 2y) \, dy$$

$$= \int_0^3 x \, [(6 - 2x)y - y^2]_0^{3-x} \, dx$$

$$= \int_0^3 x(3 - x)^2 \, dx \ = \ \int_0^3 9x - 6x^2 + x^3 \, dx \ = \ 27/4 \ .$$

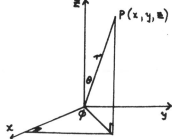

Notice: The constants, curves and surfaces mentioned in §19 are seen clearly in this example.

The x and y-limits are just the limits for a <u>double</u> integral over the triangle OAB, i.e. over the projection of the tetrahedron OABC on the xy-plane. In this connection notice that the equation of the line AB is found by setting z = 0 in the equation of the plane 2x + 2y + z = 6 to give 2x + 2y = 6, i.e. y = 3 - x.

To find the z-limits, i.e. the surfaces, draw lines through the tetrahedron parallel to and in the same direction as the positive z-axis. Such lines enter the tetrahedron on the plane OAB (i.e. on the surface z = 0) and leave it on the plane ABC (i.e. on the surface z = 6 - 2x - 2y). This fixes the z-limits as 0 and (6 - 2x - 2y).

<u>EXAMPLES TO DO:</u>   Page 30: Exs. 1, 2.

22. SPHERICAL POLAR COORDINATES IN TRIPLE INTEGRATION

In two dimensions polar coordinates are useful in integrals involving circles or functions of $(x^2 + y^2)$. Correspondingly in three dimensions spherical polar coordinates are useful in problems involving spheres or functions of $(x^2 + y^2 + z^2)$.
The point P has spherical polar coordinates (r, θ, ϕ), where r = OP and the angles θ and ϕ are shown. We can see from trigonometry that

$x = r \sin \theta \cos \phi$,

$y = r \sin \theta \sin \phi$,

$z = r \cos \theta$.

Also notice that $x^2 + y^2 + z^2 = r^2$.

The following is the rule for changing to spherical polars:

<u>RULE</u>.   For suitably well-behaved functions f,

$$\iiint_V f(x,y,z) \; dxdydz$$

$$= \iiint_V f(r \sin \theta \cos \phi, r \sin \theta \sin \phi, r \cos \theta) \; r^2 \sin \theta \; d\phi d\theta dr.$$

<u>Notice</u>:   (i) This means that we change the integrand to spherical polars and insert the factor $r^2 \sin \theta$.

(ii) It is often good policy to perform such integrals in the order

$$\int d\phi \int d\theta \int \ldots dr,$$

as in §23.

(iii) See §27 for justification of the rule.

23.   <u>EXAMPLE</u>.   Evaluate $\iiint z^2 \; dxdydz$, where the region of integration is the three dimensional region V above the plane $z = 0$ and between the spheres $x^2 + y^2 + z^2 = 1$ and $x^2 + y^2 + z^2 = 4$.

<u>Solution</u>.   The region of integration is the hemispherical shell shown. So the integral is

$$\int_0^{2\pi} d\phi \int_0^{\frac{1}{2}\pi} d\theta \int_1^2 r^2 \cos^2 \theta \; r^2 \sin \theta \; dr$$

$$= 2\pi \int_0^{\frac{1}{2}\pi} \cos^2 \theta \sin \theta \; d\theta \int_1^2 r^4 \; dr$$

$$= 2\pi \; [-\cos^3 \theta /3]_0^{\frac{1}{2}\pi} \; [r^5/5]_1^2 \; = 62\pi/15.$$

<u>Notice</u>:   (i) Drawing radius vectors out from the origin cutting through V can help in deciding the limits. The ϕ-limits are the least and greatest values of ϕ at any point in V: here ϕ runs from 0 to 2π corresponding to a complete swing round the z-axis.

For the θ-limits, remember that θ is measured <u>from</u> the z-axis, and consider the possible values of θ <u>for</u> various positions of the radius vectors mentioned above. The limit $\theta = \frac{1}{2}\pi$ corresponds to those radius vectors lying on the xy-plane.

The   r-limits are given by the surfaces on which the radius vectors enter and leave V, i.e. $x^2 + y^2 + z^2 = 1$ and $x^2 + y^2 + z^2 = 4$, which translate to $r^2 = 1$ and $r^2 = 4$, giving $r = 1$ and $r = 2$.

(ii) The θ-limits always lie between 0 and π in such problems: negative values of θ do not occur because the angle ϕ takes account of swing round the z-axis.

<u>EXAMPLES TO DO:</u> (See also §24.) Page 30: Exs. 3(a)-(d).

24. <u>EXAMPLE.</u> Evaluate $\iiint z^3 \, dxdydz$ over the region which lies outside the sphere $x^2 + y^2 + z^2 = 2bz$ but inside the sphere $x^2 + y^2 + z^2 = 2az$, where $0 < b < a$.

<u>Solution.</u> The first sphere is
$$x^2 + y^2 + (z-b)^2 = b^2,$$
which has centre $(0,0,b)$ and radius b. Similarly the second sphere has centre $(0,0,a)$ and radius a. So

$$I = \int_0^{2\pi} d\phi \int_0^{\frac{1}{2}\pi} d\theta \int_{2b\cos\theta}^{2a\cos\theta} r^3\cos^3\theta . r^2\sin\theta \, dr$$

$$= 2\pi \int_0^{\frac{1}{2}\pi} \cos^3\theta \, \sin\theta \, [r^6/6]_{2b\cos\theta}^{2a\cos\theta} \, d\theta$$

$$= \frac{\pi}{3} \int_0^{\frac{1}{2}\pi} \cos^3\theta \, \sin\theta [64a^6\cos^6\theta - 64b^6\cos^6\theta] \, d\theta$$

$$= \frac{64\pi(a^6 - b^6)}{3} \int_0^{\frac{1}{2}\pi} \cos^9\theta \, \sin\theta \, d\theta$$

$$= \frac{64\pi(a^6 - b^6)}{3} [-\frac{\cos^{10}\theta}{10}]_0^{\frac{1}{2}\pi} = \frac{32\pi}{15}(a^6 - b^6).$$

<u>Notice</u>: The r-limits are given by the equations of the two spheres bounding the region of integration. Converting $x^2 + y^2 + z^2 = 2bz$ to spherical polar coordinates gives $r^2 = 2br\cos\theta$, i.e. $r = 2b\cos\theta$.

<u>EXAMPLES TO DO:</u> Pages 30-31: Exs. 3(e)-(g), 4, 5, 9, 10.

25. AN INTERPRETATION OF TRIPLE INTEGRALS

Think of a solid V of non-uniform density in three dimensional space, the density at the point (x,y,z) being $f(x,y,z)$. Take a small part of V in the form of a cuboid of sides δx, δy, δz at the point (x,y,z). The mass of this cuboid is approximately

$$f(x,y,z) \, \delta x \delta y \delta z \, ,$$

and the mass of the whole solid is effectively the sum of

the contributions from all such cuboids in V. In the
limit this sum becomes a triple integral so that the mass
of the whole solid V is

$$\iiint_V f(x,y,z) \, dxdydz.$$

EXAMPLES TO DO: Page 31: Ex. 11.

26. CALCULATING VOLUMES BY TRIPLE INTEGRATION

According to §25 the integral

$$\iiint_R 1 \, dxdydz,$$

where R is a region in three dimensional space gives the
mass of a solid in the shape of the region R and of
uniform density one unit. Numerically the value of the
integral is therefore equal to the volume of the region R.
So we see that

$$\text{volume of region } R = \iiint_R 1 \, dxdydz.$$

(Compare $\iint_A 1 \, dxdy$ in §9.)

EXAMPLES TO DO: Page 31: Ex. 6.

27. MAKING A GENERAL CHANGE OF VARIABLES IN A TRIPLE INTEGRAL

This corresponds to the situation for double
integrals in §14. We change from x, y, z to u, v, w,
where u, v, w are independent functions of x, y, z in
the sense of §108. Under these circumstances and for
suitably well behaved functions f, the rule is:

RULE:
$$\iiint_R f(x,y,z) \, dxdydz = \iiint_S F(u,v,w) \left| \frac{\partial(x,y,z)}{\partial(u,v,w)} \right| dudvdw,$$

where F(u,v,w) is derived by substituting for x, y, z
in f in terms of u, v, w, and S is the region in
uvw-space corresponding to R in xyz-space. (For
details of the Jacobian on the right-hand side see §107.)

N.B. It is the modulus of the Jacobian that is used.

EXAMPLE. Use the rule above to confirm the rule given
in §22 for changing from x, y, z coordinates to
spherical polar coordinates.

<u>Solution.</u>   We have that

$$x = r \sin \theta \cos \phi , \quad y = r \sin \theta \sin \phi , \quad z = r \cos \theta.$$

So

$$\frac{\partial (x,y,z)}{\partial (r,\theta,\phi)} = \begin{vmatrix} \sin \theta \cos \phi & r \cos \theta \cos \phi & -r \sin \theta \sin \phi \\ \sin \theta \sin \phi & r \cos \theta \sin \phi & r \sin \theta \cos \phi \\ \cos \theta & -r \sin \theta & 0 \end{vmatrix}$$

$$= \cos \theta [r^2 \sin \theta \cos \theta (\cos^2 \phi + \sin^2 \phi)]$$
$$+ r \sin \theta [r \sin^2 \theta (\cos^2 \phi + \sin^2 \phi)]$$

$$\text{(on expanding by the last row)}$$

$$= r^2 \sin \theta (\cos^2 \theta + \sin^2 \theta) = r^2 \sin \theta.$$

Substituting this factor for the Jacobian in the above rule confirms the rule given in §22.

28. <u>EXAMPLE</u>.   Evaluate

$$\iiint_R (x^2 + y^2 + z^2) \, dxdydz ,$$

where   R   is the solid ellipsoid given by $(x/a)^2 + (y/b)^2 + (z/c)^2 \le 1$.

<u>Solution.</u>   Make the change of variables $x = au, \quad y = bv, \quad z = cw.$ So

$$\frac{\partial (x,y,z)}{\partial (u,v,w)} = \begin{vmatrix} a & 0 & 0 \\ 0 & b & 0 \\ 0 & 0 & c \end{vmatrix} = abc.$$

So, by the rule of §27,

$$I = \iiint_S (a^2 u^2 + b^2 v^2 + c^2 w^2) abc \, dudvdw,$$

where   S   is given by substituting for x,y,z   in the equation of the ellipsoid, i.e.   S   is the solid sphere given by $u^2 + v^2 + w^2 \le 1,$

$$= abc (a^2 + b^2 + c^2) \iiint_S w^2 \, dudvdw$$

(on using the symmetry of the sphere as in Ex.2.4 at the end of this chapter)

$$= \frac{4 \pi abc}{15} (a^2 + b^2 + c^2) , \quad \text{(on evaluation using spherical polars).}$$

<u>EXAMPLES TO DO</u>:   Page 31:   Exs. 12, 13.

29. CYLINDRICAL POLAR COORDINATES

The point P in three dimensional space with Cartesian coordinates (x,y,z) has cylindrical polar coordinates (ρ,ϕ,z) given by

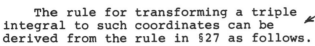

$$x = \rho \cos \phi, \quad y = \rho \sin \phi, \quad z = z.$$

The diagram shows ρ and ϕ .

The rule for transforming a triple integral to such coordinates can be derived from the rule in §27 as follows.

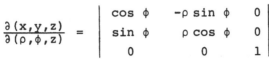

$$\frac{\partial(x,y,z)}{\partial(\rho,\phi,z)} = \begin{vmatrix} \cos \phi & -\rho \sin \phi & 0 \\ \sin \phi & \rho \cos \phi & 0 \\ 0 & 0 & 1 \end{vmatrix}$$

$$= \rho(\cos^2 \phi + \sin^2 \phi) = \rho.$$

So $\iiint f(x,y,z) \, dxdydz$

$$= \iiint f(\rho \cos \phi, \rho \sin \phi, z) \, \rho \, d\rho d\phi dz.$$

30. THE MEAN VALUE OF A FUNCTION THROUGHOUT A THREE DIMENSIONAL REGION

Definition.   The mean value of the function f (of three variables) throughout a three dimensional region V is defined to be

$$\frac{1}{\text{volume of } V} \times \iiint_V f(x,y,z) \, dxdydz.$$

A case in point is the calculation of the mean density (average density) of a solid sphere whose density varies from point to point.

EXAMPLE.   A solid sphere $x^2 + y^2 + z^2 \leq a^2$ has density $\sqrt{(x^2 + y^2)}$ at the point (x,y,z) .   Calculate its average density.

Solution.   The mass of the sphere (§25) is given by $\iiint_V \sqrt{(x^2 + y^2)} \, dxdydz$

$$= \iiint_V \sqrt{(r^2\sin^2\theta \cos^2\phi + r^2\sin^2\theta \sin^2\phi)}.r^2\sin\theta \, d\phi d\theta dr$$

$$= \iiint r^3\sin^2\theta \, d\phi d\theta dr \quad \text{(throughout the sphere)}$$

$$= \int_0^{2\pi} d\phi \int_0^{\pi} \sin^2\theta \, d\theta \int_0^a r^3 \, dr = \pi^2 a^4/4.$$

So average density = mass/volume $= (\pi^2 a^4/4)/(4\pi a^3/3) = 3\pi a/16.$

EXAMPLES TO DO: Page 31:   Exs. 7, 8, 14, 15.

31. FINDING THE CENTRE OF GRAVITY OF A SOLID

The method resembles that for a lamina in §18 except that here we consider a small cuboid of mass δm and of sides δx, δy, δz instead of the small rectangle of mass δm and of sides δx, δy, and we do triple integration instead of double integration. Many cases can of course be treated by more elementary methods.

EXAMPLES TO DO: Page 32: Exs. 16, 17.

32. FINDING THE MOMENT OF INERTIA OF A SOLID

The method illustrated in the example below resembles that for a lamina in §19 except that here cuboids replace rectangles and triple integration replaces double integration. Many cases can be treated by more elementary methods given in books on Dynamics.

EXAMPLE. A solid sphere V of mass M has uniform density ρ and radius a. Find its moment of inertia about a diameter.

Solution. Take the sphere as $x^2 + y^2 + z^2 \leq a^2$ and take the axis of rotation as the z-axis. A typical small cuboid of mass δm and at the point (x,y,z) contributes $b^2 \delta m$ to the moment of inertia (M.I.), where b is the distance from (x,y,z) to the z-axis in this case, i.e. $b^2 = x^2 + y^2$. So

$$\text{M.I.} = \Sigma(x^2 + y^2)\, \delta m = \Sigma(x^2 + y^2)\, \rho\, \delta x \delta y \delta z$$

$$= \iiint_V (x^2 + y^2)\, \rho\, dx dy dz$$

$$= \iiint_V r^2\sin^2\theta \,.\, r^2 \sin\theta \,.\, \rho\, d\phi d\theta dr$$

$$= \rho \int_0^{2\pi} d\phi \int_0^{\pi} d\theta \int_0^a r^4 \sin^3\theta\, dr$$

$$= 2\pi\rho \,.\, \frac{2.2}{3} \,.\, a^5/5 = (4\pi a^3/3)\rho \,.\, 2a^2/5 = 2Ma^2/5 \,.$$

Notice: This method will find the moment of inertia of certain solids of variable density, e.g. Ex.2.19.

EXAMPLES TO DO: Page 32: Exs. 18 - 20.

EXAMPLES 2

(In these examples a, b, c are positive constants.)

1.   In each of the following cases, evaluate the triple integral over the region R given:

(a) $\iiint yz^2\,dxdydz$ where R is the solid cube given by $0 \le x \le 1$, $0 \le y \le 1$, $0 \le z \le 1$;

(b) $\iiint y\,dxdydz$ where R is the tetrahedron given by $x \ge 0$, $y \ge 0$, $z \ge 0$ and $x+y+z \le 1$;

(c) $\iiint xy\,dxdydz$ where R is the region enclosed by the five planes $x = 0$, $x = 1$, $y = 0$, $z = 0$ and $y+z = 1$.

2.   The tetrahedron OABC has its vertices at $(0,0,0)$, $(a,0,0)$, $(0,b,0)$ and $(0,0,c)$.   Show that the equation of the plane ABC is $(x/a)+(y/b)+(z/c) = 1$ and use triple integration to show that the volume of this tetrahedron is $(abc)/6$.

3.   Use spherical polar coordinates in each of the following cases to evaluate the triple integral over the region R given:

(a) $\iiint z^2\,dxdydz$ where R is the part of the sphere $x^2+y^2+z^2 \le a^2$ in the first octant;

(b) $\iiint \sqrt{(x^2+y^2+z^2)}\,dxdydz$ where R is the part of the sphere $x^2+y^2+z^2 \le a^2$ in the first octant;

(c) $\iiint (x^2+y^2+z^2)^{-2}\,dxdydz$ where R is the region in the first octant outside the sphere $x^2+y^2+z^2 = 1$;

(d) $\iiint \sqrt{(x^2+y^2+z^2)}\,e^{-(x^2+y^2+z^2)}\,dxdydz$ where R is the interior of the unit sphere;

(e) $\iiint \dfrac{z}{\sqrt{(x^2+y^2+z^2)}}\,dxdydz$ where R is the interior of the sphere $x^2+y^2+z^2 = 2z$;

(f)   the same integrand as in (e) but where R is the volume enclosed by the sphere $x^2+y^2+z^2 = 2z$ and which lies above the plane $z = 1$;

(g) $\iiint \sqrt{(x^2+y^2+z^2)}\,dxdydz$ where R is the region which lies inside the sphere $x^2+y^2+z^2 = 2az$ but outside the sphere $x^2+y^2+z^2 = a^2$.

4.   Explain why the values of $\iiint x^2\,dxdydz$, $\iiint y^2\,dxdydz$ and $\iiint z^2\,dxdydz$ throughout the sphere $x^2+y^2+z^2 \le a^2$ are all equal.

5.   Show that $\iiint z\,dxdydz = 0$, where the integration is done throughout the solid sphere $x^2 + y^2 + z^2 \leq a^2$. Generalise this to show that, for every positive integer n,

$$\iiint z^{2n-1}\,dxdydz = 0,$$

where the integration is done throughout this sphere.

6.   Find the volume of the part of the sphere $x^2 + y^2 + z^2 \leq a^2$ that lies inside the cylinder $x^2 + y^2 = b^2$, where b < a.

7.   Show that the mean value of $\sqrt{(x^2 + y^2 + z^2)}$ throughout the sphere $x^2 + y^2 + z^2 \leq a^2$ is 3a/4.

8.   Let B be a fixed point on the surface of a solid sphere of radius a and let K be a variable point of the sphere.   Show that the mean distance BK as K moves throughout the sphere is 6a/5.   [Think carefully about how to choose your origin and sphere before starting.]

9.   Show that the point (1,0,1) lies on the cone $x^2 + y^2 = z^2$ and hence show that the cone has semi-vertical angle 45° and vertex at O and axis along the z-axis.   Show that

$$\iiint_V z^2\,dxdydz = \pi a^5 (4 - \sqrt{2})/30 ,$$

where V is the region which lies inside the cone and inside the hemisphere given by $z \geq 0$ and $x^2 + y^2 + z^2 \leq a^2$.

10.   Show that $\iiint (x^2 + y^2)\,dxdydz = 256\pi/15$, where the region of integration is the interior of the sphere $x^2 + y^2 + z^2 = 4z$.

11.   The hemisphere $x^2 + y^2 + z^2 \leq a^2$, $z \geq 0$ has density z at the point (x,y,z).   Find its mass.

12.   Show that the volume of the ellipsoid $(x/a)^2 + (y/b)^2 + (z/c)^2 \leq 1$ is $4\pi abc/3$.   (Compare $4\pi a^3/3$ for a sphere of radius a.)

13.   Evaluate $\iiint z\,dxdydz$ throughout the part of the ellipsoid $(x/a)^2 + (y/b)^2 + (z/c)^2 \leq 1$ in the first octant.

14.   Show that the mean value of $(x^2 + y^2 + z^2)$ throughout the interior of the ellipsoid in Ex.12 is $(a^2 + b^2 + c^2)/5$.

15.   Find the mean value of z throughout the region enclosed within the cone $x^2 + y^2 = z^2$ between the planes z = 1 and z = 2.   [See Ex.9 above for the geometry of the cone.   Recall that the volume of a right circular cone of height h and base radius r is $\pi r^2 h/3$.]

16. A mountain of uniform density is in the shape of the paraboloid $z = 4 - x^2 - y^2$, $z \geq 0$. Find the height of its centre of gravity. [This type of calculation may be relevant to the type of experiment done by Maskeylene in Perthshire in 1774. He tried to calculate the gravitational constant G from the deflection of a pendulum in the vicinity of the mountain Schiehallion.]

17. Find the position of the centre of gravity of a solid hemisphere of radius a and of uniform density.

18. Show that the moment of inertia of a homogeneous solid cube of mass M and of side a is

(i) $2Ma^2/3$ about an edge,
(ii) $Ma^2/6$ about the line joining the central points of two opposite faces.

19. A solid sphere of mass M and radius a has density r at points at distance r from its centre. Show that $M = \pi a^4$. Show also that the moment of inertia of this sphere of variable density about a diameter is $4Ma^2/9$.

20. Show that the moment of inertia of a homogeneous solid sphere of mass M and radius a about a tangent is $7Ma^2/5$. [Take the sphere as $x^2 + y^2 + z^2 = 2az$ and the tangent as the x-axis.]

21. Let A be a 3×3 positive definite matrix (with real entries) and let x be a 3×1 vector. The equation $x^T A x = 1$ then represents an ellipsoid in three dimensional space. From linear algebra there exists a real orthogonal matrix P such that $P^T A P = D$, where D is a diagonal matrix with positive entries. By making the change of variables $x = Py$, show that the volume of the ellipsoid is $4\pi/(3\sqrt{(\det A)})$. [Note that we have used the superscript T to denote the transpose.]

III.   BETA AND GAMMA FUNCTIONS

---

33.   DEFINITIONS OF THESE FUNCTIONS AS INTEGRALS

The values taken by these two functions are given as the values of the following two integrals:

(i) $B(p,q) = \int_0^1 x^{p-1} (1-x)^{q-1} dx,$ $(p > 0$ and $q > 0)$,

(ii) $\Gamma(k) = \int_0^\infty x^{k-1} e^{-x} dx,$ $(k > 0)$.

Demanding that these integrals exist forces the given restrictions on p, q and k.

The Beta function has two other useful forms:

(iii) $B(p,q) = 2 \int_0^{\frac{1}{2}\pi} \sin^{2p-1} y \cos^{2q-1} y \, dy$,

(iv) $B(p,q) = \int_0^\infty \dfrac{y^{p-1}}{(1+y)^{p+q}} \, dy$.

To get (iii) put $x = \sin^2 y$ in (i).   For (iv) put $x = y/(1+y)$ in (i).

Many integrals in Probability and Statistics in connection with the probability density functions of normal, t, χ^2 and Gamma random variables can be reduced to integrals of the above four types.

34.   PROPERTIES OF THE BETA AND GAMMA FUNCTIONS

A. $\Gamma(1) = 1$, $\Gamma(2) = 1$, $\Gamma(3) = 2$ and in general
   $\Gamma(n) = (n-1)!$ for every positive integer n.

B. $\Gamma(k) = (k-1)\Gamma(k-1)$ for all real numbers $k > 1$.
   Repeated use of this reduces the calculation of $\Gamma(k)$ to that of $\Gamma(k-p)$ where $0 < k-p \le 1$. For example, $\Gamma(\frac{9}{4}) = \frac{5}{4} \cdot \frac{1}{4} \cdot \Gamma(\frac{1}{4})$.

C.   For $0 < k < 1$, $\Gamma(k) \cdot \Gamma(1-k) = \pi/\sin k\pi$.
   For example, $\Gamma(\frac{1}{6}) \cdot \Gamma(\frac{5}{6}) = 2\pi$.

D. $\Gamma(\frac{1}{2}) = \sqrt{\pi}$.   (A special case of C.)

E. $B(p,q) = \dfrac{\Gamma(p)\Gamma(q)}{\Gamma(p+q)}$.

A and B are easily proved with integration by parts, while C, D and E are considerably harder.   E expresses every Beta function in terms of the Gamma function and B expresses every Gamma function in terms of $\Gamma(t)$, where $0 < t \le 1$.   The values of $\Gamma(\frac{1}{4})$ etc are given in tables.

35. In attempting to reduce a given integral to a Beta or Gamma function, decide at the outset which of the four forms in §33 you are aiming for. Then make a change of variables to achieve it. Looking at the limits of integration as well as the integrand can help in deciding what to aim for and in fixing the change of variable.

36. <u>EXAMPLE</u>. Evaluate

$$\text{(a)} \quad \int_0^\infty x^4 e^{-3x} \, dx, \qquad \text{(b)} \quad \int_0^\infty x^2 e^{-\frac{1}{2}x^2} \, dx.$$

<u>Solution</u>. (a) Put $y = 3x$. So $dy = 3\,dx$. Then

$$I = \int_0^\infty (y/3)^4 \, e^{-y} \cdot \tfrac{1}{3}\,dy \; = \; \tfrac{1}{243} \int_0^\infty y^4 e^{-y} \, dy \; = \; \tfrac{1}{243} \, \Gamma(5) \; = \; \tfrac{8}{81} \,.$$

(b) Put $y = \tfrac{1}{2}x^2$, i.e. $x = \sqrt{2}\sqrt{y}$.
So $dx = \sqrt{2} \cdot \tfrac{1}{2} y^{-\frac{1}{2}} \, dy$. It follows then that

$$I = \int_0^\infty 2y \, e^{-y} \cdot \sqrt{2} \cdot \tfrac{1}{2} y^{-\frac{1}{2}} \, dy \; = \; \sqrt{2} \int_0^\infty y^{\frac{1}{2}} e^{-y} \, dy \; = \; \sqrt{2} \, \Gamma(\tfrac{3}{2})$$

$$= \; \sqrt{2} \cdot \tfrac{1}{2} \, \Gamma(\tfrac{1}{2}) \; = \; \tfrac{1}{2} \, \sqrt{(2\pi)} \,.$$

<u>Notice</u>: In each case the impetus for the substitution made is the need to reduce the exponential to the form e^{-y}. It is no use leaving the exponential in such problems as e^{-2y} or e^{-y^2}.

<u>EXAMPLES TO DO</u>: Page 37: Exs. 1(a)-(e).

37. <u>EXAMPLE</u>. Express each of the following as a Beta function and hence evaluate them:

$$\text{(a)} \quad \int_0^1 x^2 \sqrt{(1 - x^2)} \, dx, \qquad \text{(b)} \quad \int_0^2 (2x - x^2)^{\frac{3}{2}} \, dx.$$

<u>Solution</u>. (a) Let $y = x^2$, i.e. $x = \sqrt{y}$.

This gives $dx = \tfrac{1}{2} y^{-\frac{1}{2}} \, dy$. So

$$I = \int_0^1 y \sqrt{(1 - y)} \cdot \tfrac{1}{2} y^{-\frac{1}{2}} \, dy \; = \; \tfrac{1}{2} \int_0^1 y^{\frac{1}{2}} (1 - y)^{\frac{1}{2}} \, dy \; = \; \tfrac{1}{2} B(\tfrac{3}{2}, \tfrac{3}{2})$$

$$= \; \frac{\Gamma(\tfrac{3}{2}) \, \Gamma(\tfrac{3}{2})}{2 \, \Gamma(3)} \; = \; \frac{\tfrac{1}{2}\sqrt{\pi} \cdot \tfrac{1}{2}\sqrt{\pi}}{2.2} \; = \; \frac{\pi}{16} \,.$$

(b) Write it as $\int_0^2 x^{\frac{3}{2}} (2 - x)^{\frac{3}{2}} dx$. Then let $x = 2y$.

This gives $dx = 2\,dy$. So $I = \int_0^1 (2y)^{\frac{3}{2}} (2 - 2y)^{\frac{3}{2}} \cdot 2 \, dy$

$$= 16 \int_0^1 y^{\frac{3}{2}} (1 - y)^{\frac{3}{2}} dy \; = \; 16 \, B(\tfrac{5}{2}, \tfrac{5}{2}) \; = \; 16 \cdot \frac{(3\sqrt{\pi}/4)^2}{4!} \; = \; \frac{3\pi}{8} \,.$$

<u>Notice</u>:   The impetus for each substitution is the need to produce a factor of the form $(1 - y)^k$ for the Beta function.   Other forms like $(1 - y^2)^k$ are unacceptable. In (b) the substitution is suggested by needing $(2 - x)$ equal to $(2 - 2y)$ so that the factor   2   can be taken out to leave the factor $(1 - y)$ needed for the Beta function.

<u>EXAMPLES TO DO</u>:   Pages 37-38:   Exs. 1(f)-(m).

38.   <u>EXAMPLE</u>.   Evaluate

$$I = \int_0^\infty \frac{\sqrt{y}}{16 + y^2}\, dy.$$

<u>Solution</u>.   We aim for form (iv) of §33.   The idea is to make $(16 + y^2)$ into $16(1 + u)$.   So let $y^2 = 16u$, i.e. $y = 4\sqrt{u}$.   So $dy = 2u^{-\frac{1}{2}} du$.   Then,

$$I = \int_0^\infty \frac{2u^{\frac{1}{4}} \cdot 2u^{-\frac{1}{2}}}{16 + 16u}\, du \;=\; \frac{1}{4}\int_0^\infty \frac{u^{-\frac{1}{4}}}{1 + u}\, du \;=\; \frac{1}{4}\, B(\tfrac{3}{4}, \tfrac{1}{4})\quad [\S33(iv)]$$

$$= \frac{1}{4}\, \Gamma(\tfrac{1}{4}) \cdot \Gamma(\tfrac{3}{4}) = \pi\sqrt{2}/4 \qquad \text{(from §34C).}$$

<u>EXAMPLES TO DO</u>:   Pages 38-39:   Exs. 1(n)-(s), 4 - 7.

39.   From the properties of the Beta and Gamma functions the following rule can be derived concerning the integral (iii)   of §33.

<u>RESULT</u>.   For non-negative integers   m   and   n,

$$\int_0^{\frac{1}{2}\pi} \sin^m x\, \cos^n x\, dx \;=\; \frac{(m-1)(m-3)\ldots (n-1)(n-3)\ldots}{(m+n)(m+n-2)(m+n-4)\ldots} \cdot K$$

where   K = 1   unless   m   and   n   are   both even in which case $K = \frac{1}{2}\pi$.   The dots in the product indicate that the factors continue until   1   or   2   is reached.   If   m = 0 or   m = 1,   none of the factors   (m-1), (m-3)   appears etc.

<u>EXAMPLE</u>. $\displaystyle\int_0^{\frac{1}{2}\pi} \sin^3 x \cos^6 x\, dx \;=\; \frac{2.5.3.1}{9.7.5.3.1} = \frac{2}{63}$.

$$\int_0^{\frac{1}{2}\pi} \cos^6 x\, dx \;=\; \frac{5.3.1}{6.4.2} \cdot \tfrac{1}{2}\pi \;=\; \frac{5\pi}{32}\ .$$

40.   The graphs of   sin x,   cos x,   sin²x,   cos²x   are shown on page 36.   If we recall that a definite integral calculates the area under a curve and that areas

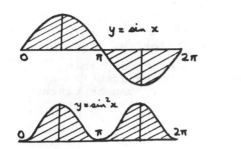

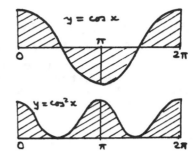

below the x-axis count as negative, we can see from the
graphs that

$$\int_0^\pi \sin x \, dx = 2 \int_0^{\frac{1}{2}\pi} \sin x \, dx; \qquad \int_0^{2\pi} \sin x \, dx = 0.$$

$$\int_0^\pi \cos x \, dx = 0; \qquad \int_0^{2\pi} \cos x \, dx = 0.$$

$$\int_0^\pi \sin^2 x \, dx = 2 \int_0^{\frac{1}{2}\pi} \sin^2 x \, dx; \quad \int_0^{2\pi} \sin^2 x \, dx = 4 \int_0^{\frac{1}{2}\pi} \sin^2 x \, dx.$$

$$\int_0^\pi \cos^2 x \, dx = 2 \int_0^{\frac{1}{2}\pi} \cos^2 x \, dx; \quad \int_0^{2\pi} \cos^2 x \, dx = 4 \int_0^{\frac{1}{2}\pi} \cos^2 x \, dx.$$

In such integrals because of relations like
$\sin(\pi - x) = \sin x$, $\sin(\pi + x) = -\sin x$, $\cos(\pi - x) = -\cos x$, $\cos(\pi + x) = -\cos x$, it follows that the area
under any of these curves in any of the intervals
$[\frac{1}{2}\pi, \pi]$, $[\pi, \frac{3}{2}\pi]$, $[\frac{3}{2}\pi, 2\pi]$ is plus or minus the area
under the curve between 0 and $\frac{1}{2}\pi$. So, for example,
to calculate the integral on $[0, 2\pi]$, you need only
decide the <u>sign</u> of the integrand on each of the four
subintervals of length $\frac{1}{2}\pi$, counting $+1$ for a positive
sign and -1 for a negative sign. The total count,
(e.g. $+1 + 1 - 1 - 1$ for $\sin x$), gives the required
multiple of the integral on the interval $[0, \frac{1}{2}\pi]$.

Similar considerations apply to integrals where the
integrand is of the form $\sin^m x \cos^n x$, where m and n
are non-negative integers, as the following example
illustrates.

<u>EXAMPLE</u>. Evaluate

(a) $I = \int_0^\pi \sin^3 x \cos^4 x \, dx$, (b) $J = \int_0^\pi \sin^3 x \cos^5 x \, dx$,

(c) $K = \int_0^{2\pi} \sin^3 x \cos^2 x \, dx$, (d) $L = \int_0^{2\pi} \sin^2 x \cos^4 x \, dx$.

<u>Solution</u>. In each case we make a table of sign first.

(a)

Quadrant	1	2
$\sin^3 x$	+	+
$\cos^4 x$	+	+
$\sin^3 x \cos^4 x$	+	+
<u>TOTAL</u> = +2		

So $I = 2 \int_0^{\frac{1}{2}\pi} \sin^3 x \cos^4 x \, dx$

$$= 2 . \frac{2.3.1}{7.5.3.1} = \frac{4}{35}.$$

(b) <u>Quadrant</u>   1   2   So J = 0.

$\sin^3 x$ +   +
$\cos^5 x$ +   −
$\sin^3 x \cos^5 x$ +   −

<u>TOTAL</u> = 0

(c) <u>Quadrant</u>   1   2   3   4

$\sin^3 x$ +   +   −   −   So K = 0.
$\cos^2 x$ +   +   +   +
$\sin^3 x \cos^2 x$ +   +   −   −

<u>TOTAL</u> = 0

(d) <u>Quadrant</u>   1   2   3   4   So,

$\sin^2 x$ +   +   +   + $L = 4\int_0^{\frac{1}{2}\pi} \sin^2 x \cos^4 x \, dx$
$\cos^4 x$ +   +   +   +
$\sin^2 x \cos^4 x$ +   +   +   + $= 4 \cdot \dfrac{1.3.1}{6.4.2} \cdot \tfrac{1}{2}\pi = \dfrac{\pi}{8}$.

<u>TOTAL</u> = 4

<u>EXAMPLES TO DO</u>:   Page 38: Exs. 2, 3.

41. THE DUPLICATION FORMULA

This is in general less useful than A, B, C, D, E
of §34.   It states that, for p > 0,

$$\Gamma(2p) \cdot \Gamma(\tfrac{1}{2}) = 2^{2p-1} \, \Gamma(p) \cdot \Gamma(p+\tfrac{1}{2}) .$$

We do not prove it here.

EXAMPLES 3
(In these examples a, m, n denote positive numbers.)

1.   Show that each of the following integrals has the
value stated by expressing it in terms of Beta or Gamma
functions:

(a) $\int_0^\infty x e^{-2x} \, dx = \tfrac{1}{4}$,   (b) $\int_0^\infty \sqrt{x} \, e^{-2x} \, dx = \dfrac{\sqrt{(2\pi)}}{8}$,

(c) $\int_0^\infty x^4 e^{-ax} \, dx = 24/a^5$,   (d) $\int_{-\infty}^\infty e^{-\frac{1}{2}x^2} \, dx = \sqrt{(2\pi)}$,

(e) $\int_0^\infty x^2 e^{-ax^2} \, dx = \sqrt{\pi}/(4a^{3/2})$,   (f) $\int_0^4 x \sqrt{(4-x)} \, dx = \dfrac{128}{15}$,

(g) $\int_0^1 \dfrac{\sqrt{x}}{\sqrt{(1-x)}} \, dx = \tfrac{1}{2}\pi$,   (h) $\int_0^1 \dfrac{x^3}{\sqrt{(1-x^2)}} \, dx = \tfrac{2}{3}$,

(i) $\int_0^2 \dfrac{x}{\sqrt{(2-x)}} \, dx = \dfrac{8\sqrt{2}}{3}$,   (j) $\int_0^1 \dfrac{\sqrt{x}}{\sqrt{(1-x^2)}} \, dx = \dfrac{\sqrt{2}}{\sqrt{\pi}} (\Gamma(\tfrac{3}{4}))^2$,

(k) $\int_0^2 \sqrt{(16x^2 - x^6)}\ dx = 2\pi,$ (l) $\int_0^2 (4 - x^2)^{3/2}\ dx = 3\pi,$

(m) $\int_0^1 \dfrac{dx}{\sqrt{(1 - x^4)}} = \dfrac{(\Gamma(\frac{1}{4}))^2}{4\ \sqrt{(2\pi)}},$ (n) $\int_0^\infty \dfrac{dx}{1 + x^4} = \dfrac{\pi\sqrt{2}}{4},$

(o) $\int_0^\infty \dfrac{dx}{(1 + x^3)^2} = \dfrac{4\pi\sqrt{3}}{27},$ (p) $\int_0^\infty \dfrac{dx}{(2 + x^2)^2} = \dfrac{\pi\sqrt{2}}{16},$

(q) $\int_{-\infty}^\infty \dfrac{x^2}{1 + x^4}\ dx = \dfrac{\pi\sqrt{2}}{2},$ (r) $\int_0^\infty \dfrac{x^3}{(1 + 8x^3)^2}\ dx = \dfrac{\pi\sqrt{3}}{216},$

(s) $\int_{-\infty}^\infty \dfrac{x}{1 + x^4}\ dx = 0.$

2. Evaluate the following:

(a) $\int_0^{\frac{1}{2}\pi} \sin^3 x\ \cos^2 x\ dx,$ (b) $\int_0^{\frac{1}{2}\pi} \sin^7 x\ \cos^3 x\ dx,$

(c) $\int_0^{\frac{1}{2}\pi} \sin^4 x\ \cos^2 x\ dx,$ (d) $\int_0^{\frac{1}{2}\pi} \sin^7 x\ dx,$

(e) $\int_0^{\frac{1}{2}\pi} \cos^6 x\ dx,$ (f) $\int_0^{\frac{1}{2}\pi} (\sin x)^{3/2} (\cos x)^{1/2}\ dx,$

(g) $\int_0^{\frac{1}{2}\pi} \sqrt{(\tan x)}\ dx.$

3. Evaluate the following:

(a) $\int_0^\pi \sin^5 x\ dx,$ (b) $\int_0^\pi \cos^5 x\ dx,$ (c) $\int_0^\pi \sin^6 x\ dx,$

(d) $\int_0^\pi \cos^6 x\ dx,$ (e) $\int_0^\pi \sin^2 x\ \cos^3 x\ dx,$

(f) $\int_0^\pi \sin^3 x\ \cos^2 x\ dx,$ (g) $\int_0^\pi \sin^4 x\ \cos^4 x\ dx,$

(h) $\int_0^{2\pi} \cos^4 x\ dx,$ (i) $\int_0^{2\pi} \sin^3 x\ \cos^2 x\ dx,$

(j) $\int_0^{2\pi} \sin^4 x\ \cos^3 x\ dx,$ (k) $\int_0^{2\pi} \sin^2 x\ \cos^6 x\ dx,$

(l) $\int_0^{2\pi} \sin^3 x\ \cos^3 x\ dx.$

4. By making suitable substitutions reduce each of the following to Beta or Gamma functions and hence find their values:

(a) $\int_0^{\frac{1}{2}\pi} \dfrac{\sqrt{(\tan x)}\ dx}{\cos^2 x + 4 \sin^2 x},$ (b) $\int_{-2}^2 \left(\dfrac{2 - x}{2 + x}\right)^{\frac{1}{2}} dx,$

(c) $\int_0^{\frac{1}{2}\pi} \dfrac{\sqrt{(\tan x)}\ dx}{(\cos x + \sin x)^2},$ (d) $\int_1^\infty \dfrac{dx}{x^2\ \sqrt{(x-1)}},$ (e) $\int_1^\infty \dfrac{(\log x)^3}{x^2}\ dx.$

5.   Express the double integral
$$\int_0^1 dx \int_0^{1-x} xy(1-x-y)^{\frac{1}{2}} \, dy$$
in terms of the Beta function and hence evaluate it.

6.   Show that
$$\int_0^\infty \frac{x^{2m-1} \, dx}{(1+x^2)^{m+n}} = \tfrac{1}{2} B(m,n).$$

7.   Show that the volume of the region given by the inequalities $x \geq 0$, $y \geq 0$, $z \geq 0$, $x^3 + y^3 + z^3 \leq 1$,

is $\frac{1}{27}(\Gamma(\tfrac{1}{3}))^3$.

8.   (The mean and variance of the Normal Distribution) Using the properties of the Gamma function show that
$$\int_{-\infty}^\infty \frac{x}{\sqrt{(2\pi)}\sigma} \, e^{-(x-\mu)^2/2\sigma^2} \, dx = \mu, \quad \int_{-\infty}^\infty \frac{(x-\mu)^2}{\sqrt{(2\pi)}\sigma} \, e^{-(x-\mu)^2/2\sigma^2} \, dx = \sigma^2,$$

where μ and σ are constants with $\sigma > 0$.   (These show that the Normal Distribution $N(\mu, \sigma^2)$ has expected value μ and variance σ^2.)

IV. DIFFERENTIAL EQUATIONS: FIRST ORDER

---

42. THE IDEA OF A DIFFERENTIAL EQUATION

Equations like

$$y' = 2xy + 1; \quad (y')^2 = y^2 + 1; \quad x^2 y'' + y = e^x,$$

are <u>differential equations</u>: y is an unknown function
of x while y' and y" denote dy/dx and d^2y/dx^2.
The order of the highest derivative appearing in the
equation is the <u>order</u> of the equation, e.g.

$$y'' - y' - 6y = e^{3x}$$

is a <u>second</u> order equation.

A <u>particular solution</u> of a differential equation is a
particular function y which satisfies the equation; in
general any given differential equation has many particular
solutions, e.g. y = 3x + 8,   y = 3x + 34,   y = 3x − 5   are
all particular solutions of the differential equation
y' = 3.

The <u>general solution</u> of the differential equation
includes all its particular solutions and as such it
generally involves arbitrary constants, e.g. y = 3x + C
is the general solution of the differential equation
y' = 3 mentioned above.   <u>Solving</u> a differential
equation means finding its general solution.

The behaviour of many biological, physical, dynamical
and electrical systems is governed by differential
equations, e.g. see Exs.4.11 – 4.13.

<u>EXAMPLE</u>.   Verify that, for every value of the real
constant C, the function y given by

$$y(x) = 3x + \frac{C}{1 + x}$$

is a solution of the differential equation

$$(1 + x)y' + y = 6x + 3.$$

<u>Solution</u>.   For the given function y we have

$$y' = 3 - \frac{C}{(1 + x)^2}.$$

So $(1 + x)y' + y = 3(1 + x) - C(1 + x)^{-1} + 3x + C(1 + x)^{-1}$

$$= 6x + 3, \quad \text{as required.}$$

43. SEPARABLE EQUATIONS

<u>EXAMPLE</u>.   Find the general solution of the equation

$$(2y^2 + 1) y' - 2xy = 0.$$

Method. Here it is possible to pull all the factors involving x to one side together with dx and to pull all the factors involving y to the other side together with dy. Each side is then integrated separately.

Solution. Write the given differential equation as

$$\frac{2y^2 + 1}{y} \frac{dy}{dx} = 2x,$$

which gives

$$\left(2y + \frac{1}{y}\right) dy = 2x\, dx.$$

Integrating each side separately then gives

$$\int 2y + \frac{1}{y}\, dy = \int 2x\, dx,$$

i.e. $y^2 + \log y = x^2 + C,$ ...(*)

where C is an arbitrary constant. This is the general solution required.

Notice: (i) This example illustrates that it may <u>not</u> always be possible to find an explicit solution of the form y = g(x). In such cases we have to be content with a general solution in which y is defined implicitly as a function of x, as in (*).

(ii) The general solution (*) in the above example can be rearranged by taking exponentials to give

$$e^{y^2} \cdot e^{\log y} = e^{x^2} \cdot e^{C},$$

i.e. $y\, e^{y^2} = K e^{x^2},$ where K is a constant,

i.e. $y\, e^{y^2 - x^2} = K,$ where K is a constant.

This is another form of the general solution. In tackling problems notice that your answer may look different from a given answer because of such rearrangements.

EXAMPLES TO DO: Page 48: Ex. 1.

44. HOMOGENEOUS EQUATIONS

EXAMPLE. Find the general solution of the differential equation

$$2xy\, y' - y^2 = x^2.$$

Method. Rewrite the equation as y' = f(x,y). Then put y = vx, where v is an unknown function of x. A homogeneous equation then becomes a separable equation in v and x, which can be solved as in §43.

Solution. Rearrangement of the given equation gives

$$\frac{dy}{dx} = \frac{x^2 + y^2}{2xy} \; .$$

Setting $y = vx$ gives

$$\frac{dy}{dx} = v + x\frac{dv}{dx} \quad \text{and} \quad \frac{x^2 + y^2}{2xy} = \frac{x^2 + x^2 v^2}{2x^2 v} \; .$$

So the given differential equation becomes

$$v + x\frac{dv}{dx} = \frac{1 + v^2}{2v} \; ,$$

$$\text{i.e.} \quad x\frac{dv}{dx} = \frac{1 - v^2}{2v} \; .$$

This is now a separable equation.   So

$$\int \frac{2v}{1 - v^2}\, dv = \int \frac{1}{x}\, dx \; ,$$

i.e. $-\log(1 - v^2) = \log x + \log C, \quad$ say,

i.e. $\log(1/(1 - v^2)) = \log Cx.$

So $Cx(1 - v^2) = 1, \quad$ i.e. $Cx(1 - (y/x)^2) = 1,$

i.e. $C(x^2 - y^2) = x.$

This is the general solution, with C as arbitrary constant.

Notice: (i)   To decide whether a given equation is homogeneous, rewrite it in the form $y' = f(x,y)$.   Theory then says that the equation is homogeneous if and only if $f(tx,ty) = f(x,y)$ for every real number t. In practice, however, many equations can be instantly recognised as homogeneous because

$$f(x,y) = \frac{g(x,y)}{h(x,y)} \; ,$$

where $g(x,y)$ and $h(x,y)$ consist entirely of terms of the same combined degree.   For example, in the above problem, $g(x,y) = x^2 + y^2$ and $h(x,y) = 2xy$, in which case all the terms are of degree 2.   Similarly the equation would be homogeneous if

$f(x,y) = (x^3 + 6xy^2)/(2x^2 y + x^3)$ [all terms of degree 3],

but not if

$f(x,y) = (x^2 + 3y)/(xy + 4y^2)$ [the term $3y$ debars it].

(ii)   The equation in the above example is not separable.

EXAMPLES TO DO: Page 48: Ex. 2.

45.   LINEAR EQUATIONS (FIRST ORDER)

EXAMPLE.   Find the general solution of the differential equation

$$(x^2 + 1)y' + xy = x(x^2 + 1).$$

Method.   Rewrite the equation in the form

$$\frac{dy}{dx} + P(x) y = Q(x), \qquad \ldots (1)$$

i.e. reduce the coefficient of dy/dx to 1.   Then multiply through in (1) by the <u>integrating factor</u> G(x) given by

$$G(x) = e^{\int P(x) \, dx}.$$

The differential equation then becomes

$$\frac{d}{dx} (y \, G(x)) = Q(x) G(x),$$

for which both sides can be integrated with respect to x. This gives the general solution.

Solution.   Rewrite the given equation as

$$\frac{dy}{dx} + \frac{x}{x^2 + 1} y = x. \qquad \ldots (2)$$

So in the notation of the method $P(x) = \frac{x}{x^2 + 1}$ and

$$\int P(x) \, dx = \int \frac{x}{x^2 + 1} \, dx = \tfrac{1}{2} \log (x^2 + 1) = \log \sqrt{(x^2 + 1)}.$$

So $G(x) = e^{\log \sqrt{(x^2 + 1)}} = \sqrt{(x^2 + 1)}.$

The equation then becomes

$$\frac{d}{dx} (y \, \sqrt{(x^2 + 1)}) = x \sqrt{(x^2 + 1)}. \qquad \text{[See (i) below.]}$$

Integrating both sides of this with respect to x gives

$$y \, \sqrt{(x^2 + 1)} = \int x \, \sqrt{(x^2 + 1)} \, dx,$$

i.e. $y \, \sqrt{(x^2 + 1)} = \tfrac{1}{3} (x^2 + 1)^{\frac{3}{2}} + C.$

The general solution is therefore

$$y = \tfrac{1}{3} (x^2 + 1) + C (x^2 + 1)^{-\frac{1}{2}}.$$

Notice: (i)   Once the integrating factor has been found as $\sqrt{(x^2 + 1)}$, we can multiply line (2) by it to obtain

$$\sqrt{(x^2 + 1)} \, \frac{dy}{dx} + \frac{x}{\sqrt{(x^2 + 1)}} y = x \sqrt{(x^2 + 1)}. \qquad \ldots (3)$$

Because of the way the theory tells us to calculate the integrating factor, the left-hand side of (3) is <u>automatically</u>

$$\frac{d}{dx} (y \, \sqrt{(x^2 + 1)}),$$

as can be verified using the product rule for different-iation.

There is therefore no need to include line (3) in the

solution: immediately the integrating factor is known
you can write the left-hand side of the equation as

$$\frac{d}{dx}(y \times (\text{integrating factor})) .$$

(ii) The lines (1) in the method and (2) in the solution are in the standard form for linear equations. In
the standard form the coefficient of dy/dx is 1: we had
to divide the given equation by $(x^2 + 1)$ to achieve this
here. It is <u>vital</u> that the equation be in this form
<u>before</u> finding the integrating factor.

(iii) Don't forget to multiply the <u>right</u>-hand side of
the equation by the integrating factor <u>before</u> integrating
both sides.

<u>EXAMPLES TO DO</u>:   Page 48: Ex. 3.

46. HOW TO RECOGNISE THE TYPES OF FIRST ORDER EQUATION: LINEAR, HOMOGENEOUS, SEPARABLE

Of the three types, linear equations may be the
hardest to solve, but they are probably the easiest to
recognise. The following scheme suggests a strategy
for settling the type of a given equation.

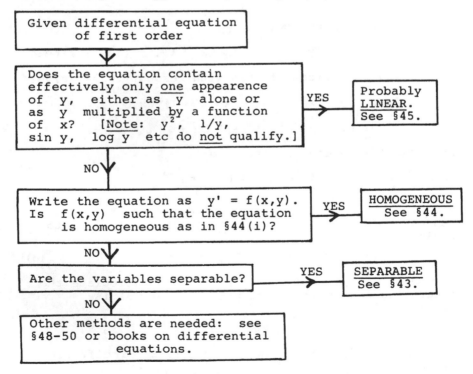

<u>EXAMPLES TO DO</u>:   Pages 48-49: Exs. 4, 5.

47. FINDING A PARTICULAR SOLUTION

EXAMPLE. Find the particular solution of the differential equation

$$y' + y = xe^{-x}$$

which satisfies the condition that $y = 2$ when $x = 0$.

Method. First find the general solution. Then determine the arbitrary constant using the given condition. This gives the particular solution satisfying this condition.

Solution. The given equation is linear with the integrating factor $e^{\int 1 \, dx} = e^x$. So the equation becomes

$$\frac{d}{dx}(y \, e^x) = x \, .$$

So the general solution is

$$ye^x = \tfrac{1}{2}x^2 + C$$

Now the given condition means that $y = 2$ when $x = 0$,

i.e. we need $2 = 0 + C$, i.e. $C = 2$.

So the particular solution satisfying the given condition

is $ye^x = \tfrac{1}{2}x^2 + 2$, i.e. $y = \tfrac{1}{2}e^{-x}(x^2 + 4)$.

Notice: In many real life situations, e.g. in Dynamics or in the theory of alternating current, a physical system is governed by a differential equation. Think of y as a function of time t. In Dynamics $y(t)$ might represent displacement from some origin at time t, while in alternating current $y(t)$ might represent the current flowing at time t. In both cases y varies as t varies. If we are given initial conditions (i.e. conditions which specify the value of y at some point in time, e.g. for $t = 0$) in addition to the differential equation governing the system, then substitution of these conditions in the general solution settles the value of the arbitrary constant. This gives that <u>particular</u> solution (i.e. y as a function of t) which fits the given initial conditions. This is the solution of the given <u>initial</u> <u>value problem</u>.

EXAMPLES TO DO: Pages 49-50: Ex. 6, 11-13.

48. EXAMPLE. Find the general solution of the differential equation

$$y' = \frac{4x + 10y + 2}{10x + y + 29} \, .$$

Method. This is a standard type of equation which as it stands is neither separable, homogeneous nor linear. It can however be made into a homogeneous equation by shifting the origin of coordinates to the point of intersection of the lines $4x + 10y + 2 = 0$ and $10x + y + 29 = 0$.

Solution.   Solve the equations

$$4x + 10y + 2 = 0 \quad \text{and} \quad 10x + y + 29 = 0$$

to see that these lines intersect at the point $(-3, 1)$.
Then let $\quad X = x + 3 \quad$ and $\quad Y = y - 1$,

i.e. $x = X - 3 \quad$ and $\quad y = Y + 1$.

The differential equation then (see (i) below) becomes

$$\frac{dY}{dX} = \frac{4(X - 3) + 10(Y + 1) + 2}{10(X - 3) + (Y + 1) + 29},$$

i.e. $\dfrac{dY}{dX} = \dfrac{4X + 10Y}{10X + Y}.$

This is now homogeneous (§44) and we put $Y = VX$.   So

$$V + X\frac{dV}{dX} = \frac{4X + 10VX}{10X + VX},$$

which gives

$$X\frac{dV}{dX} = \frac{4 - V^2}{10 + V}.$$

So

$$\int \frac{10 + V}{4 - V^2}\, dV = \int \frac{1}{X}\, dX,$$

i.e. $\displaystyle \int \frac{3}{2 - V} + \frac{2}{2 + V}\, dV = \int \frac{1}{X}\, dX,$

which on integration gives

$$(2 + V)^2 = CX(2 - V)^3.$$

Now substitute $V = Y/X$ and simplify to obtain

$$(2X + Y)^2 = C(2X - Y)^3,$$

i.e. $(2x + y + 5)^2 = C(2x - y + 7)^3,$

which is the general solution.

Notice: (i) To see that $dY/dX = dy/dx$ in the above example, suppose that $y = g(x)$.   Then $Y + 1 = g(X - 3)$. Differentiating this gives

$$\frac{dY}{dX} = g'(X - 3) = g'(x) = \frac{dy}{dx}.$$

  (ii) Look also at Ex. 4.8 which illustrates what to do in this type of problem when the two lines are parallel so that no point of intersection can be found.

EXAMPLES TO DO: Page 49: Exs. 7, 8.

49. REDUCTION OF ORDER FOR SECOND ORDER EQUATIONS WITH Y ABSENT

EXAMPLE.   Find the general solution of the equation

$$(1 + x^2)y'' - 2xy' = 60x(1 + x^2)^2.$$

Method.   Notice that this is actually a <u>second</u> order
equation.   Moreover y itself does not appear, though
its derivatives do.   The substitution y' = w reduces
such an equation to a <u>first</u> order equation which may be
amenable to the foregoing methods of solution.

Solution.   Put y' = w, so that y" = w'.   The given
equation then becomes

$$(1 + x^2)w' - 2xw = 60x(1 + x^2)^2,$$

$$\text{i.e.}\quad \frac{dw}{dx} - \frac{2x}{1 + x^2}w = 60x(1 + x^2),$$

which is linear with the integrating factor

$$e^{-\log(1 + x^2)} = e^{\log(1/(1 + x^2))} = 1/(1 + x^2).$$

$$\text{So}\quad \frac{d}{dx}\left[\frac{w}{1 + x^2}\right] = 60x,$$

$$\text{i.e.}\quad w/(1 + x^2) = 30x^2 + C,$$

$$\text{i.e.}\quad w = 30x^2(1 + x^2) + C(1 + x^2),$$

$$\text{i.e.}\quad y' = 30x^2 + 30x^4 + C(1 + x^2).$$

So, on integrating in this last line , we have

$$y = 10x^3 + 6x^5 + C(x + \tfrac{1}{3}x^3) + D,$$

where C and D are arbitrary constants.   This is the
general solution.

Notice: It is vital that y be absent from the original
equation for the technique to work.

<u>EXAMPLES TO DO</u>:   Page 49:   Ex. 9.

50.   BERNOULLI EQUATIONS

EXAMPLE.   Find the general solution of the differential
equation

$$y' + \frac{y}{x} = x^3 y^6.$$

Method.   This equation is of none of the types already
dealt with.   To solve it we divide through by y^6 and
then set $u = 1/y^5$, whereupon it becomes linear.

Solution.   Dividing through by y^6 gives

$$\frac{1}{y^6}\frac{dy}{dx} + \frac{1}{xy^5} = x^3.$$

Now set $u = 1/y^5$.   So $\frac{du}{dx} = -\frac{5}{y^6}\cdot\frac{dy}{dx}.$

The equation then becomes $-\frac{1}{5}\frac{du}{dx} + \frac{u}{x} = x^3,$

$$\text{i.e.} \quad \frac{du}{dx} - \frac{5}{x}u = -5x^3.$$

This is linear with the integrating factor $e^{-5 \log x}$,
i.e. $1/x^5$. The equation is then

$$\frac{d}{dx}\left(u \cdot \frac{1}{x^5}\right) = -\frac{5}{x^2},$$

which gives $\quad u \cdot \frac{1}{x^5} = \frac{5}{x} + C,$

from which the general solution is

$$x^4 y^5 (5 + Cx) = 1.$$

Notice: Equations of this type have the general form

$$y' + a(x)y = b(x)y^n,$$

where $a(x)$, $b(x)$ involve x only. To solve divide
throughout by y^n and put $u = 1/y^{n-1}$.

EXAMPLES TO DO: Page 50: Ex. 10.

EXAMPLES 4

1. The following differential equations are all
separable. Find their general solutions.

(a) $(1 + x)y' - 2y = 0,$ (b) $y' + 2y^2 = 2,$

(c) $(y + 1)^2 \cos^2 x \; y' = 1,$ (d) $e^{x+2y} y' = x + 1.$

2. The following differential equations are all
homogeneous. Find their general solutions.

(a) $xy y' = x^2 + y^2,$ (b) $xy' - y = x \sec(y/x),$

(c) $(x + y)y' - y = 0,$ (d) $xy' - y = 3xe^{2y/x}.$

3. The following differential equations are all
linear. Find their general solutions.

(a) $y' + 3y = (2x + 1)e^{-3x},$ (b) $(x + 1)y' + 2y = e^x,$

(c) $2xy' - y = 2 + 2\sqrt{x}.$

4. Each of the following is linear, homogeneous or
separable. Classify them into types.

(a) $xy' - 3y = x^4 \cos x,$ (b) $5x^2 y' + y^2 = -6x^2,$

(c) $y' = y(\tan x) + 1 + \cos x$,   (d) $(x + 2)y' = 4y + (x + 2)^2$,

(e) $(x^2 + 3xy + y^2)y' = 3y^2 + xy$,

(f) $(x^2 + 4)y' - xy = 6x(x^2 + 4)$,

(g) $xy^2y' - x^2 = 1$,   (h) $(x - 4y)y' - y = 4x$,

(i) $xy' - y = \sqrt{(4x^2 - y^2)}$,

(j) $(x^2 + 1)y' - 2xy = x(3x + 2)(x^2 + 1)^2$,

(k) $y \sec x\, y' - e^{-y} = 0$,   (l) $(x^2 + x)y' = 1 - 2y - 3xy$.

   5.   Find the general solution of each of the
differential equations in Ex.4 above.

   6.   For each of the following find the particular
solution which satisfies the given condition:

(a) $e^{3x}(y + 1)y' = 6$ with $y = 2$ when $x = 0$,

(b) $(x^2 + 1)y' + 2xy = 4x + 1$ with $y = 5$ when $x = 0$,

(c) $xy' - 2y = x^2 + 2x$ with $y = 1$ when $x = 1$,

(d) $(t^2 + 2)\dfrac{dy}{dt} + 4ty = 12t$ with $y = 5$ when $t = 0$.

   7.   Find the general solutions of each of the
following:

(a) $(x - 3y + 5)y' = -3x + y + 1$,   (b) $(x - y - 2)y' = x + y - 6$,

(c) $(7x - y - 2)y' = -3x + 5y - 22$.

   8.   In the differential equation

$$(3x - y + 2)y' = (3x - y + 1),$$

make the substitution $z = 3x - y$, and hence find its
general solution.   [Notice that the method of §48 does
not apply because the lines $3x - y + 2 = 0$ and
$3x - y + 1 = 0$ do not intersect.]

   9.   Find the general solution of each of the
following:

(a) $xy'' - y' = x^2$,   (b) $y'' = 1 + y'$,

(c) $x^3y'' + 3x^2y' - 12x = 6$.

10.   Find the general solution of each of the following:

(a) $y' + xy = xy^3$,   (b) $(x + 1)^2 y' - (x + 1)y = y^4$.

11.   A body falls in a medium in which the resistance is proportional to the speed of the body.   Let the speed of the body at time   t   be $v(t)$.   The motion is then governed by the differential equation

$$\frac{dv}{dt} = g - kv,$$

where   g   and   k   are constants.   If it is given that the body   falls from rest at   t = 0,   show that its speed at time   t   is given by

$$v(t) = \frac{g}{k}(1 - e^{-kt}).$$

Show that the speed of the body approaches the terminal velocity   g/k.

12.   In Ex.11 the initial conditions are now altered: the body is now fired down into the medium with initial speed   U.   Find the resulting solution for $v(t)$ and show that the terminal velocity is unaltered.

13.   A circuit containing a resistance   R   and a self-inductance   L   is connected to a battery of constant e.m.f. V   at time   t = 0.   The subsequent value of the current   I   at time   t   is governed by the differential equation

$$L\frac{dI}{dt} + RI = V.$$

Show that the integration of this equation subject to the condition that   I = 0   at   t = 0   gives the solution

$$I = \frac{V}{R}(1 - e^{-(Rt/L)}).$$

(So the current builds up to the value   V/R   asymptotically.)

V. DIFFERENTIAL EQUATIONS: SECOND ORDER

51. Our treatment of second order equations restricts
attention to equations of the form

$$p(x)y'' + q(x)y' + r(x)y = s(x),$$

where p, q, r, s are functions of certain particular
types. The general solution of such an equation contains
<u>two</u> arbitrary constants because effectively two integra-
tions are done to reach the solution.

In §52-66 we deal with equations for which the
coefficient functions p, q, r are constants. In §67-70
we deal with certain equations where p, q, r are of
more general form.

SECOND ORDER EQUATIONS WITH CONSTANT COEFFICIENTS

52. The examples of §53-55 illustrate the three possible
cases that can occur for the differential equation
of §51, when p, q, r are real constants (p $\neq$ 0) and
s = 0. The division into three cases is a consequence
of the three possible natures of the roots of the <u>auxiliary</u>
<u>equation</u>, i.e. the quadratic equation $pt^2 + qt + r = 0$,
namely the case of real roots (§53), complex conjugate
roots (§54) and repeated real roots (§55).

53. <u>EXAMPLE</u>. Find the general solution of the differential equation

$$y'' - 8y' - 20y = 0.$$

<u>Solution</u>. Form the auxilary equation $t^2 - 8t - 20 = 0$,
which has roots t = 10 and t = -2. The general
solution of the differential equation is then

$$y = Ae^{10x} + Be^{-2x},$$

where A and B are arbitrary constants.

<u>Notice</u>: (i) Making particular choices of the constants
A and B gives different particular solutions. For
example, $y = e^{10x}$ and $y = e^{-2x}$ are two particular
solutions, and these act as building blocks for the
general solution. (It is worth verifying by direct
substitution that e^{10x} and e^{-2x} are indeed particular
solutions.)

(ii) There have to be two arbitrary constants as
mentioned in §51.

54.   **EXAMPLE**.   Find the general solution of the
differential equation

$$y'' - 8y' + 25y = 0.$$

Solution.   The auxiliary equation is $t^2 - 8t + 25 = 0$,
with the roots $t = 4 \pm 3i$,   found using the formula for
the solution of a quadratic equation.   The general
solution of the differential equation is then

$$y = e^{4x}(A \cos 3x + B \sin 3x),$$

where   A   and   B   are arbitrary constants.

Notice: (i)   The particular choices $A = 1$, $B = 0$ and
$A = 0$, $B = 1$ give $e^{4x}\cos 3x$ and $e^{4x}\sin 3x$ as
particular solutions.   These act as building blocks
for the general solution.

(ii)   In contrast to the real roots of the auxiliary
equation in §53, the roots here are genuinely complex
and the method of solution seems rather different.   This
difference is not so great however as it first appears,
for if in this example we try to follow the method of §53
literally we obtain the general solution

$$y = C e^{(4+3i)x} + D e^{(4-3i)x}, \qquad \ldots (1)$$

i.e. $y = C e^{4x}(\cos 3x + i \sin 3x) + D e^{4x}(\cos 3x - i \sin 3x)$

$$= (C + D)e^{4x}\cos 3x + i(C - D)e^{4x}\sin 3x$$

$$= A e^{4x}\cos 3x + B e^{4x}\sin 3x, \quad \text{say}, \qquad \ldots (2)$$

which is just the general solution found above.

Naturally, in many applications   (2)   is easier to
work with than   (1), but both are forms of the general
solution.

55.   **EXAMPLE**.   Find the general solution of the
differential equation

$$y'' - 8y' + 16y = 0.$$

Solution.   Here the auxiliary equation is $t^2 - 8t + 16 = 0$,
with the roots $t = 4, 4$,   i.e. a repeated real root   4.
The general solution is of the differential equation is
then
$$y = (Ax + B)e^{4x},$$

where   A   and   B   are arbitrary constants.

<u>Notice</u>: (i) Particular choices of A and B give $y = e^{4x}$ and $y = xe^{4x}$ as particular solutions.

(ii) Following the method of §53 does <u>not</u> give the general solution in this case. A would-be general solution of the form

$$y = Ae^{4x} + Be^{4x} = (A + B)e^{4x}$$

fails because there is effectively only <u>one</u> arbitrary constant in it.

(iii) To see that the general solution given is correct, we can set $y = v(x)e^{4x}$ in the original equation, where v is a function to be determined. It follows that

$$y' = v'e^{4x} + 4ve^{4x},$$

$$y'' = v''e^{4x} + 8v'e^{4x} + 16ve^{4x},$$

which on substitution reduce the original equation to

$$v''e^{4x} = 0, \quad \text{i.e.} \quad v'' = 0.$$

Integrating this twice gives $v(x) = Ax + B$, where A, B are arbitrary constants. So the general solution of the original differential equation is indeed

$$y = (Ax + B)e^{4x}.$$

<u>EXAMPLES TO DO</u> (on §53-55): Page 65: Ex. 1.

56. GENERAL CONSIDERATIONS WHEN THE RIGHT HAND SIDE IS NON-ZERO

The general solution of the equation

$$py'' + qy' + ry = s(x), \qquad \qquad \text{...(1)}$$

where p, q, r are constants and s is a function, is related to the general solution of

$$py'' + qy' + ry = 0, \qquad \qquad \text{...(2)}$$

which can of course be found by the methods of §53-55. The relationship is given by the following result.

<u>RESULT</u>.

$$\begin{pmatrix} \text{General solution} \\ \text{of (1)} \end{pmatrix} = \begin{pmatrix} \text{General solution} \\ \text{of (2)} \end{pmatrix} + \begin{pmatrix} \text{Any particular} \\ \text{solution of (1)} \end{pmatrix}.$$

Notice: (i) The general solution (G.S.) of the equation (2) is called the complementary function (C.F.); it contains two arbitrary constants and it is found as in §53-55.

(ii) Any particular solution of the equation (1) is called a particular integral (P.I.); it contains no arbitrary constant. For how to find a particular integral look at §57-66.

(iii) The result above can be remembered in the form

$$G.S. = C.F. + P.I..$$

(iv) To see that the above result is reasonable, suppose that $y = g(x)$ is the general solution of equation (2) and that $y = h(x)$ is a particular solution of equation (1). Then $y = g(x) + h(x)$ contains two arbitrary constants, and furthermore it is a solution of equation (1) because

$$p(g(x) + h(x))'' + q(g(x) + h(x))' + r(g(x) + h(x))$$

$$= (pg''(x) + qg'(x) + rg(x)) + (ph''(x) + qh'(x) + rh(x))$$

$$= 0 + s(x) = s(x).$$

(v) The equation (2) is called the homogeneous equation (not the same use of the word as in §44), while the equation (1) is called the non-homogeneous equation.

57. FINDING A PARTICULAR INTEGRAL

In §58-66 methods for finding particular integrals of equations

$$py'' + qy' + ry = s(x) \qquad (p, q, r \text{ constants}, p \neq 0)$$

are suggested only for cases in which $s(x)$ is of certain particular forms and further particular forms are considered in Chapter 13. Still further methods (e.g. variation of parameters) are also available but more advanced books will have to be consulted for these.

58. FINDING A PARTICULAR INTEGRAL WHEN THE RIGHT HAND SIDE IS A MULTIPLE OF e^{kx}

The scheme on page 55 applies to the equation

$$py'' + qy' + ry = Me^{kx},$$

where M and k are non-zero constants, and p, q, r are as in §57. How the scheme works in practice is illustrated in the examples in §59-60.

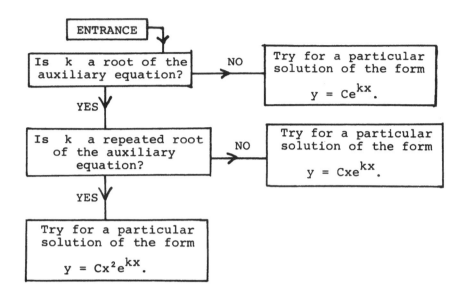

59. **EXAMPLE.** Find the general solutions of

$$\text{(a)} \quad y'' - y' - 12y = 36e^{-5x},$$

$$\text{(b)} \quad y'' - y' - 12y = 21e^{-3x}.$$

Solution. Both equations have the auxiliary equation $t^2 - t - 12 = 0$ with the roots $t = 4$ and $t = -3$. So the complementary function for both equations is given by

$$\text{C.F.} = Ae^{4x} + Be^{-3x},$$

where A and B are constants.

For (a), note that -5 is not a root of the auxiliary equation; so we try $y = De^{-5x}$ as a particular integral. This gives $y' = -5De^{-5x}$, $y'' = 25De^{-5x}$.

So $y = De^{-5x}$ is a particular integral of (a) if and only if

$$25De^{-5x} + 5De^{-5x} - 12De^{-5x} = 36e^{-5x},$$

i.e. $18De^{-5x} = 36e^{-5x}$, i.e. $D = 2$.

So $y = 2e^{-5x}$ is a particular integral, and from §56, the G.S. of (a) is $y = Ae^{4x} + Be^{-3x} + 2e^{-5x}$.

For (b), we note from the scheme of §58 that because −3 is a root of the auxiliary equation our trial particular integral is $y = Dxe^{-3x}$ (not De^{-3x}). This gives

$$y' = D(e^{-3x} - 3xe^{-3x}) \quad \text{and} \quad y'' = D(-6e^{-3x} + 9xe^{-3x}).$$

So $y = Dxe^{-3x}$ is a particular integral if and only if

$$D(-6e^{-3x} + 9xe^{-3x}) - D(e^{-3x} - 3xe^{-3x}) - 12Dxe^{-3x} = 21e^{-3x},$$

i.e. if and only if $-7De^{-3x} = 21e^{-3x}$,

i.e. if and only if $D = -3$.

So a particular integral is $y = -3xe^{-3x}$. So, from §56, the G.S. of (b) is $y = Ae^{4x} + Be^{-3x} - 3xe^{-3x}$.

Notice: In (b) it would be a sheer waste of time to try for a particular solution of the form $y = De^{-3x}$, because e^{-3x} already appears in the complementary function and this means that taking $y = De^{-3x}$ is certain to make the left hand side of the differential equation equal to zero and so not equal to $21e^{-3x}$: in this situation the scheme of §58 tells us to multiply De^{-3x} by x and try for a P.I. of that form. This works.

   In the equation (a) on the other hand, the need to multiply by x does not arise because e^{-5x} is not part of the complementary function.

EXAMPLES TO DO: Page 65: Exs. 2(a),(b).

60.   EXAMPLE.   Find the general solutions of

(a) $y'' + 6y' + 9y = -32e^{5x}$,

(b) $y'' + 6y' + 9y = e^{-3x}$.

Solution.   The auxiliary equation for both equations is $t^2 + 6t + 9 = 0$, which has the roots $t = -3, -3$, (i.e. a repeated root). So the complementary function for both equations is given by

$$\text{C.F.} = (Ax + B)e^{-3x}.$$

For (a), the scheme of §58 tells us to try $y = De^{5x}$ as a particular integral. This gives $y' = 5De^{5x}$ and $y'' = 25De^{5x}$. So this is a particular integral if and only if

$$De^{5x}(25 + 30 + 9) = -32e^{5x}, \quad \text{i.e.} \quad D = -\tfrac{1}{2}.$$

So the general solution of (a) is

$$y = (Ax + B)e^{-3x} - \tfrac{1}{2}e^{5x}.$$

For (b), the scheme of §58 tells us to try $y = Dx^2e^{-3x}$ as a particular integral. This gives

$$y' = D(-3x^2 + 2x)e^{-3x} \quad \text{and} \quad y'' = D(9x^2 - 12x + 2)e^{-3x}.$$

So this is a particular integral if and only if

$$De^{-3x}(9x^2 - 12x + 2 - 18x^2 + 12x + 9x^2) = e^{-3x},$$

$$\text{i.e. if and only if} \quad 2De^{-3x} = e^{-3x},$$

$$\text{i.e. if and only if} \quad D = \tfrac{1}{2}.$$

So the general solution of (b) is

$$y = (Ax + B)e^{-3x} + \tfrac{1}{2}x^2e^{-3x}.$$

Notice: In (b) it is futile to try for a particular integral of either of the forms $y = De^{-3x}$ or $y = Dxe^{-3x}$ because both these already appear as parts of the complementary function and so they both make the left hand side of the differential equation equal to zero and so not equal to e^{-3x}. In this case §58 tells us to try for a particular integral $y = Dx^2e^{-3x}$, which does succeed.

In contrast, equation (a) is straightforward because e^{5x} is not part of the complementary function.

EXAMPLES TO DO: Page 65: Exs. 2(c)-(i).

61. INITIAL VALUE PROBLEMS

These were mentioned in §47. For second order equations there are two constants to be determined and so two initial conditions are needed: often these are given as the values of y and y' for some particular value of x. In many problems the independent variable is t (time) not x, and the values of y and y' are given for $t = 0$, i.e. at the start of the action.

<u>EXAMPLE</u>. Find the solution of the differential equation

$$y'' + 6y' + 9y = e^{-3x}$$

for which $y(0) = 2$ and $y'(0) = 1$.

<u>Method</u>.   There are two stages:
1. Find the G.S. of the given differential equation.
2. Determine the constants A and B using the given initial conditions.

<u>Solution</u>.   The equation is actually (b) in §60 and we have already found the G.S. there as

$$y = (Ax + B)e^{-3x} + \tfrac{1}{2}x^2 e^{-3x}.$$

From this $y' = Ae^{-3x} - 3(Ax + B)e^{-3x} - \tfrac{3}{2}x^2 e^{-3x} + xe^{-3x}.$

Using the given conditions in these two lines (i.e. putting x = 0) gives the two equations

$$B = 2 \quad \text{and} \quad A - 3B = 1.$$

Solving these gives A = 7 and B = 2.
So the required solution, which satisfies the given conditions, is

$$y = (7x + 2)e^{-3x} + \tfrac{1}{2}x^2 e^{-3x}.$$

<u>EXAMPLES TO DO</u>:   Page 66:   Ex.3.

62. FINDING A PARTICULAR INTEGRAL WHEN THE RIGHT HAND SIDE IS A LINEAR COMBINATION OF COSINE AND SINE

The following scheme applies to the equation

$$py'' + qy' + ry = K \cos \beta x + L \sin \beta x,$$

where p, q, r are as in §57 and the right hand side does not degenerate to a constant.   The examples in §63 illustrate its use.

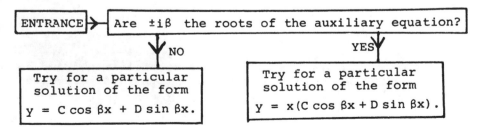

63. **EXAMPLE.** Find the general solutions of the differential equations

$$\text{(a)} \quad 2y'' - y' - 6y = 21 \sin 3x,$$

$$\text{(b)} \quad y'' + 9y = 12 \cos 3x - 6 \sin 3x.$$

Solution. (a) The auxiliary equation is $2t^2 - t - 6 = 0$, with the roots $t = -\tfrac{3}{2}$ and $t = 2$, giving the complementary function

$$\text{C.F.} = Ae^{-\frac{3}{2}x} + Be^{2x}.$$

For a particular integral §62 tells us to try

$$y = C \cos 3x + D \sin 3x,$$

$$\text{for which} \quad y' = -3C \sin 3x + 3D \cos 3x$$

$$\text{and} \quad y'' = -9C \cos 3x - 9D \sin 3x.$$

When these are substituted in equation (a) it becomes

$$(-24C - 3D) \cos 3x + (3C - 24D) \sin 3x = 21 \sin 3x .$$

So we get a P.I. if

$$-24C - 3D = 0 \quad \text{and} \quad 3C - 24D = 21,$$

$$\text{i.e.} \quad C = \frac{7}{65} \quad \text{and} \quad D = -\frac{56}{65} \quad \text{(on solving).}$$

So the general solution is

$$y = Ae^{-\frac{3}{2}x} + Be^{2x} + \frac{1}{65}\left[7 \cos 3x - 56 \sin 3x\right].$$

(b) Here the auxiliary equation is $t^2 + 9 = 0$, which has the roots $t = \pm 3i$. So the complementary function is

$$\text{C.F.} = A \cos 3x + B \sin 3x.$$

To find a particular integral notice that $\pm 3i$ are roots of the auxiliary equation and so by §62 we try for a P.I.

$$y = x(C \cos 3x + D \sin 3x),$$

with $y' = (C \cos 3x + D \sin 3x) + x(-3C \sin 3x + 3D \cos 3x)$
and $y'' = (-6C - 9Dx) \sin 3x + (6D - 9Cx) \cos 3x.$

On substitution of these in the given differential equation we see that this gives a solution if and only if $C = 1$ and $D = 2$. So the general solution is

$$y = (A \cos 3x + B \sin 3x) + x(\cos 3x + 2 \sin 3x).$$

Notice: (i)   In (a), even though the right hand side does
not involve the cosine, the trial particular integral must
still involve both the sine and the cosine.

(ii)   In (b) it would be folly to try for a P.I. of
the form   y = C cos 3x + D sin 3x,   since this already
appears in the complementary function, and so makes the
left hand side of the differential equation zero and not
12 cos 3x - 6 sin 3x.

(iii)   It may be a help to decide that you will always
take the letter   C   (and not   D) as the coefficient of
the   cos   term in your trial particular integral.   This
means that you don't have to look back to check which is
which later.

EXAMPLES TO DO: Page 66:   Ex. 4.

64.   FINDING A PARTICULAR INTEGRAL WHEN THE RIGHT HAND SIDE IS A POLYNOMIAL IN X

EXAMPLE.   Find the general solution of the differential
equation

$$y'' + 4y' + 8y = 16x^2 + 4 .$$

Solution.   The complementary function is

$$\text{C.F.} = e^{-2x}(A \cos 2x + B \sin 2x).$$

Try for a particular integral $y = Cx^2 + Dx + E$, (i.e.   a
polynomial of the same degree as the polynomial on the
right hand side of the given equation).   This gives

$$y' = 2Cx + D \quad \text{and} \quad y'' = 2C.$$

So this is a particular integral if and only if

$$2C + 4(2Cx + D) + 8(Cx^2 + Dx + E) = 16x^2 + 4 .$$

Equating coefficients of the various powers of   x   gives

$$C = 2, \quad D = -2, \quad E = 1$$

so that a P.I. is $2x^2 - 2x + 1$.   So the general solution

is $y = e^{-2x}(A \cos 2x + B \sin 2x) + (2x^2 - 2x + 1)$.

Notice: The particular integral is of the same degree
as the right hand side of the original differential
equation , unless the left hand side is degenerate with
the result that   1   or   x   appears as part of the
complementary function (e.g. see Ex.5.1(h) and Ex.5.5(c));
in such a case the particular integral has to be of
higher degree.

EXAMPLES TO DO: Page 66:   Ex. 5.

65. THE SUM OF PARTICULAR INTEGRALS

To find a particular integral for

$$py'' + qy' + ry = f(x) + g(x),$$

it is enough to find particular integrals for

$$py'' + qy' + ry = f(x) \quad \text{and} \quad py'' + qy' + ry = g(x)$$

separately and then add them.   It is easy to justify this.

EXAMPLES TO DO: Page 65: Ex. 2(e),(i).

66. FINDING A PARTICULAR INTEGRAL: A SUMMARY

For the differential equation

$$py'' + qy' + ry = s(x),$$

where p, q, r are constants with $p \neq 0$ and s is a function of the types mentioned in §58-64, the particular integral is in general of the same form as s(x), unless s(x) or part of s(x) already appears in the complementary function, in which case the particular integral contains an extra factor x or x^2.   Similar considerations apply also to certain other forms of s . Chapter 13 deals with some of these harder cases.

CERTAIN SECOND ORDER EQUATIONS
WITH NON-CONSTANT COEFFICIENTS

67. EQUATIONS FOR WHICH ONE SOLUTION OF THE HOMOGENEOUS EQUATION IS KNOWN

Suppose that the given equation is

$$p(x)y'' + q(x)y' + r(x)y = s(x). \qquad \dots(1)$$

If we can guess or find otherwise any one solution $y = g(x)$ of the corresponding homogeneous equation, i.e.

$$p(x)y'' + q(x)y' + r(x)y = 0 , \qquad \dots(2)$$

then (1) can be reduced to an equation of first order by setting $y = g(x)v(x)$, where v is a function to be determined.   The example which follows illustrates the method.

EXAMPLE.   Find the general solution of

$$x^2(x + 1)y'' + x(3x - 2)y' - (3x - 2)y = 10x^3$$

by first guessing a solution of the homogeneous equation.

<u>Solution</u>.   We can guess the solution   y = x   of

$$x^2(x+1)y" + x(3x-2)y' - (3x-2)y = 0.$$

Now set   y = xv   in the given equation, where   v   is an unknown function of   x.   So

$$y' = xv' + v \quad \text{and} \quad y" = xv" + 2v'.$$

The given equation then becomes

$$x^2(x+1)(xv" + 2v') + x(3x-2)(xv' + v) - (3x-2)xv = 10x^3,$$

$$\text{i.e.} \quad x^3(x+1)v" + 5x^3v' = 10x^3$$

> [<u>Note</u>:   The term in   v   has gone - a characteristic of this situation.]

Rearrange and set   v' = w   as in §49 to obtain

$$w' + \frac{5}{x+1}w = \frac{10}{x+1}.$$

This equation is linear with integrating factor $(x+1)^5$, so that on integration we have

$$w(x+1)^5 = 2(x+1)^5 + C,$$

$$\text{i.e.} \quad v' = 2 + C(x+1)^{-5}.$$

So

$$v = 2x + D(x+1)^{-4} + E. \quad \text{(D, E   constants)}$$

The general solution of the original equation is therefore   y = xv,   i.e.

$$y = 2x^2 + Ex + Dx(x+1)^{-4},$$

where   D   and   E   are arbitrary constants.

<u>Notice</u>:   In guessing a particular solution try x, x^2, e^x, e^{-x}, etc in the first instance.   If the sum of the coefficients on the left hand side of the equation is zero then e^x is a particular solution, e.g. Ex.5.7.

<u>EXAMPLES TO DO</u>:   Page 66:   Exs. 7 - 9.

68. EULER EQUATIONS

These are of the form

$$ax^2y" + bxy' + cy = s(x),$$

where   a, b, c   are constants and   a ≠ 0.   There are two methods of solution:

<u>Method 1.</u>   Determine by direct substitution a real number
k such that $y = x^k$ is a solution of the corresponding
homogeneous equation, i.e. the equation

$$ax^2y'' + bxy' + cy = 0.$$

The order of the original equation can then be reduced
(as in §67) by setting $y = vx^k$.

<u>Method 2.</u>   Put $x = e^t$ in the original equation thereby
reducing the original equation to one with constant
coefficients which may be amenable to the methods of
§52-66.

The examples of §69 and §70 illustrate the two methods.
Be warned that in some cases (e.g. Ex.5.11) method 1 fails
because no real number k can be found.

69.   <u>EXAMPLE</u>.   Find the general solution of the differential equation

$$x^2y'' - 7xy' + 16y = 6x^4.$$

<u>Solution.</u>   (<u>Method 1 of §68</u>)   Try, by substitution, for
a solution $y = x^k$ of

$$x^2y'' - 7xy' + 16y = 0. \qquad \qquad ...(*)$$

This means $(k(k-1) - 7k + 16)x^k = 0,$

i.e. $k^2 - 8k + 16 = 0,$ i.e. $k = 4, 4.$

So $y = x^4$ is one solution of (*).

Now let $y = vx^4$ in the given equation, thereby reducing
it, as in §67, to

$$x^2v'' + xv' = 6.$$

Then, as in §49, let $u = v'$ and solve the linear equation

$$x^2u' + xu = 6,   \text{etc.}$$

This gives $v = 3(\log x)^2 + A(\log x) + B,$ and the general
solution of the original equation is then $y = vx^4$, i.e.

$$y = 3x^4(\log x)^2 + Ax^4(\log x) + Bx^4.$$

<u>Notice</u>:   If the quadratic equation derived above from (*)
had had complex roots then the above method would have
failed.   In such a case the method illustrated in §70
might still succeed, e.g. Ex.5.11.

70. **EXAMPLE.** Find the general solution of

$$x^2 y'' - 7xy' + 16y = 6x^4.$$

Solution. (Method 2 of §68) Let $x = e^t$. So

$$\frac{dy}{dt} = \frac{dy}{dx} \cdot \frac{dx}{dt} = \frac{dy}{dx} \cdot e^t = x\frac{dy}{dx},$$

and

$$\frac{d^2y}{dt^2} = \frac{d}{dt}\left(x\frac{dy}{dx}\right) = \frac{d}{dx}\left(x\frac{dy}{dx}\right) \cdot \frac{dx}{dt}$$

$$= \left(\frac{dy}{dx} + x\frac{d^2y}{dx^2}\right) \cdot e^t = x\frac{dy}{dx} + x^2\frac{d^2y}{dx^2}.$$

So $\quad x\dfrac{dy}{dx} = \dfrac{dy}{dt}\quad$ and $\quad x^2\dfrac{d^2y}{dx^2} = \dfrac{d^2y}{dt^2} - \dfrac{dy}{dt}.$

Substitution of these in the given equation reduces it to

$$\frac{d^2y}{dt^2} - 8\frac{dy}{dt} + 16y = 6e^{4t},$$

which has constant coefficients and by the methods of §52–66 this has the solution

$$y = (At + B)e^{4t} + 3t^2 e^{4t},$$

i.e. $\quad y = (A \log x + B)x^4 + 3x^4 (\log x)^2 ,$

as in §69.

EXAMPLES TO DO (on §68-70):   Page 67: Exs. 10, 11.

71. **SIMULTANEOUS LINEAR DIFFERENTIAL EQUATIONS**

EXAMPLE. Find the general solution of the simultaneous differential equations

$$\dot{x} - x + 6y = 6t - 4, \qquad\qquad \ldots(1)$$

$$\dot{y} - x + 4y = 4t - 3, \qquad\qquad \ldots(2)$$

where x and y are functions of t and $\dot{x}$, $\dot{y}$ denote dx/dt, dy/dt. (You can think of $x(t)$ and $y(t)$ as being the coordinates of a moving point at time t.)

Solution. Differentiate equation (1) with respect to t to give

$$\ddot{x} - \dot{x} + 6\dot{y} = 6, \qquad\qquad \ldots(3)$$

where $\ddot{x}$ denotes d^2x/dt^2.

Now eliminate y and $\dot{y}$ as follows. First take

$2 \times (1) - 3 \times (2)$ to eliminate y.   This gives

$$2\dot{x} - 3\dot{y} + x = 1. \qquad \ldots (4)$$

Then take $(3) + 2 \times (4)$ to eliminate $\dot{y}$.   This gives

$$\ddot{x} + 3\dot{x} + 2x = 8, \qquad \ldots (5)$$

which has (by the methods of §52-66) the general solution

$$x = Ae^{-t} + Be^{-2t} + 4. \qquad \ldots (6)$$

Substituting this in (1) gives

$$y = \tfrac{1}{3}Ae^{-t} + \tfrac{1}{2}Be^{-2t} + t. \qquad \ldots (7)$$

Together (6) and (7) give the general solution.

Notice: The guiding idea here is to produce a differential equation like (5) which involves only x and its
derivatives or only y and its derivatives.   Differentiating one of the given equations usually helps to
achieve this.
    Other methods for tackling systems of simultaneous
linear differential equations are given in §81 and
in Chapter 15.
EXAMPLES TO DO: Page 67: Exs. 12, 13.

EXAMPLES 5

    1.   Find the general solutions of the following
differential equations:

(a) $y'' - 6y' + 8y = 0$,   (b) $y'' + y' - 6y = 0$,

(c) $y'' - 2y' + 26y = 0$,   (d) $y'' + 4y = 0$,

(e) $y'' + 4y' + 4y = 0$,   (f) $2y'' + y' - 6y = 0$,

(g) $y'' - 4y' + 29y = 0$,   (h) $y'' - 3y' = 0$,

(i) $y'' - 12y' + 36y = 0$,   (j) $y'' + a^2 y = 0$ $(a > 0)$.

    2.   Find the general solutions of the following
differential equations:

(a) $y'' - 2y' - 8y = 10e^{-x}$,   (b) $y'' + y = 15e^{-3x}$,

(c) $y'' - 4y' + 4y = 4e^{3x}$,   (d) $y'' - 3y' + 2y = 8e^{2x}$,

(e) $y'' + 2y' + 17y = 8e^{-x} + 10e^{-3x}$,

(f) $y'' - 4y' + 4y = 6e^{2x}$,   (g) $2y'' - 15y' + 7y = 7e^{\frac{1}{2}x}$,

(h) $y'' + 2y' + y = 6e^{-x}$,   (i) $y'' + 4y' + 4y = 36 \cosh x$.

3.   Find the particular solution of each of the following which satisfies the given conditions:

(a) $y'' - y' - 12y = 0$ with $y(0) = 1$ and $y'(0) = \frac{1}{2}$;

(b) $y'' - 4y' + 3y = 60e^{-2x}$ with $y(0) = 2$ and $y'(0) = -6$;

(c) $y'' - 2y' + 10y = 26e^{-x}$ with $y(0) = -2$ and $y'(0) = 0$;

(d) $\frac{d^2y}{dt^2} + 25y = 0$ with $y = 12$ and $\frac{dy}{dt} = 0$ when $t = 0$;

(e) $\frac{d^2y}{dt^2} + 2\frac{dy}{dt} + y = 10e^{-t}$ with $y = 0$, $\frac{dy}{dt} = 2$ for $t = 0$.

4.   Find the general solution of each of the following:

(a) $y'' - 6y' + 5y = 6\cos x + 22\sin x$,

(b) $y'' - y' - 2y = 60\sin 2x$,

(c) $y'' + y = 6\sin x$,   (d) $y'' + 9y = -6\sin 3x - 24\cos 3x$.

5.   Find the general solutions of the following:

(a) $y'' + 8y' + 17y = 51x + 58$,

(b) $y'' + 8y' + 16y = 16x^2 + 26$,   (c) $y'' + y' = 6x$.

6.   For each of the following find the particular solution which satisfies the given conditions:

(a) $y'' - 11y' + 28y = 30e^{2x}$ with $y(0) = 5$, $y'(0) = 11$;

(b) $y'' - 2y' - 3y = 10\cos x$ with $y(0) = 0$, $y'(0) = 5$;

(c) $y'' - y = e^{-x}$ with $y(0) = 1$ and $y(x) \to 0$ as $x \to \infty$;

(d) $y'' - 6y' + 10y = 250x^2$ with $y(0) = 15$, $y'(0) = 36$.

7.   Show that $y = e^x$ is a particular solution of the differential equation

$$xy'' - (2x + 1)y' + (1 + x)y = 0$$

and hence find the general solution of

$$xy'' - (2x + 1)y' + (1 + x)y = e^x.$$

8.   By guessing particular solutions of the corresponding homogeneous equations, find the general solutions of the following:

(a) $x^2y'' + x(2x - 2)y' - (2x - 2)y = 0$,

(b) $(x + 1)y'' - 2xy' + (x - 1)y = 3e^x(x + 1)$,

(c) $x^2(x - 1)y'' + 2xy' - 2y = 2x^3$.

9. Find a solution of the form $y = ax + b$, where a and b are constants, for the equation

$$(x + 4)^2y'' - (x + 4)y' + y = 0,$$

and hence find the general solution of

$$(x + 4)^2y'' - (x + 4)y' + y = (x + 4)^3.$$

10. Find the general solutions of

(a) $x^2y'' - 2xy' - 10y = 24x$, (b) $x^2y'' - 2y = 2x + 1$.

11. Solve the equation

$$x^2y'' - xy' + 2y = 2(\log x)^2 + 2.$$

12. (Simultaneous equations) In the following x and y are functions of t and $\dot{x}$ and $\dot{y}$ denote dx/dt and dy/dt respectively. In each case find the general solution of the pair of equations:

(a) $\dot{x} + \dot{y} + 2x - y = 0$, (b) $\dot{x} + \dot{y} + x - 3y = 0$,

  $\dot{y} + x + 7y = 0$; $\dot{x}$ $-9x - y = 0$;

(c) $3x - 3y$ $-2\dot{y} = 3t - 8$,

  $5x - y + 2\dot{x}$ $= 9t + 2$;

(d) $x - 2y - 3\dot{x}$ $= 4 \cos t + 8 \sin t - 1$,

  $3x$ $- \dot{x} + 2\dot{y} = 16 \cos t + 4 \sin t - 3$.

13. Find the general solution of the simultaneous equations

$$\dot{x} + 2\dot{y} - x = -4t \quad \text{and} \quad \dot{y} + x + 2y = 0$$

and find also the particular solution that satisfies the conditions $x(0) = 1$ and $y(0) = 0$.

14. Look in any good book on Electricity for the theory of L, C, R circuits. For a circuit containing an inductance L, a condenser of capacitance C and a resistor of resistance R and with no applied voltage, the current I at time t is governed by the equation

$$L\frac{d^2I}{dt^2} + R\frac{dI}{dt} + \frac{1}{C}I = 0,$$

i.e. a second order equation with constant coefficients.

VI. LAPLACE TRANSFORMS

72. ELEMENTARY IDEAS

Suppose that we have a problem involving functions f, g etc, and that in the given form the problem is difficult to solve. It may be possible to change the setting of the problem completely by applying a transformation process to all the functions involved, f being transformed to F, g being transformed to G and so on. If we can then find a solution for this new problem (for F, G etc) we may then be able to reverse the transformation process to produce a solution for the original problem for f, g etc.

The Laplace transform provides such a transformation process, which can help in the solution of certain differential and integral equations.

Definition. The Laplace transform of a given function f is the function F defined for real numbers s by

$$F(s) = \int_0^\infty f(x)e^{-sx}\, dx,$$

provided that this integral exists. (Notations for the Laplace transform of f are $L(f; s)$ and $\bar{f}$. We shall use both of these.)

For the functions dealt with in this book we find that though $L(f; s)$ does not exist for all s, it does exist provided that s is positive and sufficiently large. Accordingly throughout this chapter we think of s as a large positive number.

73. THE LAPLACE TRANSFORMS OF SOME ELEMENTARY FUNCTIONS

Page 245 gives a table of the Laplace transforms of some common functions. We calculate some of them here:

(a) $L(1; s) = \int_0^\infty e^{-sx}\, dx = [-e^{-sx}/s]_0^\infty = 1/s.$

(b) $L(x^k; s) = \int_0^\infty x^k e^{-sx}\, dx$ (for $k > -1$)

$$= (1/s^{k+1}) \int_0^\infty u^k e^{-u}\, du, \text{ on setting } u = sx,$$

$$= \Gamma(k+1)/s^{k+1} \quad \text{(from §33).}$$

In particular, $L(x^n; s) = n!/s^{n+1}$ (n a positive integer).

(c) $L(e^{kx}; s) = \int_0^\infty e^{-(s-k)x}\, dx = 1/(s-k).$ [We need $s > k$ for convergence.]

(d) $L(\cos ax; s) = \int_0^\infty e^{-sx}\cos ax\, dx = \dfrac{s}{s^2 + a^2}.$

(e) $L(\sin ax; s) = \int_0^\infty e^{-sx}\sin ax\, dx = \dfrac{a}{s^2 + a^2}$.

The integration by parts required in (d) and (e) can be found in books on elementary calculus.

74.   LAPLACE TRANSFORMS OF RELATED FUNCTIONS

RESULT.   Suppose that f and g are functions with the Laplace transforms $\bar{f}$ and $\bar{g}$.   Then the Laplace transforms of the functions in the left-hand column of the following table are given in the right hand column.   (In parts (d), (e) and (f) there are restrictions on the function f :   we shall assume that f has appropriate derivatives and that

$$f(x)e^{-sx}, \quad f'(x)e^{-sx}, \quad f''(x)e^{-sx}, \quad \dots$$

all tend to zero as $x \to \infty$.)

	function	Laplace transform	
(a)	$kf(x)$	$k\bar{f}$	(k a constant)
(b)	$f(x) + g(x)$	$\bar{f} + \bar{g}$	
(c)	$e^{kx}f(x)$	$L(f; (s-k))$	(k a constant)
(d)	$f'(x)$	$s\bar{f} - f(0)$	
(e)	$f''(x)$	$s^2\bar{f} - sf(0) - f'(0)$	
(f)	$f^{(n)}(x)$	$s^n\bar{f} - s^{n-1}f(0) - s^{n-2}f'(0) - \dots - f^{(n-1)}(0)$	
(g)	$x^n f(x)$	$(-1)^n \dfrac{d^n}{ds^n}(\bar{f})$	(n a positive integer)

Proof: (c) $L(e^{kx}f(x); s) = \int_0^\infty f(x)e^{kx}e^{-sx}\, dx$

$$= \int_0^\infty f(x)e^{-(s-k)x}\, dx = L(f; (s-k)).$$

(d) $L(f'(x);s) = \int_0^\infty f'(x)e^{-sx}\, dx$

$$= [f(x)e^{-sx}]_0^\infty + \int_0^\infty s f(x)e^{-sx}\, dx$$
$$\text{(on integration by parts)}$$
$$= -f(0) + s\bar{f}, \quad \text{as required.}$$

For (e) and (f) apply (d) repeatedly.   For example,

$L(f''; s) = sL(f'; s) - f'(0)$ [treating f" as (f')'
                                               and using part (d)]

$$= s(s\bar{f} - f(0)) - f'(0) = s^2\bar{f} - sf(0) - f'(0).$$

For (g), differentiate the equation

$$\int_0^\infty f(x)e^{-sx}\ dx = \bar{f}$$

n times with respect to s. This involves differentiation under the integral sign on the left hand side.

Notice: Parts (d),(e),(f),(g) of the above result are useful in solving certain differential equations, e.g. in §77-81. The use of (c) and (g) is illustrated in the following example.

EXAMPLE. Find the Laplace transforms of x^2e^{6x}, $e^{6x}\cos 2x$, $e^{6x}\sin 2x$, $x\sin 2x$.

Solution. Part (c) of the above result tells us that the first three of these can be found from the Laplace transforms of x^2, cos 2x and sin 2x by replacing s by (s-6). So

$$L(x^2e^{6x};\ s) = 2!/(s-6)^3 = 2/(s-6)^3,$$

$$L(e^{6x}\cos 2x;\ s) = \frac{(s-6)}{(s-6)^2 + 4} = \frac{(s-6)}{s^2 - 12s + 40},$$

$$L(e^{6x}\sin 2x;\ s) = \frac{2}{(s-6)^2 + 4} = \frac{2}{s^2 - 12s + 40}.$$

For x sin 2x we use part (g) with k = 1:

$$L(x\sin 2x;\ s) = -\frac{d}{ds}(L(\sin 2x;\ s))$$

$$= -\frac{d}{ds}\left(\frac{2}{s^2 + 4}\right) = \frac{4s}{(s^2 + 4)^2}.$$

EXAMPLES TO DO: Page 76: Ex. 1.

75. LAPLACE TRANSFORMS: INVERSION

It is beyond the scope of this book to give a general method for reversing the transformation process described in §72, i.e. a method for recovering the original function f from a given Laplace transform $\bar{f}$. In this book we rely on recognising any given Laplace transform using the table on page 245 together with the ideas of §74. We use the notation L^{-1} to denote the inverse of a Laplace transform, e.g.

$$L^{-1}\left(\frac{s}{s^2 + 4}\right) = \cos 2x.$$

The following example illustrates what can be done with these methods.

EXAMPLE.   Find

(a) $L^{-1}\left[\frac{1}{(s+5)^3}\right]$,   (b) $L^{-1}\left[\frac{3s^2+25s-2}{(s-1)(s^2-4s+29)}\right]$.

Solution.   (a) $L(x^2; s) = 2!/s^3 = 2/s^3$.   The given transform contains $(s+5)^3$ instead of s^3 but §74(c) tells us that this indicates the presence of a factor e^{-5x}.   So

$$L^{-1}\left[\frac{1}{(s+5)^3}\right] = \tfrac{1}{2}x^2 e^{-5x}.$$

(b)   Using partial fractions we obtain

$$\frac{3s^2+25s-2}{(s-1)(s^2-4s+29)} = \frac{1}{s-1} + \frac{2s+31}{s^2-4s+29}$$

$$= \frac{1}{s-1} + \frac{2(s-2)}{(s-2)^2+25} + \frac{35}{(s-2)^2+25}$$

$$= \frac{1}{s-1} + \frac{2(s-2)}{(s-2)^2+5^2} + \frac{7.5}{(s-2)^2+5^2}.$$

So $L^{-1}(.) = e^x + 2e^{2x}\cos 5x + 7e^{2x}\sin 5x$,   by §74(c) together with the Laplace transforms of e^x, $\cos 5x$ and $\sin 5x$.

EXAMPLES TO DO: Page 76:   Ex. 2.

76.   SOLVING DIFFERENTIAL EQUATIONS USING LAPLACE TRANSFORMS

We illustrate with some examples in §77-79.   Notice that the method applies to situations where initial conditions are given, i.e. it does not find the general solution.   Notice also that for some equations the methods of the previous two chapters may in fact be shorter.

77.   EXAMPLE.   Find the solution of the differential equation

$$\frac{d^2y}{dt^2} + 6\frac{dy}{dt} + 9y = 24te^{-3t},$$

where y is a function of t,   and $y(0) = 0$ and $y'(0) = 1$.   (You can think of t as time.)

Solution.   Take Laplace transforms throughout the equation (using §74(e)and(d) on the LHS and using §74(c) on the RHS) to obtain

$$(s^2\bar{y} - sy(0) - y'(0)) + 6(s\bar{y} - y(0)) + 9\bar{y} = \frac{24}{(s+3)^2},$$

On insertion of the values of $y(0)$ and $y'(0)$ this

becomes $\qquad (s^2 + 6s + 9)\bar{y} - 1 = \dfrac{24}{(s+3)^2}$,

i.e. $\qquad \bar{y} = \dfrac{1}{(s+3)^2} + \dfrac{24}{(s+3)^4}$.

So, on inverting the Laplace transforms, we have

$$y = te^{-3t} + 4t^3 e^{-3t}$$

as the solution of the given problem.

78. **EXAMPLE.** Find the solution of the differential equation

$$\frac{d^2 y}{dt^2} + \frac{dy}{dt} - 2y = -20e^{-3t}\cos 2t,$$

where y is a function of t with $y(0) = 0$, $y'(0) = 4$.

Solution. Take Laplace transforms throughout the equation using the results of §73-74. This gives

$$(s^2\bar{y} - 4) + s\bar{y} - 2\bar{y} = \frac{-20(s+3)}{(s+3)^2 + 4} ,$$

i.e. $\qquad (s^2 + s - 2)\bar{y} = 4 - \dfrac{20(s+3)}{s^2 + 6s + 13}$,

i.e. $\qquad (s^2 + s - 2)\bar{y} = \dfrac{4s^2 + 4s - 8}{s^2 + 6s + 13}$.

So, on cancelling the factor $(s^2 + s - 2)$ on each side,

we have $\bar{y} = \dfrac{4}{s^2 + 6s + 13}$, which on inversion gives

$$y = 2e^{-3t}\sin 2t.$$

79. **EXAMPLE.** Use Laplace transforms to solve the differential equation

$$\frac{d^2 y}{dt^2} + 8\frac{dy}{dt} + 15y = 4e^{-3t},$$

where y is a function of t and subject to the conditions $y(0) = 0$ and $y'(0) = 4$.

Solution. Taking Laplace transforms gives

$$(s^2\bar{y} - 4) + 8(s\bar{y}) + 15\bar{y} = \frac{4}{s+3} ,$$

i.e. $\qquad (s^2 + 8s + 15)\bar{y} = 4 + \dfrac{4}{s+3} = \dfrac{4s+16}{s+3}$.

So, $\bar{y} = \dfrac{4s + 16}{(s + 3)^2 (s + 5)} = \dfrac{2}{(s + 3)^2} + \dfrac{1}{s + 3} - \dfrac{1}{s + 5}$.

On inversion this gives the solution as

$$y = 2te^{-3t} + e^{-3t} - e^{-5t}.$$

80.   While the Laplace transform method does work well in the examples of §77-79, do be warned that in some cases the work involved in finding the partial fractions can become heavy: the possibility of arithmetical error may then be a factor of significance.   In the above examples the fact that some of the initial values are 0 (e.g. $y(0) = 0$) helps to keep the work reasonably simple.

EXAMPLES TO DO (on §77-80):   Pages 76-77:   Exs. 3, 5, 6.

81.   SOLVING CERTAIN SIMULTANEOUS LINEAR DIFFERENTIAL EQUATIONS USING LAPLACE TRANSFORMS

Laplace transforms provide an alternative to the methods of §71 for solving simultaneous linear differential equations if initial conditions are given.   The following example illustrates the method.

EXAMPLE.   Find x and y (functions of t) such that

$$x + 3y + \dot{x} = 5 \cos t, \qquad \ldots (1)$$
$$y + 2\dot{x} + 2\dot{y} = -5 \sin t, \qquad \ldots (2)$$

where $x(0) = 1$ and $y(0) = 2$.

Solution.   Taking Laplace transforms throughout the equations using §74(d) together with the initial conditions gives

$$\bar{x} + 3\bar{y} + s\bar{x} - x(0) = \dfrac{5s}{s^2 + 1} ,$$

and $\bar{y} + 2(s\bar{x} - x(0)) + 2(s\bar{y} - y(0)) = \dfrac{-5}{s^2 + 1}$,

i.e. $(s + 1)\bar{x} + 3\bar{y} = \dfrac{s^2 + 5s + 1}{s^2 + 1}$ $\ldots (3)$

and $2s\bar{x} + (2s + 1)\bar{y} = \dfrac{6s^2 + 1}{s^2 + 1}$. $\ldots (4)$

Multiplying (3) by $(2s + 1)$ and (4) by 3 and then subtracting the resulting equations gives

$$(2s^2 - 3s + 1)\bar{x} = \dfrac{2s^3 - 7s^2 + 7s - 2}{s^2 + 1} ,$$

i.e. $\quad \bar{x} = \dfrac{(s-1)(2s-1)(s-2)}{(2s-1)(s-1)(s^2+1)} = \dfrac{s-2}{s^2+1}$

$\qquad\quad = \dfrac{s}{s^2+1} - \dfrac{2}{s^2+1}$.

On inversion this gives

$$x = \cos t - 2\sin t.$$

Substituting this in equation (1) gives

$$y = 2\cos t + \sin t.$$

Notice: For this pair of equations there is a minor advantage gained by solving (3) and (4) for $\bar{x}$ rather than $\bar{y}$, because substitution of x and $\dot{x}$ in equation (1) gives y immediately.   In contrast if we first solve (3) and (4) for $\bar{y}$ and so determine y, we do not immediately recover x by substituting y and $\dot{y}$ in (1) and (2).   In some cases such considerations may merit attention.

EXAMPLES TO DO: Page 77:   Ex. 4.

82.   LAPLACE TRANSFORMS: CONVOLUTION

§74(b) tells us that the Laplace transform of the sum of two functions is the sum of the two Laplace transforms.   There is however no corresponding result for the Laplace transform of a product: for given functions f and g, the function which has $\overline{fg}$ as its Laplace transform is in general not fg, but rather a function derived from f and g (as explained below) and called the convolution of f and g.

For two given functions f and g, the convolution of f and g is the function f ∗ g where

$$(f \ast g)(x) = \int_0^x f(t)g(x-t)\ dt,$$

when this integral exists.   (If you think about the evaluation of this integral you soon see that the final answer does indeed involve x only, i.e. it is a function of x.)   It is the function f ∗ g which has $\overline{fg}$ as its Laplace transform, where $\bar{f}$ and $\bar{g}$ are L(f; s) and L(g; s) respectively.   This is the message of the following result.

RESULT.   In the above notation,

$$L(f \ast g; s) = L(f; s)L(g; s).$$

Proof. $L(f \ast g; s) = \int_0^\infty \left[\int_0^x f(t)g(x-t)\ dt \right] e^{-sx}\ dx$

$$= \int_0^\infty dx \int_0^x f(y) g(x-y) e^{-sx} dy$$

(on writing y instead of t)

$$= \int_0^\infty dy \int_y^\infty f(y) g(x-y) e^{-sx} dx$$

(on changing the order of integration)

$$= \int_0^\infty f(y) e^{-sy} dy \int_y^\infty g(x-y) e^{-s(x-y)} dx$$

$$= \int_0^\infty f(y) e^{-sy} dy \int_0^\infty g(u) e^{-su} du$$

(on setting u = x - y)

$= L(f; s) L(g; s)$ (because the two integrals are now independent of each other and so can be evaluated separately).

83. SOLVING CERTAIN INTEGRAL EQUATIONS WITH LAPLACE TRANSFORMS

Typically a <u>differential</u> equation is an equation involving the <u>derivative</u> (or derivatives) of an unknown function y; solving the equation means determining y as a function of the independent variable x. In a similar way an <u>integral</u> equation involves the <u>integral</u> of an unknown function y; solving the equation means determining y as a function of the independent variable x.

The Laplace transform (and in particular the idea of convolution) allows us to solve certain integral equations, including Abel's integral equation (Ex.6.8). The following example illustrates the method.

<u>EXAMPLE</u>.   Solve tne integral equation

$$\int_0^x (x - t)^2 y(t) \, dt = \tfrac{1}{3} x^3 + x - \sin x,$$

(i.e. determine the function y).

<u>Solution</u>.   (Here the LHS of the equation is the convolution $f * g$, where $f(t) = y(t)$ and $g(t) = t^2$.) Taking Laplace transforms throughout the equation using the convolution result on the LHS gives

$$\bar{y} \cdot \frac{2}{s^3} = \frac{6}{3s^4} + \frac{1}{s^2} - \frac{1}{s^2 + 1} .$$

So $\bar{y} = \dfrac{1}{s} + \dfrac{s}{2} - \dfrac{s^3}{2(s^2 + 1)} = \dfrac{1}{s} + \dfrac{s}{2(s^2 + 1)}$, which on inversion of transforms gives the solution $y(t) = 1 + \tfrac{1}{2} \cos t.$

<u>EXAMPLES TO DO</u>:   Pages 77-78: Exs. 7, 8.

EXAMPLES 6

1. Using the table of Laplace transforms (page 245) together with the results of §74 give the Laplace transforms of the following:

(a) $\sin 3x$, (b) x^3, (c) $x^2 - 3x + 6$, (d) $\sqrt{x}$,

(e) e^{4x}, (f) $e^{-x}\sin 3x$, (g) $e^{4x}\cos x$, (h) $x^3 e^{-x}$,

(i) $(x + 1)^2$, (j) $e^{5x}\cos 5x$, (k) $e^{-2x}(x^2 + 4x)$,

(l) $x \cos 2x$, (m) $x^2 \sin 4x$.

2. Find the functions of which the following are the Laplace transforms:

(a) $\frac{1}{s}$, (b) $\frac{1}{s^3}$, (c) $\frac{s^2 + 2}{s^3}$, (d) $\frac{1}{s - 2}$, (e) $\frac{1}{(s - 2)^2}$,

(f) $\frac{2s - 5}{(s - 2)^2}$, (g) $\frac{s}{s^2 + 1}$, (h) $\frac{1}{s^2 + 1}$, (i) $\frac{1}{s^2 + 4}$,

(j) $\frac{s + 1}{s^2 + 2s + 5}$, (k) $\frac{2s + 4}{s^2 - 8s + 17}$, (l) $\frac{1}{s^2 - 8s + 15}$,

(m) $\frac{2s^2 + s}{(s - 2)(s^2 + 1)}$, (n) $\frac{48 - s}{(s + 2)(s^2 + 2s + 50)}$,

(o) $\frac{s^2 - 4s - 1}{(s - 2)^3}$, (p) $\frac{s - 2}{s^2(s + 2)}$, (q) $\frac{3s^2 + 3}{s^3 + 1}$.

3. For each of the following, use Laplace transforms to find the solution $y(t)$ of the differential equation subject to the given conditions:

(a) $y'' + 2y' - 3y = -6$ with $y(0) = 0$ and $y'(0) = 6$;

(b) $y'' + 8y' + 16y = 6te^{-4t}$ with $y(0) = y'(0) = 0$;

(c) $y'' + 4y' + 3y = -6e^{-2t}\sin t$ with $y(0) = 0$, $y'(0) = 3$;

(d) $y'' + y' + y = 2t^2$ with $y(0) = 0$, $y'(0) = -4$;

[Note: $(s^3 - 1) = (s - 1)(s^2 + s + 1)$.]

(e) $y'' + 2y' + 10y = -10$ with $y(0) = 0$, $y'(0) = -1$;

(f) $y'' + y' - 2y = 4t - 4$ with $y(0) = y'(0) = 0$;

(g) $y'' - 4y' + 5y = 10t - 8$ with $y(0) = 0$, $y'(0) = 3$.

4.   (<u>Simultaneous equations</u>)   In each of the
following pairs   of simultaneous equations   x   and   y   are
functions of   t.   Use Laplace transforms to find the
solution of each pair satisfying the given conditions:

(a) $2\dot{x} + \dot{y} + y = 4$ and $\dot{y} - 4x - y = 4t^2 - 4t$

with $x(0) = 1$ and $y(0) = 0$;

(b) $\dot{x} + 2\dot{y} - 2x = 0$ and $2\ddot{y} - 4\dot{x} + 3x = 3e^{-2t} - 9$

with $x(0) = \dot{x}(0) = y(0) = \dot{y}(0) = 0$;

(c) $2\ddot{x} - \ddot{y} = -18e^{3t}$ and $\dot{y} - 3y - 8\dot{x} = 0$

with $x(0) = 0, \ \dot{x}(0) = 1, \ y(0) = 0, \ \dot{y}(0) = 8$;

(d) $x + y + 2\ddot{x} = 2t + 4$ and $\ddot{x} + \ddot{y} + 2\dot{x} = 4$

with $x(0) = \dot{x}(0) = 0, \ y(0) = 4, \ \dot{y}(0) = 2$;

(e) $\dot{y} + 2x + y = 2$ and $2\dot{y} + \dot{x} + 5x = 5$

with $x(0) = 1$ and $y(0) = 1$.

5.   For each of the following use the Laplace
transform to find the solution $y(x)$ of the differential
equation subject to the given conditions.   (You will
need §74(g) here.)

(a) $xy'' + (6 - 9x)y = 0$ with $y(0) = 0$ and $y'(0) = 4$;

(b) $xy'' - 2y' - (x + 4)y = 0$ with $y(0) = 0$ and $y(1) = 4e$.

6.   Show that

$$L(f'''(x); s) = s^3\bar{f} - s^2 f(0) - sf'(0) - f''(0).$$

Use this to solve the differential equation

$$y''' + y'' + y' + y = 2,$$

where   y   is a function of   x, subject to the conditions
$y(0) = 0, \ y'(0) = 0, \ y''(0) = 2.$ [Note that
$a^3 + a^2 + a + 1 = (a + 1)(a^2 + 1)$.]

7.   Use Laplace transforms to solve the following
integral equations (i.e. in each case find the function   y):

(a) $\int_0^x (x - t)^2 \, y(t) \ dt = 2 \sin x - 2x$;

(b) $\int_0^x (x - t)^3 y(t) \, dt = x^5 + 3x^4$;

(c) $y(x) = 6x + \int_0^x y(t) \sin(x - t) \, dt$;

(d) $y(x) = e^{3x} + \int_0^x y(t) e^{x-t} \, dt$;

(e) $\displaystyle\int_0^x \frac{y(t)}{\sqrt{(x - t)}} \, dt = 4x$.

[In (d) verify your solution by direct evaluation.]

8.   Abel's integral equation has the form

$$\int_0^x \frac{y(t)}{(x - t)^k} \, dt = f(x), \qquad \ldots (*)$$

where k is a constant with $0 < k < 1$, f is a given function and y is the unknown function that is to be determined.   (Ex.7(e) above is a special case.)   Solve the equation (*) when $f(x) = x^{2-k}$.

VII. PARTIAL DIFFERENTIATION

---

84. PARTIAL DERIVATIVES

Many physical quantities depend on more than one variable. For example the surface area S of a closed rectangular tank with sides x, y, z is given by

$$S(x,y,z) = 2xy + 2yz + 2zx.$$

The <u>partial derivative</u> of such a function S with respect to one of the variables is found by differentiating the formula for S with respect to the variable in question while treating the other variables as constants. The partial derivatives with respect to x, y, z are denoted by $\frac{\partial S}{\partial x}$, $\frac{\partial S}{\partial y}$, $\frac{\partial S}{\partial z}$ or by S_x, S_y, S_z respectively. So, in the above example,

$$\frac{\partial S}{\partial x} = 2y + 2z, \qquad \frac{\partial S}{\partial y} = 2x + 2z, \qquad \frac{\partial S}{\partial z} = 2y + 2x.$$

The examples of §85-87 illustrate how the Chain Rule (function of a function rule), the Product Rule and the idea of implicit differentiation all extend easily to partial differentiation.

The value of $\frac{\partial S}{\partial x}$ at a point (a,b,c) gives a measure of how fast the function S increases as we move away from the point (a,b,c) on a vector parallel to the x-axis, in much the same way that for a function f of <u>one</u> variable x the value of $\frac{df}{dx}$ at a point a gives a measure of the rate of increase of f as we move away from the point a in the direction of the x-axis. In the case of three variables x, y and z however it is possible to move away from (a,b,c) not only parallel to the x-axis, but also parallel to the y-axis and parallel to the z-axis. The rates of increase of S in these directions are given by $\frac{\partial S}{\partial y}$ and $\frac{\partial S}{\partial z}$ respectively.

(In fact we could consider the rate of increase along a vector in <u>any</u> direction: this is dealt with in §126.)

85. EXAMPLE. (To illustrate the Chain Rule)

Let $g(x,y) = \sin(x^2 + 3xy + 4y^2)$. Find $\frac{\partial g}{\partial x}$, $\frac{\partial g}{\partial y}$.

<u>Solution.</u> $\quad \frac{\partial g}{\partial x} = (2x + 3y)\cos(x^2 + 3xy + 4y^2)$

and $\quad \frac{\partial g}{\partial y} = (3x + 8y)\cos(x^2 + 3xy + 4y^2)$.

Notice: This is just an extension of the Chain Rule (function of a function rule) for ordinary differentiation. Here we see that

$$\frac{\partial}{\partial x}(f(u)) \ , \quad \text{where} \quad u = x^2 + 3xy + 4y^2$$

is given by

$$\frac{\partial}{\partial x}(f(u)) \ = \ f'(u).\frac{\partial u}{\partial x} \ .$$

Similarly,

$$\frac{\partial}{\partial y}(f(u)) \ = \ f'(u).\frac{\partial u}{\partial y} \ .$$

86. <u>EXAMPLE</u>. (<u>To illustrate the Product Rule</u>)
Let $g(x,y) = (2x + 7y) \sin(3x^2 + 5y)$. Find $\frac{\partial g}{\partial x}$, $\frac{\partial g}{\partial y}$.

<u>Solution</u>. $\frac{\partial g}{\partial x} = 2 \sin(3x^2 + 5y) + (2x + 7y).6x \cos(3x^2 + 5y)$

and $\frac{\partial g}{\partial y} = 7 \sin(3x^2 + 5y) + (2x + 7y).5 \cos(3x^2 + 5y)$.

Notice: This is just an extension of the Product Rule for ordinary differentiation. In practice it means that

$$\frac{\partial}{\partial x}(\phi(x,y)\psi(x,y)) \ = \ \phi(x,y)\frac{\partial\psi}{\partial x} + \psi(x,y)\frac{\partial\phi}{\partial x} \ .$$

<u>EXAMPLES TO DO</u> (on §85-86): Page 98: Ex. 1.

87. The following example illustrates that the idea of implicit differentiation can be carried over from ordinary differentiation to partial differentiation also.

EXAMPLE. (<u>To illustrate implicit partial differentiation</u>)
Let $r^2 = x^2 + y^2$ and let g be defined as a function of x and y by the equation

$$g(x,y) = \frac{xy^3}{r} \ .$$

Prove that $x\frac{\partial g}{\partial x} + y\frac{\partial g}{\partial y} = 3g$.

<u>Solution</u>. Differentiate both sides of the equation $r^2 = x^2 + y^2$ partially with respect to x and with respect to y to obtain

$$2r\frac{\partial r}{\partial x} = 2x \quad \text{and} \quad 2r\frac{\partial r}{\partial y} = 2y,$$

i.e. $\frac{\partial r}{\partial x} = \frac{x}{r}$ and $\frac{\partial r}{\partial y} = \frac{y}{r}$ . ...(*)

Now partially differentiate g with respect to x treating the function as the product of xy^3 and $1/r$. So the Product Rule gives

$$\frac{\partial g}{\partial x} = y^3 \cdot \frac{1}{r} + xy^3 \cdot \left(\frac{-1}{r^2}\right)\frac{\partial r}{\partial x}$$

$$= \frac{y^3}{r} - \frac{x^2 y^3}{r^3} \qquad \text{(on using (*))} .$$

Similarly,

$$\frac{\partial g}{\partial y} = \frac{3xy^2}{r} + xy^3\left(\frac{-1}{r^2}\right)\frac{\partial r}{\partial y}$$

$$= \frac{3xy^2}{r} - \frac{xy^4}{r^3} \qquad \text{(on using (*))} .$$

So $\quad x\frac{\partial g}{\partial x} + y\frac{\partial g}{\partial y} = \frac{xy^3}{r} - \frac{x^3 y^3}{r^3} + \frac{3xy^3}{r} - \frac{xy^5}{r^3}$

$$= \frac{4xy^3}{r} - \frac{xy^3(x^2 + y^2)}{r^3}$$

$$= \frac{4xy^3}{r} - \frac{xy^3 r^2}{r^3} = \frac{3xy^3}{r} = 3g ,$$

$$\text{as required.}$$

EXAMPLES TO DO: Page 98:   Ex. 2.

88.   HIGHER ORDER PARTIAL DERIVATIVES: THE COMMUTATIVE PROPERTY

Just as for functions of one variable there may exist derivatives of the second or higher orders, so also for functions of more than one variable there may exist partial derivatives of the second or higher orders.   For example, if f is a function of two variables x and y, we may have the higher order partial derivatives

$$\frac{\partial^2 f}{\partial x^2} = \frac{\partial}{\partial x}\left(\frac{\partial f}{\partial x}\right), \qquad \frac{\partial^2 f}{\partial y^2} = \frac{\partial}{\partial y}\left(\frac{\partial f}{\partial y}\right),$$

$$\frac{\partial^2 f}{\partial x \partial y} = \frac{\partial}{\partial x}\left(\frac{\partial f}{\partial y}\right), \qquad \frac{\partial^2 f}{\partial y \partial x} = \frac{\partial}{\partial y}\left(\frac{\partial f}{\partial x}\right), \qquad \frac{\partial^3 f}{\partial x^3} = \frac{\partial}{\partial x}\left(\frac{\partial^2 f}{\partial x^2}\right) \quad \text{etc.}$$

(Alternative notations are f_{xx}, f_{yy}, f_{xy}, f_{yx}, f_{xxx} respectively.)

So, for example, if $\quad f(x,y) = x^3 y^5 + 4x + 7y^2$, then

$f_x = 3x^2 y^5 + 4$, $\quad f_y = 5x^3 y^4 + 14y$, $\quad f_{xx} = 6xy^5$,

$f_{yy} = 20x^3 y^3 + 14$, $\quad f_{xy} = 15x^2 y^4$, $\quad f_{yx} = 15x^2 y^4$.

Notice here that the equality of f_{xy} and f_{yx} is <u>not</u> just chance but is rather evidence of the <u>commutative</u> <u>property of partial differentiation</u>, which states that for suitably well behaved functions

$$f_{xy} = f_{yx} .$$

In particular if f_{xy} and f_{yx} are both continuous on an open set then they are equal on that set. In most practical applications these conditions are fulfilled. We shall use this property without comment from now on.

89. **EXAMPLE.** Find the real numbers n for which the function f defined by

$$f(x,y) = xe^{2x}/y^n$$

satisfies the partial differential equation

$$3x \frac{\partial^2 f}{\partial x^2} - xy^2 \frac{\partial^2 f}{\partial y^2} = 12f.$$

<u>Solution.</u> We have

$$f_x = \frac{1}{y^n}\left(e^{2x} + 2x e^{2x}\right) \quad \text{and} \quad f_y = x e^{2x}\left(\frac{-n}{y^{n+1}}\right) ,$$

i.e. $f_x = \frac{(2x+1)}{y^n} e^{2x}$ and $f_y = \frac{-nx}{y^{n+1}} e^{2x}.$

Further partial differentiation then gives

$$f_{xx} = \frac{2}{y^n} e^{2x} + \frac{2(2x+1)}{y^n} e^{2x} = \frac{(4x+4)}{y^n} e^{2x} ,$$

$$f_{yy} = \frac{n(n+1)x}{y^{n+2}} e^{2x} .$$

For f to satisfy the given equation we therefore need

$$\frac{3x(4x+4)}{y^n} e^{2x} - \frac{n(n+1)x^2}{y^n} e^{2x} = \frac{12x}{y^n} e^{2x} ,$$

i.e. $3x(4x+4) - n(n+1)x^2 = 12x ,$

So we need $(12 - n(n+1))x^2 = 0$ for all values of x.

So $12 - n(n+1) = 0,$ i.e. $n^2 + n - 12 = 0,$

i.e. $(n+4)(n-3) = 0,$ i.e. $n = -4$ or $3.$

These are the required values.

<u>EXAMPLES TO DO</u>: Pages 98-99: Exs. 5, 6.

90. **EXAMPLE.** Let $z = g(y^2/x)$, where g is a twice differentiable function of one variable. Prove that

$$\text{(a)} \qquad 2x\,\frac{\partial z}{\partial x} + y\,\frac{\partial z}{\partial y} = 0,$$

and deduce that

$$\text{(b)} \qquad 4x^2\,\frac{\partial^2 z}{\partial x^2} + 4xy\,\frac{\partial^2 z}{\partial x \partial y} + y^2\,\frac{\partial^2 z}{\partial y^2} + 2x\,\frac{\partial z}{\partial x} = 0.$$

[If you are unclear about the meaning of $g(y^2/x)$ look at (i) after the solution of this example.]

<u>Solution.</u> (a) Let $u = y^2/x$. Then with $z = g(u)$, we apply the rule mentioned in §85 to see that

$$\frac{\partial z}{\partial x} = g'(u)\,\frac{\partial u}{\partial x} = -\frac{y^2}{x^2}\,g'(u) \quad \text{and} \quad \frac{\partial z}{\partial y} = g'(u)\,\frac{\partial u}{\partial y} = \frac{2y}{x}\,g'(u).$$

So, $2x\,\dfrac{\partial z}{\partial x} + y\,\dfrac{\partial z}{\partial y} = -\dfrac{2y^2}{x}\,g'(u) + \dfrac{2y^2}{x}\,g'(u) = 0$, as required.

(b) Differentiate (a) partially, first with respect to x and then with respect to y, to obtain

$$2x\,\frac{\partial^2 z}{\partial x^2} + 2\,\frac{\partial z}{\partial x} + y\,\frac{\partial^2 z}{\partial x \partial y} = 0 \quad \text{and} \quad 2x\,\frac{\partial^2 z}{\partial y \partial x} + y\,\frac{\partial^2 z}{\partial y^2} + \frac{\partial z}{\partial y} = 0.$$

Multiply these by $2x$ and y respectively and add the results to obtain

$$4x^2\,\frac{\partial^2 z}{\partial x^2} + 4xy\,\frac{\partial^2 z}{\partial x \partial y} + y^2\,\frac{\partial^2 z}{\partial y^2} + 4x\,\frac{\partial z}{\partial x} + y\,\frac{\partial z}{\partial y} = 0.$$

Using (a) to simplify the last two terms of this gives (b).

<u>Notice</u>: (i) This example means that every function of x and y in which x and y appear only in the combination y^2/x is a solution of the partial differential equations (a) and (b). So, for example,

$$\sin(y^2/x), \qquad \frac{3y^4}{x^2} - \frac{4y^2}{x} + 1 \quad \text{and} \quad 2\log y - \log x$$

are all solutions.

(ii) To do (b) we could alternatively find all the required second derivatives separately and then substitute them into equation (b), e.g.

$$\frac{\partial^2 z}{\partial x^2} = \frac{\partial}{\partial x}\left(-\frac{y^2}{x^2}\,g'(u)\right) = \frac{2y^2}{x^3}\,g'(u) - \frac{y^2}{x^2}\,g''(u).\left(-\frac{y^2}{x^2}\right), \quad \text{etc.}$$

The solution above shows however that it may be easier to build up the second order equation (b) by suitable partial differentiation of a first order equation like (a).

<u>EXAMPLES TO DO</u>: Pages 98-99: Exs. 3, 4, 7, 8, 9.

91. DIFFERENTIATION OF FUNCTIONS OF TWO OR MORE VARIABLES: THE CHAIN RULE

Many functions are defined by functions of one or more variables which are themselves functions of one or more variables, e.g. take the functions F, G, H defined by:

$$F(x,y) = f(u), \text{ where } u = x^2 + 3xy + 4y^2,$$

$$G(t) = g(u,v), \text{ where } u = t^2, v = t^3,$$

$$H(x,y) = h(u,v), \text{ where } u = xy, v = x/y.$$

Here F is a function of <u>two</u> variables because it ultimately depends on the independent variables x and y, though the link is through the function f which is of a single variable.

G is a function of <u>one</u> variable because it ultimately depends only on the variable t, though the link is through the function g, which is a function of two variables.

H is a function of <u>two</u> variables because it ultimately depends on the independent variables x and y, the link being through a function of two variables.

An immediate issue is how to find

$$\frac{\partial F}{\partial x}, \frac{\partial F}{\partial y}, \frac{dG}{dt}, \frac{\partial H}{\partial x}, \frac{\partial H}{\partial y}.$$

(Notice that dG/dt is an <u>ordinary</u> derivative because G is a function of <u>one</u> variable only.)

For $\frac{\partial F}{\partial x}$ and $\frac{\partial F}{\partial y}$ the linking function f is a function of <u>one</u> variable and the rule is just an extension of the Chain Rule for functions of one variable and has already been given and used in §85, namely

$$(1) \qquad \frac{\partial F}{\partial x} = \frac{df}{du} \cdot \frac{\partial u}{\partial x} \quad \text{and} \quad \frac{\partial F}{\partial y} = \frac{df}{du} \cdot \frac{\partial u}{\partial y}.$$

For $\frac{dG}{dt}$, $\frac{\partial H}{\partial x}$ and $\frac{\partial H}{\partial y}$ the linking functions g and h are functions of <u>two</u> variables and we have the following forms of the <u>Chain Rule for functions of two variables</u>:

$$(2) \qquad \frac{dG}{dt} = \frac{\partial g}{\partial u} \frac{du}{dt} + \frac{\partial g}{\partial v} \frac{dv}{dt},$$

$$(3) \qquad \frac{\partial H}{\partial x} = \frac{\partial h}{\partial u} \frac{\partial u}{\partial x} + \frac{\partial h}{\partial v} \frac{\partial v}{\partial x} \quad \text{and} \quad \frac{\partial H}{\partial y} = \frac{\partial h}{\partial u} \frac{\partial u}{\partial y} + \frac{\partial h}{\partial v} \frac{\partial v}{\partial y}.$$

Essentially the same rule applies in case (2) and in case (3): ordinary derivatives appear in (2) instead of partial derivatives because in this case G, u and v are functions of a single variable. The examples of §92 and §93 illustrate the rules (2) and (3) respectively.

92.   <u>EXAMPLE</u>.   Let $G(t) = u^2 \sin v$,   where $u = t^2$ and $v = t^3$.   Find $\dfrac{dG}{dt}$.

<u>Solution</u>.   Here $G(t) = g(u,v)$,   where $g(u,v) = u^2 \sin v$ and $u = t^2$, $v = t^3$.   So, from (2) in §91,

$$\frac{dG}{dt} = \frac{\partial g}{\partial u}\frac{du}{dt} + \frac{\partial g}{\partial v}\frac{dv}{dt} = 2u \sin v \cdot 2t + u^2 \cos v \cdot 3t^2$$

$$= 2t^2 \sin(t^3) \cdot 2t + t^4 \cos(t^3) \cdot 3t^2$$

$$= 4t^3 \sin(t^3) + 3t^6 \cos(t^3).$$

[That this is indeed correct can be checked directly by noting that $G(t) = t^4 \sin(t^3)$ and differentiating this.]

93.   FINDING FIRST ORDER PARTIAL DERIVATIVES UNDER A CHANGE OF VARIABLES

<u>EXAMPLE</u>.   Let $H(x,y) = h(u,v)$,   where $u = xy$, $v = y/x$. Find $\dfrac{\partial H}{\partial x}$ and $\dfrac{\partial H}{\partial y}$ in terms of $\dfrac{\partial h}{\partial u}$ and $\dfrac{\partial h}{\partial v}$.

<u>Solution</u>.   By the Chain Rule ((3) of §91),

$$\frac{\partial H}{\partial x} = \frac{\partial h}{\partial u}\frac{\partial u}{\partial x} + \frac{\partial h}{\partial v}\frac{\partial v}{\partial x} = y\frac{\partial h}{\partial u} - \frac{y}{x^2}\frac{\partial h}{\partial v},$$

$$\frac{\partial H}{\partial y} = \frac{\partial h}{\partial u}\frac{\partial u}{\partial y} + \frac{\partial h}{\partial v}\frac{\partial v}{\partial y} = x\frac{\partial h}{\partial u} + \frac{1}{x}\frac{\partial h}{\partial v} .$$

<u>Notice</u>:   Here   x   and   y   are independent variables and by writing $\dfrac{\partial H}{\partial x}$ we tacitly understand that it is   y   that is held constant in the differentiation (<u>not</u>   u   or   v).   It is occasionally useful to emphasise this by writing

$$\left(\frac{\partial H}{\partial x}\right)_y \quad \text{instead of just} \quad \frac{\partial H}{\partial x}.$$

Similarly   u   and   v   are independent variables and in writing $\dfrac{\partial h}{\partial u}$ we tacitly assume that it is   v   (and <u>not</u>   x   or   y) that is being held constant in the differentiation.

This whole matter is taken further in §98, where we consider the problem of how to obtain similar expressions for the <u>second</u> order partial derivatives.

94. PARTIAL DIFFERENTIAL EQUATIONS: GENERAL AND PARTICULAR SOLUTIONS

An equation like

$$x \frac{\partial f}{\partial x} + y \frac{\partial f}{\partial y} = 3f, \qquad \ldots (*)$$

which involves partial derivatives of a function of two or more variables, is called a <u>partial differential equation</u>, often shortened to <u>p.d.e.</u>. A <u>particular solution</u> of such an equation is any function which satisfies the equation. For example, $f(x,y) = x^2 y$ is easily checked to be a particular solution of the equation $(*)$.

Usually a partial differential equation has many particular solutions. The <u>general solution</u> of the p.d.e. includes all its particular solutions as special cases and as such it usually involves an arbitrary function or functions. <u>Solving a p.d.e.</u> means finding its general solution.

95. SOLUTION OF SIMPLE PARTIAL DIFFERENTIAL EQUATIONS

<u>EXAMPLE</u>. Find the general solution of the p.d.e.

$$\frac{\partial f}{\partial x} = 2x + y + 3,$$

where f is a function of the two independent variables x and y.

<u>Solution</u>. We can integrate this directly with respect to x, treating y as a constant in the integration, i.e.

$$f(x,y) = \int (2x + y + 3) \, dx$$

$$= x^2 + xy + 3x + \phi(y),$$

where $\phi(y)$ is an arbitrary function of y.

<u>Notice</u>: Here the arbitrary function $\phi(y)$ corresponds to the arbitrary constant which occurs in the general solution of a first order differential equation. It may help to verify by partial differentiation that, for example, $x^2 + xy + 3x + y^3 + 7\sqrt{y} + 4$ and $x^2 + xy + 3x + \sin^2 y$ are both particular solutions of the given p.d.e..

<u>EXAMPLE</u>. Find the general solution of the p.d.e.

$$\frac{\partial^2 f}{\partial x \partial y} = 2.$$

<u>Solution</u>. Write the equation in the form

$$\frac{\partial}{\partial x}\left(\frac{\partial f}{\partial y}\right) = 2.$$

Integrate this with respect to x to obtain

$$\frac{\partial f}{\partial y} = \int 2\ dx = 2x + \phi(y)\ , \qquad \ldots(1)$$

where ϕ is an arbitrary function.

Now integrate equation (1) with respect to y.   So

$$f(x,y) = \int (2x + \phi(y))\ dy \qquad \ldots(2)$$

$$\text{i.e.} \quad f(x,y) = 2xy + \psi(y) + \tau(x), \qquad \ldots(3)$$

where ψ and τ are arbitrary functions.   This is the general solution.   [So, for example, one particular solution is $f(x,y) = 2xy + y^4 + x^2 \log x + 1$.]

Notice: (i)   It is y that is held constant in the integration in line (1).   So the constant of integration is any arbitrary function of y.

On the other hand it is x that is held constant in the integration in line (2).   So the constant of integration is an arbitrary function of x.

(ii)   We have denoted $\int \phi(y)\ dy$ by $\psi(y)$, since this integral is effectively another arbitrary function of y.

EXAMPLES TO DO: Page 99: Exs. 10, 11.

96. PARTIAL DIFFERENTIAL EQUATIONS: THE IDEA OF SOLUTION BY CHANGE OF VARIABLES

The methods exemplified in §95 are far too weak for solving partial differential equations in general.   Some equations can however by a suitable change of variables be reduced to a form to which the methods of §95 will apply.   The method of deciding on which particular change of variables to make lies beyond the scope of this book, but the examples of §97 (for first order equations) and §99 (for second order equations) illustrate what can be done if a suitable change of variables is known.

97. SOLUTION OF A FIRST ORDER PARTIAL DIFFERENTIAL EQUATION

EXAMPLE.   Make the change of variables $u = xy$, $v = y$ in the p.d.e.

$$x\frac{\partial f}{\partial x} - y\frac{\partial f}{\partial y} = 3xy^2$$

and hence find its general solution.

Solution.   (Here we shall for convenience use the same letter f to denote the solution as a function of x and y _and_ as a function of u and v, even though we should strictly speaking use different letters as in §93. The solution found finally is unaffected by this decision.)

The Chain Rule gives

$$\frac{\partial f}{\partial x} = \frac{\partial f}{\partial u}\frac{\partial u}{\partial x} + \frac{\partial f}{\partial v}\frac{\partial v}{\partial x} = y\frac{\partial f}{\partial u} ,$$

$$\frac{\partial f}{\partial y} = \frac{\partial f}{\partial u}\frac{\partial u}{\partial y} + \frac{\partial f}{\partial v}\frac{\partial v}{\partial y} = x\frac{\partial f}{\partial u} + \frac{\partial f}{\partial v} .$$

Under this change of variables the given equation becomes

$$xy\frac{\partial f}{\partial u} - y\left(x\frac{\partial f}{\partial u} + \frac{\partial f}{\partial v}\right) = 3xy^2 ,$$

i.e. $\dfrac{\partial f}{\partial v} = -3xy,$ i.e. $\dfrac{\partial f}{\partial v} = -3u.$

This equation can be treated by the methods of §95:

$$f(u,v) = \int -3u\,dv = -3uv + \phi(u),$$

where ϕ is an arbitrary function.

Substituting for u and v gives the general solution as

$$f(x,y) = -3xy^2 + \phi(xy).$$

Notice: $\phi(xy)$ contains x and y only in the combination xy, e.g. $x^2y^2 + 4xy + 3$ and $\sin(xy)$ qualify to play $\phi(xy)$ but $(x + y)$ does not.

EXAMPLES TO DO: Page 100: Ex. 12 and page 217: Exs. 1, 2.

98. FINDING SECOND ORDER PARTIAL DERIVATIVES UNDER A CHANGE OF VARIABLES

We illustrate by an example, which is effectively a continuation of the example in §93. The only tools needed are the Product Rule (§86) together with the formula (3) of §91.

EXAMPLE. Let $F(x,y) = f(u,v)$, where $u = xy$, $v = y/x$. Find $\dfrac{\partial^2 F}{\partial x^2}$, $\dfrac{\partial^2 F}{\partial y^2}$ and $\dfrac{\partial^2 F}{\partial x\partial y}$.

Solution. As in §93, we have

$$\frac{\partial F}{\partial x} = y\frac{\partial f}{\partial u} - \frac{y}{x^2}\frac{\partial f}{\partial v} , \qquad \ldots(1)$$

$$\frac{\partial F}{\partial y} = x\frac{\partial f}{\partial u} + \frac{1}{x}\frac{\partial f}{\partial v} . \qquad \ldots(2)$$

[Before proceeding notice that the coefficients in (1) and (2) depend only on u and v (and _not_ on F and f) so that these formulae apply to _every_ pair of functions that correspond as F and f do. We can therefore write

$$\frac{\partial}{\partial x}(*) = y\frac{\partial}{\partial u}(*) - \frac{y}{x^2}\frac{\partial}{\partial v}(*) \qquad \ldots (1A)$$

and

$$\frac{\partial}{\partial y}(*) = x\frac{\partial}{\partial u}(*) + \frac{1}{x}\frac{\partial}{\partial v}(*) \qquad \ldots (2A)]$$

Then

$$\frac{\partial^2 F}{\partial x^2} = \frac{\partial}{\partial x}\left(\frac{\partial F}{\partial x}\right) = \frac{\partial}{\partial x}\left(y\frac{\partial f}{\partial u} - \frac{y}{x^2}\frac{\partial f}{\partial v}\right) = \frac{\partial}{\partial x}\left(y\frac{\partial f}{\partial u}\right) - \frac{\partial}{\partial x}\left(\frac{y}{x^2}\frac{\partial f}{\partial v}\right)$$

$$= y\frac{\partial}{\partial x}\left(\frac{\partial f}{\partial u}\right) - \left(-\frac{2y}{x^3}\frac{\partial f}{\partial v} + \frac{y}{x^2}\frac{\partial}{\partial x}\left(\frac{\partial f}{\partial v}\right)\right)$$

(on using the Product Rule for differentiation)

$$= y\left(y\frac{\partial}{\partial u}\left(\frac{\partial f}{\partial u}\right) - \frac{y}{x^2}\frac{\partial}{\partial v}\left(\frac{\partial f}{\partial u}\right)\right)$$

$$+ \frac{2y}{x^3}\frac{\partial f}{\partial v} - \frac{y}{x^2}\left(y\frac{\partial}{\partial u}\left(\frac{\partial f}{\partial v}\right) - \frac{y}{x^2}\frac{\partial}{\partial v}\left(\frac{\partial f}{\partial v}\right)\right)$$

(on using (1A) to find $\frac{\partial}{\partial x}\left(\frac{\partial f}{\partial u}\right)$ and $\frac{\partial}{\partial x}\left(\frac{\partial f}{\partial v}\right)$)

$$= y^2\frac{\partial^2 f}{\partial u^2} - \frac{y^2}{x^2}\frac{\partial^2 f}{\partial u\partial v} + \frac{2y}{x^3}\frac{\partial f}{\partial v} - \frac{y^2}{x^2}\frac{\partial^2 f}{\partial u\partial v} + \frac{y^2}{x^4}\frac{\partial^2 f}{\partial v^2}$$

$$= y^2\frac{\partial^2 f}{\partial u^2} - \frac{2y^2}{x^2}\frac{\partial^2 f}{\partial u\partial v} + \frac{y^2}{x^4}\frac{\partial^2 f}{\partial v^2} + \frac{2y}{x^3}\frac{\partial f}{\partial v}. \qquad \ldots (3)$$

In a similar way,

$$\frac{\partial^2 F}{\partial x\partial y} = \frac{\partial}{\partial x}\left(x\frac{\partial f}{\partial u} + \frac{1}{x}\frac{\partial f}{\partial v}\right) = \frac{\partial f}{\partial u} + x\frac{\partial}{\partial x}\left(\frac{\partial f}{\partial u}\right) - \frac{1}{x^2}\frac{\partial f}{\partial v} + \frac{1}{x}\frac{\partial}{\partial x}\left(\frac{\partial f}{\partial v}\right)$$

(on using the Product Rule)

$$= \frac{\partial f}{\partial u} + x\left(y\frac{\partial}{\partial u}\left(\frac{\partial f}{\partial u}\right) - \frac{y}{x^2}\frac{\partial}{\partial v}\left(\frac{\partial f}{\partial u}\right)\right)$$

$$- \frac{1}{x^2}\frac{\partial f}{\partial v} + \frac{1}{x}\left(y\frac{\partial}{\partial u}\left(\frac{\partial f}{\partial v}\right) - \frac{y}{x^2}\frac{\partial}{\partial v}\left(\frac{\partial f}{\partial v}\right)\right)$$

(on using (1A) from above)

$$= xy\frac{\partial^2 f}{\partial u^2} - \frac{y}{x^3}\frac{\partial^2 f}{\partial v^2} + \frac{\partial f}{\partial u} - \frac{1}{x^2}\frac{\partial f}{\partial v} \qquad \ldots (4)$$

(on collecting terms).

Also, (and in this case the easiest of the three),

$$\frac{\partial^2 f}{\partial y^2} = \frac{\partial}{\partial y}\left(x\frac{\partial f}{\partial u} + \frac{1}{x}\frac{\partial f}{\partial v}\right) = x\frac{\partial}{\partial y}\left(\frac{\partial f}{\partial u}\right) + \frac{1}{x}\frac{\partial}{\partial y}\left(\frac{\partial f}{\partial v}\right)$$

$$= x \left[x \frac{\partial}{\partial u}\left(\frac{\partial f}{\partial u}\right) + \frac{1}{x} \frac{\partial}{\partial v}\left(\frac{\partial f}{\partial u}\right) \right] + \frac{1}{x} \left[x \frac{\partial}{\partial u}\left(\frac{\partial f}{\partial v}\right) + \frac{1}{x} \frac{\partial}{\partial v}\left(\frac{\partial f}{\partial v}\right) \right]$$

(on using formula (2A) above)

$$= x^2 \frac{\partial^2 f}{\partial u^2} + 2 \frac{\partial^2 f}{\partial u \partial v} + \frac{1}{x^2} \frac{\partial^2 f}{\partial v^2} . \qquad \dots (5)$$

Remarks: (i) In calculating the second derivatives here it is important to apply the Product Rule <u>before</u> using the formulae (1A) or (2A). For example, in the calculation of $\frac{\partial^2 f}{\partial x^2}$ it is vital that the force of the $\frac{\partial}{\partial x}$ is applied not only to $\frac{\partial f}{\partial u}$ and $\frac{\partial f}{\partial v}$ but also to any coefficient functions like $-\frac{y}{x^2}$ which involve x. If this is not done then terms may be lost.

(ii) The second stage uses the "operator formulae" (1A) and (2A) to produce the second order partial derivatives.

<u>EXAMPLES TO DO</u>: Page 100: Ex. 13.

99. SOLUTION OF A SECOND ORDER PARTIAL DIFFERENTIAL EQUATION BY CHANGE OF VARIABLES

Recall this idea from §96. We illustrate with the following example.

EXAMPLE. By changing the variables from x, y to u, v where u = xy and v = y/x, find the general solution of the partial differential equation

$$x^2 \frac{\partial^2 F}{\partial x^2} - y^2 \frac{\partial^2 F}{\partial y^2} + x \frac{\partial F}{\partial x} - y \frac{\partial F}{\partial y} = 0.$$

<u>Solution</u>. Let F(x,y) = f(u,v). Normally if you are given this type of problem you must start by calculating expressions for F_{xx}, F_{yy}, F_x, F_y in terms of f_u, f_v, f_{uu}, f_{uv}, f_{vv}, but we have already done this in §98. So, on substituting from the formulae (1), (2), (3) and (5) in §98, the given p.d.e. becomes

$$x^2 \left(y^2 f_{uu} - 2\frac{y^2}{x^2} f_{uv} + \frac{y^2}{x^4} f_{vv} + \frac{2y}{x^3} f_v \right)$$

$$- y^2 \left(x^2 f_{uu} + 2 f_{uv} + \frac{1}{x^2} f_{vv} \right)$$

$$+ x \left(y f_u - \frac{y}{x^2} f_v \right) - y \left(x f_u + \frac{1}{x} f_v \right) = 0,$$

which reduces to

$$-4y^2 \, f_{uv} = 0 \text{ , for every value of } y.$$

So we conclude that $\dfrac{\partial^2 f}{\partial u \partial v} = 0.$ ...(*)

Integrating this by the methods exhibited in §95 gives

$$\frac{\partial f}{\partial v} = \int 0 \, du = \phi(v).$$

Integrating again gives

$$f(u,v) = \int \phi(v) \, dv + \psi(u)$$

$$= \tau(v) + \psi(u), \quad \text{say,}$$

where τ and ψ are arbitrary functions of one variable. So the general solution of the given p.d.e. is

$$f(x,y) = \tau(y/x) + \psi(xy).$$

Notice: (i) The change of variables reduces the given equation to the simple form (*) which can be solved by the elementary methods of §95.

(ii) The form of the general solution means that, for example, the function f given by

$$f(x,y) = \sin(xy) + \left(\frac{y}{x}\right)^2 + 6\left(\frac{y}{x}\right) + 30$$

is a solution of the given p.d.e..

EXAMPLES TO DO: Page 100: Ex. 14 and page 217: Exs. 3 – 5.

100. A COMMON SOURCE OF TROUBLE IN SOLVING SECOND ORDER PARTIAL DIFFERENTIAL EQUATIONS

The method of §99 succeeds in giving the solution of the p.d.e. only because the change of variables simplifies the equation dramatically, e.g. to (*) in §99.

If in doing such an example you find that after the appropriate change of variables your new equation still contains unwanted terms, then it is possible that you have not understood Remark (i) in §98 and consequently you have lost terms that are needed for cancellation.

101. A MORE SPECIALISED METHOD FOR CERTAIN SECOND ORDER PARTIAL DIFFERENTIAL EQUATIONS

The method illustrated in the example which follows is worth noticing but it is rather specialised.

EXAMPLE. Show that if $u = x/y$ and $v = y$ then

$$x \frac{\partial z}{\partial x} + y \frac{\partial z}{\partial y} = v \frac{\partial z}{\partial v} . \qquad \ldots (1)$$

Deduce that

$$x^2 \frac{\partial^2 z}{\partial x^2} + 2xy \frac{\partial^2 z}{\partial x \partial y} + y^2 \frac{\partial^2 z}{\partial y^2} = v^2 \frac{\partial^2 z}{\partial v^2} .$$

Hence solve the partial differential equation

$$x^2 \frac{\partial^2 z}{\partial x^2} + 2xy \frac{\partial^2 z}{\partial x \partial y} + y^2 \frac{\partial^2 z}{\partial y^2} = 0 .$$

Solution. We use the Chain Rule ((3) of §91) to find

$$\frac{\partial z}{\partial x} = \frac{1}{y} \frac{\partial z}{\partial u} \quad \text{and} \quad \frac{\partial z}{\partial y} = -\frac{x}{y^2} \frac{\partial z}{\partial u} + \frac{\partial z}{\partial v} .$$

So
$$x \frac{\partial z}{\partial x} + y \frac{\partial z}{\partial y} = \frac{x}{y} \frac{\partial z}{\partial u} - \frac{x}{y} \frac{\partial z}{\partial u} + y \frac{\partial z}{\partial v}$$

$$= v \frac{\partial z}{\partial v} \quad \text{as required.}$$

In terms of operators this means that

$$x \frac{\partial}{\partial x}(*) + y \frac{\partial}{\partial y}(*) = v \frac{\partial}{\partial v}(*) ,$$

where * represents any function we care to choose. It follows from this and (1) that

$$\left(x \frac{\partial}{\partial x} + y \frac{\partial}{\partial y} \right) \left(x \frac{\partial z}{\partial x} + y \frac{\partial z}{\partial y} \right) = \left(v \frac{\partial}{\partial v} \right) \left(v \frac{\partial z}{\partial v} \right)$$

i.e.
$$x \left(\frac{\partial z}{\partial x} + x \frac{\partial^2 z}{\partial x^2} + y \frac{\partial^2 z}{\partial x \partial y} \right)$$

$$+ y \left(x \frac{\partial^2 z}{\partial x \partial y} + \frac{\partial z}{\partial y} + y \frac{\partial^2 z}{\partial y^2} \right) = v \left(\frac{\partial z}{\partial v} + v \frac{\partial^2 z}{\partial v^2} \right)$$

On multiplying out and using (1) to cancel two terms on the left with one term on the right, we find this gives

$$x^2 \frac{\partial^2 z}{\partial x^2} + 2xy \frac{\partial^2 z}{\partial x \partial y} + y^2 \frac{\partial^2 z}{\partial y^2} = v^2 \frac{\partial^2 z}{\partial v^2} , \quad \text{as required.}$$

It follows that under the given change of variables the given p.d.e. reduces to

$$\frac{\partial^2 z}{\partial v^2} = 0 .$$

So
$$\frac{\partial z}{\partial v} = \phi(u) \quad \text{and} \quad z = \int \phi(u) \, dv + \psi(u) ,$$

$$\text{i.e.} \quad z = v\,\phi(u) + \psi(u).$$

$$\text{So} \quad z(x,y) = y\,\phi(x/y) + \psi(x/y),$$

where ϕ and ψ are arbitrary functions.

EXAMPLES TO DO: Page 100:   Ex. 15.

102. THE CHAIN RULE FOR FUNCTIONS OF MORE THAN TWO VARIABLES

The following rules give natural extensions of the rules (2) and (3) of §91:

(1)   If $G(t) = g(u_1, u_2, \ldots, u_n)$,   where $u_1, u_2, \ldots, u_n$ are functions of the single variable t,   then

$$\frac{dG}{dt} = \frac{\partial g}{\partial u_1}\frac{du_1}{dt} + \frac{\partial g}{\partial u_2}\frac{du_2}{dt} + \ldots + \frac{\partial g}{\partial u_n}\frac{du_n}{dt}.$$

(2)   If $H(x_1, x_2, \ldots, x_m) = h(u_1, u_2, \ldots, u_n)$, where $u_1, u_2, \ldots, u_n$ are functions of $x_1, x_2, \ldots, x_m$,   then, for each i with $1 \le i \le m$,

$$\frac{\partial H}{\partial x_i} = \frac{\partial h}{\partial u_1}\frac{\partial u_1}{\partial x_i} + \frac{\partial h}{\partial u_2}\frac{\partial u_2}{\partial x_i} + \ldots + \frac{\partial h}{\partial u_n}\frac{\partial u_n}{\partial x_i}.$$

103. EXAMPLE. (The change to polar coordinates)
Let $x = r\cos\theta$, $y = r\sin\theta$.   Suppose that

$$f(x,y) = g(r,\theta).$$

Find expressions for $\partial f/\partial x$ and $\partial f/\partial y$ in terms of the partial derivatives of g with respect to r and θ.

Solution.   (This is radically different from and rather harder than the example in §93 despite the superficial similarity.   Here you have to find $\partial f/\partial x$ and $\partial f/\partial y$, where the change of variables is given in the form $x = \ldots$, $y = \ldots$.   There (i.e. in §93) you are also asked to find $\partial f/\partial x$ and $\partial f/\partial y$, but it is the other variables (u and v) that are given in the form $u = \ldots$, $v = \ldots$ and x and y appear on the right hand side of these formulae.)

Here, rather than make a direct assault on $\partial f/\partial x$ and $\partial f/\partial y$, we find it easier to calculate $\partial g/\partial r$ and $\partial g/\partial \theta$ with the Chain Rule.   (This is easier because the change of variables is given as $x = \ldots$, $y = \ldots$.)

So $\quad\dfrac{\partial g}{\partial r} = \dfrac{\partial f}{\partial x}\dfrac{\partial x}{\partial r} + \dfrac{\partial f}{\partial y}\dfrac{\partial y}{\partial r}\quad$ (θ constant)

i.e. $\quad\dfrac{\partial g}{\partial r} = \cos\theta\,\dfrac{\partial f}{\partial x} + \sin\theta\,\dfrac{\partial f}{\partial y},\qquad$ ...(1)

and $\quad\dfrac{\partial g}{\partial\theta} = \dfrac{\partial f}{\partial x}\dfrac{\partial x}{\partial\theta} + \dfrac{\partial f}{\partial y}\dfrac{\partial y}{\partial\theta}\quad$ (r constant)

i.e. $\quad\dfrac{\partial g}{\partial\theta} = -r\sin\theta\,\dfrac{\partial f}{\partial x} + r\cos\theta\,\dfrac{\partial f}{\partial y}.\qquad$ ...(2)

Solving (1) and (2) as a pair of simultaneous equations in $\partial f/\partial x$ and $\partial f/\partial y$ (either by inverting a 2×2 matrix or directly) gives

$$\dfrac{\partial f}{\partial x} = \cos\theta\,\dfrac{\partial g}{\partial r} - \dfrac{\sin\theta}{r}\dfrac{\partial g}{\partial\theta},\qquad \text{...(3)}$$

$$\dfrac{\partial f}{\partial y} = \sin\theta\,\dfrac{\partial g}{\partial r} + \dfrac{\cos\theta}{r}\dfrac{\partial g}{\partial\theta},\qquad \text{...(4)}$$

as required.

Notice: In <u>this</u> case we <u>could</u> alternatively use the method of §93 if we <u>first</u> solve the given equations $x = r\cos\theta$, $y = r\sin\theta$ to obtain $r = \sqrt{(x^2 + y^2)}$ and $\theta = \tan^{-1}(y/x) + k\pi$ ($k = 0$, 1 or -1), and then let these equations take over the roles of the equations $u = xy$, $v = y/x$ in §93. Be warned however that in some cases the equations $x = \ldots$, $y = \ldots$ may be impossible to solve explicitly and the method of solution illustrated in the example above cannot then be avoided.

EXAMPLES TO DO: Page 101: Ex. 17.

104. THE TWO DIMENSIONAL LAPLACIAN IN POLAR COORDINATES

The equation

$$\dfrac{\partial^2 f}{\partial x^2} + \dfrac{\partial^2 f}{\partial y^2} = 0,\qquad\qquad \text{...(*)}$$

where f is a function of x and y is called <u>Laplace's equation in two dimensions</u>. We change the variables to polar coordinates r and θ. To this end, notice that (3) and (4) in §103 can be used (look at Ex.18 on page 101) to obtain expressions for $\partial^2 f/\partial x^2$ and $\partial^2 f/\partial y^2$:

$$\dfrac{\partial^2 f}{\partial x^2} = \cos^2\theta\,\dfrac{\partial^2 g}{\partial r^2} - \dfrac{2\sin\theta\cos\theta}{r}\dfrac{\partial^2 g}{\partial r\partial\theta} + \dfrac{\sin^2\theta}{r^2}\dfrac{\partial^2 g}{\partial\theta^2}$$

$$+ \dfrac{\sin^2\theta}{r}\dfrac{\partial g}{\partial r} + \dfrac{2\sin\theta\cos\theta}{r^2}\dfrac{\partial g}{\partial\theta}$$

and $\dfrac{\partial^2 f}{\partial y^2} = \sin^2\theta \dfrac{\partial^2 g}{\partial r^2} + \dfrac{2\sin\theta\cos\theta}{r}\dfrac{\partial^2 g}{\partial r\partial\theta} + \dfrac{\cos^2\theta}{r^2}\dfrac{\partial^2 g}{\partial\theta^2}$

$$+ \dfrac{\cos^2\theta}{r}\dfrac{\partial g}{\partial r} - \dfrac{2\sin\theta\cos\theta}{r^2}\dfrac{\partial g}{\partial\theta}.$$

From these it is easy to see that Laplace's equation (*) in polar coordinates takes the form

$$\dfrac{\partial^2 g}{\partial r^2} + \dfrac{1}{r}\dfrac{\partial g}{\partial r} + \dfrac{1}{r^2}\dfrac{\partial^2 g}{\partial\theta^2} = 0 .$$

Notice that there is a similar treatment of the three dimensional Laplace equation

$$\dfrac{\partial^2 f}{\partial x^2} + \dfrac{\partial^2 f}{\partial y^2} + \dfrac{\partial^2 f}{\partial z^2} = 0. \qquad \ldots (**)$$

The equations (*) and (**) are often written in the form

$$\nabla^2 f = 0,$$

where ∇^2 denotes the Laplacian operator.

EXAMPLES TO DO: Page 101: Exs. 16, 18.

105.   EXAMPLE.   Suppose that a suitably well behaved function F of three variables satisfies the equation $F(x,y,z) = 0$ on some open set. Suppose further that the equation defines z as a function of x and y on this open set. By writing $z = z(x,y)$, find expressions for $\partial z/\partial x$ and $\partial z/\partial y$ in terms of $\partial F/\partial x$, $\partial F/\partial y$ and $\partial F/\partial z$, where this is possible.

Solution.   We have

$$F(x,y,z(x,y)) = 0. \qquad \ldots(*)$$

Differentiate (*) partially first with respect to x and then with respect to y (using §102) to find

$$\dfrac{\partial F}{\partial x} + \dfrac{\partial F}{\partial z}\dfrac{\partial z}{\partial x} = 0 \quad \text{and} \quad \dfrac{\partial F}{\partial y} + \dfrac{\partial F}{\partial z}\dfrac{\partial z}{\partial y} = 0.$$

So $\quad \dfrac{\partial z}{\partial x} = -\dfrac{\partial F}{\partial x}\Big/\dfrac{\partial F}{\partial z} \quad$ and $\quad \dfrac{\partial z}{\partial y} = -\dfrac{\partial F}{\partial y}\Big/\dfrac{\partial F}{\partial z}$,

provided that $\partial F/\partial z \neq 0$.

Notice: Similarly, when y is defined implicitly as a function of x by a suitable equation $G(x,y) = 0$, we can prove that

$$\dfrac{dy}{dx} = -\dfrac{\partial G}{\partial x}\Big/\dfrac{\partial G}{\partial y}, \quad \text{provided that } \dfrac{\partial G}{\partial y} \neq 0.$$

106. IS $\frac{\partial x}{\partial z}$ THE RECIPROCAL OF $\frac{\partial z}{\partial x}$?

The rule is that the answer is YES <u>provided that</u> the same variable(s) is being held constant in both differentiations <u>and</u> $\partial z/\partial x$ is non-zero. (To deal with the matter fully <u>is</u> however beyond the scope of this book.) As an illustration, suppose that x, y, z and t are related by the two equations

$$x = y + 4z \quad \text{and} \quad y = zt.$$

If we differentiate the first equation partially first with respect to x and then with respect to z <u>holding y constant</u> in both differentiations, we find

$$1 = 4\left(\frac{\partial z}{\partial x}\right)_y \quad \text{and} \quad \left(\frac{\partial x}{\partial z}\right)_y = 4.$$

So $\quad \left(\frac{\partial z}{\partial x}\right)_y = \frac{1}{4} \quad$ and $\quad \left(\frac{\partial x}{\partial z}\right)_y = 4,$

which illustrates the rule. (Recall that the subscripts y denote that y is being held constant in the differentiations.)

Similarly if we take the original two equations and eliminate y we have

$$x = zt + 4z.$$

If we now differentiate <u>this</u> equation partially first with respect to x and then with respect to z <u>but</u> now <u>holding t constant</u>, we find that

$$1 = t\left(\frac{\partial z}{\partial x}\right)_t + 4\left(\frac{\partial z}{\partial x}\right)_t \quad \text{and} \quad \left(\frac{\partial x}{\partial z}\right)_t = t + 4.$$

So $\quad \left(\frac{\partial z}{\partial x}\right)_t = \frac{1}{t+4} \quad$ and $\quad \left(\frac{\partial x}{\partial z}\right)_t = t + 4,$

which illustrates the rule again.

Do notice however that this example also has something <u>negative</u> to say: it demonstrates that (in general)

$$\left(\frac{\partial z}{\partial x}\right)_y \neq \left(\frac{\partial z}{\partial x}\right)_t.$$

An indication of the proof of the rule is given in Ex. 7.20.

<u>EXAMPLES TO DO:</u> Page 101: Exs. 19, 20.

107. JACOBIANS

Suppose that u and v are functions of two variables x and y. Then, provided that the partial derivatives exist, we define the <u>Jacobian</u> $\frac{\partial(u,v)}{\partial(x,y)}$ by

$$\frac{\partial(u,v)}{\partial(x,y)} = \frac{\partial u}{\partial x}\frac{\partial v}{\partial y} - \frac{\partial v}{\partial x}\frac{\partial u}{\partial y} ,$$

or, equivalently, by

$$\frac{\partial(u,v)}{\partial(x,y)} = \det \begin{bmatrix} \partial u/\partial x & \partial u/\partial y \\ \partial v/\partial x & \partial v/\partial y \end{bmatrix} ,$$

where det denotes the determinant of the matrix.
Similarly for functions of more than two variables, e.g. if
u, v, w are suitable functions of three variables x, y, z,
we define

$$\frac{\partial(u,v,w)}{\partial(x,y,z)} = \det \begin{bmatrix} \partial u/\partial x & \partial u/\partial y & \partial u/\partial z \\ \partial v/\partial x & \partial v/\partial y & \partial v/\partial z \\ \partial w/\partial x & \partial w/\partial y & \partial w/\partial z \end{bmatrix} .$$

The following is the only property of Jacobians that
concerns us in this book.

<u>RESULT</u>. Suppose that u, v are functions of x and y,
and that x, y are themselves functions of u and v.
Then, provided that the partial derivatives involved exist,

$$\frac{\partial(x,y)}{\partial(u,v)} \cdot \frac{\partial(u,v)}{\partial(x,y)} = 1.$$

<u>Proof</u>. By differentiating each of the equations

$$x = x(u(x,y),v(x,y)) \quad \text{and} \quad y = y(u(x,y),v(x,y))$$

partially with respect to x and with respect to y we
obtain the four equations

$$1 = \left(\frac{\partial x}{\partial u}\right)_v \left(\frac{\partial u}{\partial x}\right)_y + \left(\frac{\partial x}{\partial v}\right)_u \left(\frac{\partial v}{\partial x}\right)_y , \quad 0 = \left(\frac{\partial x}{\partial u}\right)_v \left(\frac{\partial u}{\partial y}\right)_x + \left(\frac{\partial x}{\partial v}\right)_u \left(\frac{\partial v}{\partial y}\right)_x ,$$

$$0 = \left(\frac{\partial y}{\partial u}\right)_v \left(\frac{\partial u}{\partial x}\right)_y + \left(\frac{\partial y}{\partial v}\right)_u \left(\frac{\partial v}{\partial x}\right)_y , \quad 1 = \left(\frac{\partial y}{\partial u}\right)_v \left(\frac{\partial u}{\partial y}\right)_x + \left(\frac{\partial y}{\partial v}\right)_u \left(\frac{\partial v}{\partial y}\right)_x .$$

These can be written in matrix notation as

$$\begin{bmatrix} \partial x/\partial u & \partial x/\partial v \\ \partial y/\partial u & \partial y/\partial v \end{bmatrix} \begin{bmatrix} \partial u/\partial x & \partial u/\partial y \\ \partial v/\partial x & \partial v/\partial y \end{bmatrix} = \begin{bmatrix} 1 & 0 \\ 0 & 1 \end{bmatrix} .$$

Taking determinants in this gives the result at once.

108. FUNCTIONAL DEPENDENCE

In changing the variables from x, y to u, v in a
double integral (as in §14), the new variables u, v <u>must</u>
be independent. In general terms this means that

u and v must have the ability to vary independently of each other. For example, a would-be change of variables like

$$u = xy, \quad v = 2(xy)^3 + 4$$

would <u>not</u> be acceptable because the value of u fixes the value of v and vice versa. Such functions u and v are <u>functionally dependent</u>. (More advanced books deal with functional dependence and functional independence in more detail.) For our purposes it will be enough to note that if $\frac{\partial(u,v)}{\partial(x,y)} = 0$ for all points (x,y) in some open set in two dimensional space then u and v are functionally dependent, e.g. for the case above of

u = xy and v = 2(xy)³ + 4 , we have

$$\frac{\partial(u,v)}{\partial(x,y)} = \det \begin{bmatrix} y & x \\ 6x^2y^3 & 6x^3y^2 \end{bmatrix} = 6x^3y^3 - 6x^3y^3 = 0.$$

This confirms that u and v are functionally dependent in this case.

EXAMPLES 7

1. (a) For $u(x,y) = x^2 - y^2$ and $v(x,y) = 2xy$, show that $\frac{\partial u}{\partial x}\frac{\partial v}{\partial y} - \frac{\partial v}{\partial x}\frac{\partial u}{\partial y} = 4(x^2 + y^2)$.

(b) Let $f(x,y) = xy^2\sin(y/x)$. Prove that

$$x\frac{\partial f}{\partial x} + y\frac{\partial f}{\partial y} = 3f .$$

2. Let $f(x,y,z) = (xyz)/r^2$, where $r^2 = x^2 + y^2 + z^2$. Prove that $x\frac{\partial f}{\partial x} + y\frac{\partial f}{\partial y} + z\frac{\partial f}{\partial z} = f$.

3. Let $\phi(x,y) = f(u)$, where $u = x^2y^3$ and f is a twice differentiable function of one variable. Show that

$$\frac{\partial\phi}{\partial x} = 2xy^3 f'(u) \quad \text{and} \quad \frac{\partial^2\phi}{\partial x^2} = 4x^2y^6 f''(u) + 2y^3 f'(u).$$

Find similar expressions for $\partial\phi/\partial y$ and $\partial^2\phi/\partial y^2$. Hence show that $9x^2\frac{\partial^2\phi}{\partial x^2} - 4y^2\frac{\partial^2\phi}{\partial y^2} + 3x\frac{\partial\phi}{\partial x} = 0$.

4. Let $\phi(x,y) = f(r)$, where $r^2 = x^2 + y^2$ and f is a twice differentiable function of one variable. Show that

$$\frac{\partial^2\phi}{\partial x^2} + \frac{\partial^2\phi}{\partial y^2} = f''(r) + \frac{1}{r}f'(r) .$$

5. Determine a positive integer n such that the

function $z(x,y) = \sin(nx) \cdot \cos(y^2)$ satisfies the partial differential equation $y^3 \frac{\partial^2 z}{\partial x^2} - y \frac{\partial^2 z}{\partial y^2} + \frac{\partial z}{\partial y} = 0$.

6. Determine the values of n such that the function $2xy + x^n y^{2n}$ is a solution of the partial differential equation $2x^2 \frac{\partial^2 f}{\partial x^2} - y^2 \frac{\partial^2 f}{\partial y^2} + 18f = 36xy$.

7. Let $z(x,y) = e^x g(y - 4x)$, where g is an arbitrary twice differentiable function of one variable. Show that

$$\frac{\partial z}{\partial x} + 4 \frac{\partial z}{\partial y} = z.$$

By taking suitable partial derivatives of this equation, show that $\frac{\partial^2 z}{\partial x^2} + 8 \frac{\partial^2 z}{\partial x \partial y} + 16 \frac{\partial^2 z}{\partial y^2} = z$.

8. Let $z(x,y) = (x + y)^2 + h(xy)$, where h is an arbitrary twice differentiable function of one variable. Show that $x \frac{\partial z}{\partial x} - y \frac{\partial z}{\partial y} = 2(x^2 - y^2)$. Deduce that

$$x^2 \frac{\partial^2 z}{\partial x^2} - y^2 \frac{\partial^2 z}{\partial y^2} = 2(x^2 - y^2).$$

9. Let $f(x,y) = 3r^2 + 2 \log r$, where $r^2 = x^2 + y^2$.

Evaluate $\partial f/\partial x$ and $\partial f/\partial y$ and prove that

$$\frac{\partial^2 f}{\partial x^2} + \frac{\partial^2 f}{\partial y^2} = 12.$$

By suitable partial differentiation of this equation, deduce that

$$\frac{\partial^4 f}{\partial x^4} + 2 \frac{\partial^4 f}{\partial x^2 \partial y^2} + \frac{\partial^4 f}{\partial y^4} = 0.$$

10. Find the general solution of each of the following partial differential equations:

(a) $\frac{\partial f}{\partial x} = 4xy$, (b) $\frac{\partial f}{\partial y} = 3x^2 + 3y^2$, (c) $\frac{\partial^2 f}{\partial x \partial y} = 0$,

(d) $\frac{\partial^2 f}{\partial x^2} = 0$, (e) $\frac{\partial^2 f}{\partial y^2} = 0$, (f) $\frac{\partial^2 f}{\partial x^2} = 6xy + 2$.

11. Find the general solution of the p.d.e.

$\frac{\partial f}{\partial x} - 2f = 0$, by treating it like the differential equation $f' - 2f = 0$ - i.e. find an integrating factor remembering that y is constant in the integration.

12. (First order partial differential equations)
In each of the following cases find the general solution of the given p.d.e. by making the change of variables indicated:

(a) $2x \frac{\partial f}{\partial x} - y \frac{\partial f}{\partial y} = 2xy$. Change to $u = xy^2$, $v = y$.

(b) $x \frac{\partial f}{\partial x} + y \frac{\partial f}{\partial y} = 3y(y^2 - x^2)$. Change to $u = x$, $v = y/x$.

(c) $y \frac{\partial f}{\partial x} + x \frac{\partial f}{\partial y} = 2xyf$. Change to $u = x^2 - y^2$, $v = y$.

(d) $x \frac{\partial z}{\partial x} - 2 \cos^2 y \frac{\partial z}{\partial y} = z$. Change to $u = x^2 e^{\tan y}$, $v = y$.

[Further similar examples are available on page 217.]

13. Suppose that $F(x,y) = f(u,v)$, where $u = x^2 + y^2$ and $v = y$. Find expressions for $\partial F/\partial x$ and $\partial F/\partial y$ (as in §93) and also expressions for $\partial^2 F/\partial x^2$ and $\partial^2 F/\partial y^2$ (as in §98) in terms of the partial derivatives of f with respect to u and v.

14. (Second order partial differential equations)
In each of the following cases find the general solution of the given p.d.e. by making the change of variables indicated:

(a) $4 \frac{\partial^2 f}{\partial x^2} - \frac{\partial^2 f}{\partial y^2} = 0$. Change to $u = x - 2y$, $v = x + 2y$.

(b) $\frac{\partial^2 f}{\partial x^2} - 2 \frac{\partial^2 f}{\partial x \partial y} + \frac{\partial^2 f}{\partial y^2} = 0$. Change to $u = x + y$, $v = y$.

(c) $x \frac{\partial^2 f}{\partial x^2} - y \frac{\partial^2 f}{\partial x \partial y} + \frac{\partial f}{\partial x} = 0$. Change to $u = xy$, $v = y$.

(d) $x^2 \frac{\partial^2 f}{\partial x^2} + 2xy \frac{\partial^2 f}{\partial x \partial y} + y^2 \frac{\partial^2 f}{\partial y^2} = 0$. Change to $u = x/y$, $v = y$.

(e) $4y^3 \frac{\partial^2 z}{\partial x^2} - 9y \frac{\partial^2 z}{\partial y^2} + 9 \frac{\partial z}{\partial y} = 0$. Change to $u = 3x + y^2$, $v = 3x - y^2$.

[Note: Equation (a) is a particular case of the Wave Equation. For more examples like (a) - (e) see p.217.]

15. Suppose that $f(x,y) = z(u,v)$, where $u = x/y^2$ and $v = y$. Prove that

$$2x \frac{\partial f}{\partial x} + y \frac{\partial f}{\partial y} = v \frac{\partial z}{\partial v} .$$

Deduce from this that

$$4x^2 \frac{\partial^2 f}{\partial x^2} + 4xy \frac{\partial^2 f}{\partial x \partial y} + y^2 \frac{\partial^2 f}{\partial y^2} + 2x \frac{\partial f}{\partial x} = v^2 \frac{\partial^2 z}{\partial v^2} .$$

Hence find the general solution of the partial differential equation

$$4x^2 \frac{\partial^2 f}{\partial x^2} + 4xy \frac{\partial^2 f}{\partial x \partial y} + y^2 \frac{\partial^2 f}{\partial y^2} + 2x \frac{\partial f}{\partial x} = 6x.$$

16. Let r and θ be polar coordinates in two dimensions, i.e. $x = r \cos \theta$, $y = r \sin \theta$. Show that if f is defined by

$$f(r,\theta) = A \log r + B,$$

where A and B are constants, then f is a solution of the two dimensional Laplace Equation (§104).

17. Let $x = u + v$, $y = uv$. Show that if $f(x,y) = g(u,v)$ then

$$\frac{\partial f}{\partial x} = \frac{1}{(u - v)} \left(u \frac{\partial g}{\partial u} - v \frac{\partial g}{\partial v} \right) , \quad \frac{\partial f}{\partial y} = \frac{-1}{(u - v)} \left(\frac{\partial g}{\partial u} - \frac{\partial g}{\partial v} \right) .$$

18. Carry out the work to find $\partial^2 f / \partial x^2$ and $\partial^2 f / \partial y^2$ in §104 and so verify that

$$\frac{\partial^2 f}{\partial x^2} + \frac{\partial^2 f}{\partial y^2} = \frac{\partial^2 g}{\partial r^2} + \frac{1}{r} \frac{\partial g}{\partial r} + \frac{1}{r^2} \frac{\partial^2 g}{\partial \theta^2} .$$

19. Let x, y, r, θ be related by $x = r \cos \theta$ and $y = r \sin \theta$. Find

$$\left(\frac{\partial x}{\partial r} \right)_\theta , \quad \left(\frac{\partial x}{\partial r} \right)_y , \quad \left(\frac{\partial r}{\partial x} \right)_\theta , \quad \left(\frac{\partial r}{\partial x} \right)_y .$$

Would you expect the first two to be equal? Would you expect the last two to be equal? Which pairs would you expect to be reciprocals of each other?

20. Suppose that a suitably well behaved function F of three variables satisfies the equation $F(x,y,z) = 0$ on some open set. Suppose further that this equation defines z as a function of x and y and also defines x as a function of y and z on this open set. Find expressions for

$$\left(\frac{\partial z}{\partial x} \right)_y \quad \text{and} \quad \left(\frac{\partial x}{\partial z} \right)_y$$

in terms of $\partial F / \partial x$, $\partial F / \partial y$, $\partial F / \partial z$, and hence show that they are reciprocals of each other (subject to certain partial derivatives that occur in denominators being non-zero). [This provides some confirmation of the statements made in §106.]

VIII.   ERRORS AND EXACT DIFFERENTIALS

---

109.   THE FORM OF A DIFFERENTIAL

For a function of three variables, say the function u   where

$$u(x,y,z) = xyz^3 + 4y^2,$$

we define the differential of   u   as

$$du = \frac{\partial u}{\partial x} dx + \frac{\partial u}{\partial y} dy + \frac{\partial u}{\partial z} dz ,$$

so that in this case

$$du = yz^3 dx + (xz^3 + 8y) dy + 3xyz^2 dz .$$

Notice that   dx, dy, dz   act only as markers in much the same way as in a vector like (3,6,7) the brackets and commas act as markers.   There is no suggestion that   dx, dy, dz   are numbers.   Similarly for a function   u   of any number of variables   n,   we can write

$$du = \frac{\partial u}{\partial x_1} dx_1 + \frac{\partial u}{\partial x_2} dx_2 + \ldots + \frac{\partial u}{\partial x_n} dx_n .$$

(These definitions are of course subject to the existence of the partial derivatives.)

This representation of a differential is sufficient for understanding and working all the results and examples on the topic in this book.   There is however a more sophisticated view of the concept but we do not deal with it here.

110.   THE DIFFERENTIAL OF A FUNCTION OF A FUNCTION

This is related to the differential of the given function.

To illustrate, suppose that   u   is a function of three variables   x, y, z   and that   du   exists in a certain region.   The differentials of functions of   u   (e.g. u^2, u^3, log u, etc)   are then related to the differential of   u.   Suppose that we are looking for the differential of   f(u),   where   f   is a function of one variable and that f   is differentiable on the relevant region.   Then, from the definition of §109,

$$d(f(u)) = \frac{\partial}{\partial x}(f(u)) dx + \frac{\partial}{\partial y}(f(u)) dy + \frac{\partial}{\partial z}(f(u)) dz$$

$$= \frac{df}{du} \frac{\partial u}{\partial x} dx + \frac{df}{du} \frac{\partial u}{\partial y} dy + \frac{df}{du} \frac{\partial u}{\partial z} dz \quad [\text{from §91(1)}]$$

$$= f'(u) \left[\frac{\partial u}{\partial x} dx + \frac{\partial u}{\partial y} dy + \frac{\partial u}{\partial z} dz\right] = f'(u) du.$$

The conclusion is that provided the differentials and derivatives involved exist,

$$d(f(u)) = f'(u)\,du\,. \qquad\qquad \ldots (1)$$

In the above argument we took u as a function of three variables. Clearly however a similar argument justifies (1), when u is a function of any number of variables. As examples of the use of (1), notice that

$$d(u^2) = 2u\,du, \qquad d(u^3 + 4u) = (3u^2 + 4)\,du,$$

$$d(1/u) = (-1/u^2)\,du, \qquad d(\log u) = (1/u)\,du.$$

111. TAYLOR'S THEOREM

Under suitable conditions the one dimensional form of Taylor's theorem allows certain functions of one real variable to be expanded in a neighbourhood of a point $x = a$ in the form

$$f(a + h) = f(a) + \frac{h}{1!}f'(a) + \frac{h^2}{2!}f''(a) + \ldots \,.$$

Similarly, under suitable conditions certain functions f of two real variables can be expanded in a neighbourhood of a point (a,b) using the two dimensional form of Taylor's theorem, namely,

$$f(a+h,b+k) = f(a,b) + \frac{1}{1!}\left[h\frac{\partial}{\partial x} + k\frac{\partial}{\partial y}\right]f(a,b)$$

$$+ \frac{1}{2!}\left[h\frac{\partial}{\partial x} + k\frac{\partial}{\partial y}\right]^2 f(a,b) + \ldots$$

$$= f(a,b) + \left[h\frac{\partial f}{\partial x} + k\frac{\partial f}{\partial y}\right]$$

$$+ \frac{1}{2}\left[h^2\frac{\partial^2 f}{\partial x^2} + 2hk\frac{\partial^2 f}{\partial x\partial y} + k^2\frac{\partial^2 f}{\partial y^2}\right] + \ldots \,,$$

where the partial derivatives are evaluated at the point (a,b).

Similarly for suitable functions of n real variables

$$f(a_1+h_1, \ldots, a_n+h_n)$$

$$= f(a_1, \ldots, a_n) + (h_1\frac{\partial f}{\partial x_1} + \ldots + h_n\frac{\partial f}{\partial x_n}) + \ldots \,,$$

where the partial derivatives are evaluated at the point $(a_1,a_2, \ldots, a_n)$.

112. ESTIMATION OF ERRORS

Suppose that we measure the sides of a rectangle in an attempt to calculate its area. Suppose that the true lengths of the sides are x and y, but that errors in measurement give measured values $x + \delta x$ and $y + \delta y$. The value then calculated for the area will be $(x + \delta x)(y + \delta y)$, i.e. the calculated area is

$$xy + y \, \delta x + x \, \delta y + \delta x \, \delta y \, ,$$

so that the error in the value calculated for the area is $(y \, \delta x + x \, \delta y + \delta x \, \delta y)$. In practice, if δx and δy are small, then the term $\delta x \, \delta y$ contributes relatively little, so that a first approximation to the error is $(y \, \delta x + x \, \delta y)$.

Clearly the above reasoning can be generalised to the calculation of any quantity f which is a function of two or more measured variables. For example, suppose that the quantity f is to be calculated from the formula

$$f = f(x,y,z) \, ,$$

where x, y, z are measured. Suppose further that at the point where the measurements are made the true values of the variables are (x,y,z) but that errors in measurement give measured values $(x + \delta x, y + \delta y, z + \delta z)$. The value of f then calculated from the formula will be $f(x + \delta x, y + \delta y, z + \delta z)$, and Taylor's theorem (§111) tells us that (subject to suitable differentiability conditions)

$$f(x + \delta x, y + \delta y, z + \delta z)$$
$$= f(x,y,z) + \left[\frac{\partial f}{\partial x} \delta x + \frac{\partial f}{\partial y} \delta y + \frac{\partial f}{\partial z} \delta z \right] + \ldots \, ,$$

where the partial derivatives are evaluated at (x,y,z). It follows that a first approximation to the error in f is then

$$\frac{\partial f}{\partial x} \delta x + \frac{\partial f}{\partial y} \delta y + \frac{\partial f}{\partial z} \delta z \, , \qquad \ldots (1)$$

where the partial derivatives are evaluated at (x,y,z).

Notice that (1) is of the same form as the differential in §109, apart from the fact that the numbers δx, δy, δz replace the markers dx, dy, dz. (Actually in practice in examples (§113, §114) we shall write dx, dy, dz instead of δx, δy, δz but this is only a matter of convenience.)

The idea is of course not restricted to functions of three variables: for a function f of two variables the first approximation to the error is

$$\frac{\partial f}{\partial x} \delta x + \frac{\partial f}{\partial y} \delta y \qquad \ldots (2)$$

and for a function f of n variables the corresponding expression is

$$\frac{\partial f}{\partial x_1} \delta x_1 + \frac{\partial f}{\partial x_2} \delta x_2 + \ldots + \frac{\partial f}{\partial x_n} \delta x_n \, . \qquad \ldots (3)$$

113. **EXAMPLE.** The volume of a cylindrical tank with a circular base is given by $V = \pi x^2 y$, where x is its base radius and y is its height. Find an estimate of the maximum possible percentage error in its volume if the measurements of x and y are subject to errors of ±3% and ±2% respectively.

Solution. (First method) Writing dx, dy, dz instead of δx, δy, δz, we see from (2) of §112 that

$$dV = \frac{\partial V}{\partial x} dx + \frac{\partial V}{\partial y} dy ,$$

i.e. $\quad dV = (2\pi xy) dx + (\pi x^2) dy .$ $\qquad \ldots (*)$

The percentage error in V is $(dV \times 100)/V$. To introduce it into the problem we multiply through in (*) by 100/V.

So $\qquad \dfrac{dV}{V} \times 100 = (2\pi xy\, dx + \pi x^2 dy) \times \dfrac{100}{V}$

$$= \frac{(2\pi xy\, dx + \pi x^2 dy)}{\pi x^2 y} \times 100$$

$$= 2 \left(\frac{dx}{x} \times 100 \right) + \left(\frac{dy}{y} \times 100 \right).$$

(Notice that $\left(\dfrac{dx}{x} \times 100 \right)$ and $\left(\dfrac{dy}{y} \times 100 \right)$ which have conveniently appeared are the percentage errors in x and y.) So an estimate of the maximum possible value of $\left(\dfrac{dV}{V} \times 100 \right)$

$$= 2(+3) + 2 = 8,$$

while an estimate of its minimum possible value

$$= 2(-3) - 2 = -8.$$

So we estimate that V is subject to an error of ±8%.

Solution. (Second method) Take logarithms in the original formula to find

$$\log V = \log \pi + 2 \log x + \log y .$$

Take differentials of each side to find

$$\frac{1}{V} dV = 2 \frac{dx}{x} + \frac{dy}{y} .$$

Multiplying by 100 conveniently introduces all the percentage errors desired, i.e.

$$\left(\frac{dV}{V} \times 100 \right) = 2 \left(\frac{dx}{x} \times 100 \right) + \left(\frac{dy}{y} \times 100 \right).$$

So the estimated percentage error in $V = 2(\pm 3)\% + (\pm 2)\%$

$$= \pm 8\% .$$

Notice: The taking of logarithms in the second method has the great advantage of introducing the percentage errors

more easily.   Their introduction in the first method is
less natural.   The taking of logarithms is <u>particularly</u>
successful if the formula involves only a <u>product</u> or
<u>quotient</u> of variables, as in this case.   A combination of
both methods may however be needed as in the example in
§114.

114.   EXAMPLE.   The quantity V is calculated using the
          formula
$$V = \frac{\sqrt{(x^2 - y)}}{z} \; ,$$
where the quantities x, y, z are measured as 3.0, 6.5
and 2.1 respectively. The possible percentage errors in
these measurements of x, y, z are ±1%, ±2% and ±1%
respecively.   Make an estimate of the range of percentage
error for the calculated value of V.

<u>Solution</u>.   It is advantageous to take logarithms first.
This will dispose of the square root sign and the quotient.

So $\log V = \frac{1}{2}\log(x^2 - y) \; - \; \log z$.

Now take differentials to find
$$\frac{dV}{V} = \frac{1}{2(x^2 - y)} \; d(x^2 - y) \; - \; \frac{dz}{z} \; ,$$
i.e. $\dfrac{dV}{V} = \dfrac{1}{2(x^2 - y)} \; (2x\,dx \; - \; dy) \; - \; \dfrac{dz}{z}$.

Multiply by 100 in an attempt to introduce percentage
errors.   So
$$\left(\frac{dV}{V} \times 100\right) = \frac{1}{2(x^2 - y)}(2x\,dx \; - \; dy) \times 100 \; - \; \left(\frac{dz}{z} \times 100\right).$$
This has introduced the percentage errors for V and z.
Those for x and y must however be introduced by brute
force as follows:
$$\left(\frac{dV}{V} \times 100\right) = \frac{1}{2(x^2 - y)}\left(2x^2\left(\frac{dx}{x} \times 100\right) \; - \; y\left(\frac{dy}{y} \times 100\right)\right)$$
$$- \left(\frac{dz}{z} \times 100\right) \; \ldots (*)$$

So the percentage error for V
$$= \frac{1}{2(9.0 - 6.5)}[18.0\,(\pm 1\%) \; - \; 6.5\,(\pm 2\%)] \; - \; [\pm 1\%] \; .$$
Choosing suitable signs to achieve the maximum and minimum
possible estimates of the percentage error in V gives
$$\pm\left(\frac{1}{5}(31) \; + \; 1\right)\%, \quad \text{i.e. } \pm 7.2\% \; .$$

N.B.   There are two points to notice here.
        Firstly, as mentioned in §112, this estimate of the
error is by first order terms only.   The percentage

errors must therefore in some sense be "small", so that terms of higher order can be neglected.

Secondly, the theory tells us to substitute the <u>true</u> values of x, y, z in (*) in the above example, and <u>not</u> the measured ones.   We substituted the measured ones because we did not know the true ones.   In many cases this will make little difference to the final answer, but be warned that in some circumstances it might lead to trouble.

<u>EXAMPLES TO DO</u>:   Pages 112-113: Exs. 1 - 7.

115.   EXACT DIFFERENTIALS

For a function of two variables like f given by

$$f(x,y) = x^4 + x^3y + 3y^4 - 12$$

we can calculate the differential of f as

$$df = \frac{\partial f}{\partial x} dx + \frac{\partial f}{\partial y} dy ,$$

$$= (4x^3 + 3x^2y) dx + (x^3 + 12y^3) dy.$$

There is however the possibility of trying to reverse the process, i.e. being given an expression like

$$(4x^3y^4 + 15x^2) dx + (4x^4y^3 - 12y^2) dy$$

and being asked to find the function f for which this is df.

Notice at the outset that this reversal is <u>not</u> always possible, i.e. not all expressions of the form

$$P(x,y) dx + Q(x,y) dy \qquad \ldots (1)$$

can be written as df for some function f.   Expressions of the form (1) which <u>can</u> be written as df for some function f are called <u>exact differentials</u>.

For the <u>types of function dealt with in this book</u> we have the following useful result:

<u>RESULT</u>. $P(x,y) dx + Q(x,y) dy$ is an exact differential if and only if $\frac{\partial P}{\partial y} = \frac{\partial Q}{\partial x}$.

We omit the proof that if $\frac{\partial P}{\partial y} = \frac{\partial Q}{\partial x}$ then $P dx + Q dy$ is exact, but we can prove that if $P dx + Q dy$ is exact then $\frac{\partial P}{\partial y} = \frac{\partial Q}{\partial x}$ as follows:

Suppose that $P dx + Q dy$ is exact.   So $P = \frac{\partial F}{\partial x}$

and $Q = \frac{\partial F}{\partial y}$ for some function F.   So $\frac{\partial P}{\partial y} = \frac{\partial^2 F}{\partial y \partial x}$ and

$\frac{\partial Q}{\partial x} = \frac{\partial^2 F}{\partial x \partial y}$.   The commutative property of partial differentiation (§88) then shows that (subject to F being a suitably well behaved function) we have $\frac{\partial P}{\partial y} = \frac{\partial Q}{\partial x}$, as required.

As examples of the use of the above result notice the following.   On one hand

$$(4x^3y^4 + 15x^2)\, dx \; + \; (4x^4y^3 - 12y^2)\, dy \qquad \ldots (2)$$

is exact, because

$$\frac{\partial P}{\partial y} = 16x^3y^3 \quad \text{and} \quad \frac{\partial Q}{\partial x} = 16x^3y^3$$

and we can therefore seek f for which (2) is df.
On the other hand

$$(3y - 3y^2)\, dx \; + \; (2x - 3xy)\, dy \qquad \ldots (3)$$

is not exact, because

$$\frac{\partial P}{\partial y} = 3 - 6y \quad \text{and} \quad \frac{\partial Q}{\partial x} = 2 - 3y$$

and these are in general unequal.   So it is futile to search for a function g for which (3) is dg.

The example of §116 illustrates the method of finding the function f in cases like (2).

116.   HOW TO FIND f FROM df

EXAMPLE.   Show that $(4x^3 - 4y + 3)\, dx + (4y^3 - 4x)\, dy$ is an exact differential df, and find a suitable function f.

Solution.   Writing the given differential as P dx + Q dy, notice that

$$\frac{\partial P}{\partial y} = -4 \quad \text{and} \quad \frac{\partial Q}{\partial x} = -4.$$

So the given differential is exact and we know that it can be written as $\frac{\partial f}{\partial x}\, dx + \frac{\partial f}{\partial y}\, dy$ for a suitable f.   So, in particular, we must then have

$$\frac{\partial f}{\partial y} = 4y^3 - 4x .$$

This equation can be integrated just as we integrated other partial differential equations in §95.   So

$$f(x,y) = \int (4y^3 - 4x)\, dy = y^4 - 4xy + \phi(x),$$

where ϕ is an arbitrary function of x.   For this f to be correct however, $\frac{\partial f}{\partial x}$ calculated from it must tally with the coefficient of dx in the given differential. So we must have

$$-4y + \phi'(x) = 4x^3 - 4y + 3,$$
$$\text{i.e.} \quad \phi'(x) = 4x^3 + 3.$$

So $\phi(x) = x^4 + 3x + C$ (on integration), where C is a genuine constant. So we can conclude that

$$f(x,y) = y^4 - 4xy + x^4 + 3x + C.$$

So $f(x,y) = y^4 - 4xy + x^4 + 3x$ gives a suitable function.

<u>Notice</u>: The strategy of what happens once the differential is known to be exact is shown in the following diagram:

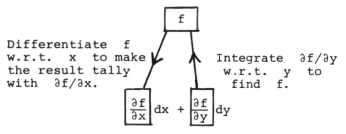

Differentiate f
w.r.t. x to make
the result tally
with $\partial f/\partial x$.

Integrate $\partial f/\partial y$
w.r.t. y to
find f.

In the above problem the following strategy would have worked equally well:

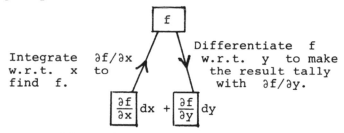

Integrate $\partial f/\partial x$
w.r.t. x to
find f.

Differentiate f
w.r.t. y to make
the result tally
with $\partial f/\partial y$.

In some problems (e.g. Ex.8.8(d), Ex.8.8(f)) one of strategies may be much better than the other because the integration involved is easier.

<u>EXAMPLES TO DO</u>: Page 114: Ex. 8.

117. EXPRESSIONS P dx + Q dy THAT CAN BE MADE EXACT BY USE OF AN INTEGRATING FACTOR

Though a given expression P dx + Q dy may not be exact, it can happen that multiplying throughout by some function of x and/or y (a so-called <u>integrating factor</u>) will make it exact. The following example illustrates the situation.

EXAMPLE. Show that $2xy\,dx - (4x^2 + 5y^3)\,dy$ is <u>not</u> exact. Find an integrating factor of the form y^n and hence find a function f such that

$$df = y^n(2xy\,dx - (4x^2 + 5y^3)\,dy).$$

<u>Solution.</u> For the given expression $\dfrac{\partial P}{\partial y} = 2x$, $\dfrac{\partial Q}{\partial x} = -8x$. So this is not exact as it stands since these are unequal.

For $y^n(2xy)\,dx - y^n(4x^2 + 5y^3)\,dy$ to be exact we need

$$\frac{\partial}{\partial y}\left(2xy^{n+1}\right) = \frac{\partial}{\partial x}\left(-4x^2y^n - 5y^{n+3}\right),$$

i.e. $2(n+1)xy^n = -8xy^n$,

i.e. $2n + 2 = -8$, i.e. $n = -5$.

So $\dfrac{2x}{y^4}\,dx - \left(\dfrac{4x^2}{y^5} + \dfrac{5}{y^2}\right)dy$ is exact. $\qquad \ldots(*)$

To find a function f for which this is df, we want

$$\frac{\partial f}{\partial x} = \frac{2x}{y^4}.$$

Integrating with respect to x gives

$$f(x,y) = \frac{x^2}{y^4} + \phi(y), \quad \text{for some function } \phi.$$

For this to tally with the form in line $(*)$ we need

$$\frac{\partial f}{\partial y} = -\frac{4x^2}{y^5} - \frac{5}{y^2},$$

i.e. $-\dfrac{4x^2}{y^5} + \phi'(y) = -\dfrac{4x^2}{y^5} - \dfrac{5}{y^2}$,

i.e. $\phi'(y) = -\dfrac{5}{y^2}$, i.e. $\phi(y) = \dfrac{5}{y} + C$.

So $f(x,y) = \dfrac{x^2}{y^4} + \dfrac{5}{y} + C$. So take $f(x,y) = \dfrac{x^2}{y^4} + \dfrac{5}{y}$.

118. **EXAMPLE.** Show that
$$y^3\,dx - (x^2 + xy^2)\,dy$$
is <u>not</u> exact, but that it has an integrating factor of the form $g(xy)$, where g is a function of one variable. Then find a function f such that

$$df = y^3 g(xy)\,dx - (x^2 + xy^2)g(xy)\,dy.$$

<u>Solution.</u> The given form is not exact because

$$\frac{\partial}{\partial y}\left(y^3\right) = 3y^2 \quad \text{and} \quad \frac{\partial}{\partial x}\left(-x^2 - xy^2\right) = -2x - y^2,$$

and these are unequal.

For $y^3 g(xy) dx - (x^2 + xy^2)g(xy) dy$ to be exact we need

$$\frac{\partial}{\partial y}\left[y^3 g(xy)\right] = \frac{\partial}{\partial x}\left[-(x^2 + xy^2)g(xy)\right],$$

i.e. $3y^2 g(u) + y^3 xg'(u) = -(2x + y^2)g(u) - (x^2 + xy^2)yg'(u)$,

(where $u = xy$),

i.e. $(x^2 y + 2y^3 x)g'(u) + (2x + 4y^2)g(u) = 0$,

i.e. $xy(x + 2y^2)g'(u) + 2(x + 2y^2)g(u) = 0$,

i.e. $ug'(u) + 2g(u) = 0$.

This is a separable (also linear) differential equation, which can be solved as in Chapter 4 to obtain the general solution $g = A/u^2$, where A is an arbitrary constant. Choosing $A = 1$ gives $g(u) = 1/u^2$, i.e. an integrating factor is $1/(xy)^2$.

So the form

$$\frac{y^3}{x^2 y^2} dx - \frac{x^2 + xy^2}{x^2 y^2} dy, \quad \text{i.e.} \quad \frac{y}{x^2} dx - \left(\frac{1}{y^2} + \frac{1}{x}\right) dy$$

is exact. This gives

$$\frac{\partial f}{\partial x} = \frac{y}{x^2} \quad \text{and} \quad f(x,y) = -\frac{y}{x} + \phi(y).$$

We then need

$$\frac{\partial f}{\partial y} = -\frac{1}{y^2} - \frac{1}{x}, \quad \text{i.e.} \quad -\frac{1}{x} + \phi'(y) = -\frac{1}{y^2} - \frac{1}{x},$$

which gives $\phi(y) = \frac{1}{y} + C$. So we then have

$$f(x,y) = -\frac{y}{x} + \frac{1}{y} + C. \quad \text{So take} \quad f(x,y) = -\frac{y}{x} + \frac{1}{y}.$$

EXAMPLES TO DO: Page 114: Ex. 9.

119. EXACT DIFFERENTIAL EQUATIONS

The same working as in the example in §116 can be used to find the solution of the differential equation

$$\frac{dy}{dx} = \frac{4x^3 - 4y + 3}{4x - 4y^3},$$

which is not amenable to the methods of Chapter 4. This differential equation can be rewritten formally as

$$(4x^3 - 4y + 3)dx + (4y^3 - 4x)dy = 0. \quad \ldots(*)$$

A differential equation written in the form

$$P(x,y)dx + Q(x,y)dy = 0$$

is called exact if the left hand side is an exact differential, i.e. the left hand side can be expressed as df for some function f. It follows from §115 that the differential equation is exact if and only if

$$\frac{\partial P}{\partial y} = \frac{\partial Q}{\partial x} \, .$$

The general solution is then $f = C$, where C is an arbitrary constant. The thinking behind the method is explained in §120. To illustrate it we solve (*) as the following example.

EXAMPLE. Show the differential equation (*) above is exact and find its general solution.

Solution. For (*), $\partial P / \partial y = -4$ and $\partial Q / \partial x = -4$. So the equation is exact. Now proceed as in the example in §116 to find $f(x,y) = y^4 - 4xy + x^4 + 3x$. The G.S. of (*) is then $y^4 - 4xy + x^4 + 3x = C$.

Notice: As in §117 and §118 you may have to multiply through by an integrating factor before solving.

EXAMPLES TO DO: Page 114: Ex. 10.

120. Suppose the equation $f(x,y) = C$ defines y as a function of x. Then the Chain Rule (§91) gives

$$\frac{\partial f}{\partial x} + \frac{\partial f}{\partial y} \cdot \frac{dy}{dx} = 0,$$

which we can **formally** rearrange as

$$\frac{\partial f}{\partial x} \, dx + \frac{\partial f}{\partial y} \, dy = 0, \quad \text{i.e.} \quad df = 0.$$

This is the thinking behind §119. (Compare also §105.)

EXAMPLES 8

1. The quantity z is calculated from measured values x and y using the formula

$$z = 4x^{1/2} \, y^{5/2} \, .$$

Estimate the percentage error in z if the measured values of x and y are subject to errors of $\pm 1\%$.

2. The quantity R is calculated from measured quantities x and y with the formula

$$R = 5xe^{-2y}.$$

Show that if the percentage errors in x and y are $p\%$ and $q\%$ respectively, then the percentage error in the calculated value of R is approximately $(p - 2qy)\%$. (Assume that p and q are both small.)

3. The quantity z is calculated from the formula

$$z = \frac{x}{x^2 + y^2} \, .$$

Show that if small percentage errors of $p\%$ and $q\%$ respectively are made in measuring x and y, then the approximate percentage error in the calculated value of z is given by

$$[p(y^2 - x^2) - 2qy^2]/(x^2 + y^2).$$

Deduce that if both x and y are overestimated by p% then z will be underestimated by p% (approximately).

4. For certain types of cargo ship an estimate of the height (H feet) of the bow breaker (i.e. the wave thrown up at the bow) in still water is given by the formula

$$H = 0.083 \frac{BV^2}{E},$$

where V is the speed of the ship in knots, B is its beam (width) in feet and E is the length of its entrance in feet. (In general terms, the length of entrance is the distance back from the bow at which the hull broadens out to its full width.) In a slight modification of an existing type of ship it is proposed to make an increase of p% in its beam and an increase of q% in its speed. Find approximately what percentage increase in the length of entrance is required if the height of the bow breaker is to be unchanged.

5. (a) Notice that $\sqrt{(8^2 + 4^2 + 1^2)} = 9$. Use differentials to estimate the values of

$$\sqrt{(8.03^2 + 3.98^2 + 1.04^2)} \quad \text{and} \quad \sqrt{(7.992^2 + 4.013^2 + 0.968^2)}.$$

Calculate the exact values with a calculator and compare.

(b) Use differentials to estimate $\sqrt{(x^2 + 5y^3)}$, when x = 1.994 and y = 1.004. Try a calculator too.

6. The quantity P is calculated using the formula

$$P = x + \frac{4}{1 + y^2}.$$

The measured values of x and y are 3.2 and 2.0 respectively and these are subject to small percentage errors of ±p% and ±q% respectively. Find an estimate (in terms of p and q only) for the maximum possible percentage error in P.

7. The quantity C is calculated from measured quantities x, y, z using the formula

$$C = xyz^2/(x - 4y + z)^2,$$

where the measurements of x, y, z are subject to errors of ±1%. Make estimates of the maximum possible percentage error in C when the true value of (x,y,z) is (a) (7, 1, 7), (b) (3, 1, 2). In each case state explicit values of x, y, z (within the ±1% error limits) intended to give the maximum possible positive percentage error in C. Use a calculator to find the actual percentage errors in C given by these values. Compare.

8. In each of the following cases show that the given expression is an exact differential and find a function f for which the given expression is df :

(a) $(4x - 7y) dx + (-7x + 12y) dy$,

(b) $(3x^2 + 4xy + 4y^2) dx + (2x^2 + 8xy - 3y^2) dy$,

(c) $(2x + y) dx + (x + 6y + 12y^2) dy$,

(d) $(ye^x(\cos x + \sin x) + 3y^2) dx + (e^x \sin x + 6xy) dy$,

(e) $(1 + \log x + 2x \log y) dx + \left[\dfrac{x^2}{y} - 2y\right] dy$,

(f) $\dfrac{(3x^2 + y^2)}{x(x^2 + y^2)} dx + \dfrac{2y}{(x^2 + y^2)} dy$.

9. In each of the following cases, show that the given form is not exact but find an integrating factor of the stated form and find a function f for which the resulting form is df:

(a) $(6x^5 + 3y^2) dx - 2xy\, dy$,   (integrating factor of

the form x^n);

(b) $2y^2 e^{2x} dx + (4ye^{2x} + e^{-y}) dy$,   (integrating factor of

the form y^n);

(c) $(y^3 + y \cos x) dx + (5xy^2 + 3 \sin x) dy$,   (integrating

factor of the form y^n);

(d) $2(y + 4) dx + 3(2x + 1) dy$,   (integrating factor of the

form $g(y)$) .

10. Show that each of the following differential equations is either exact or can be made exact by an integrating factor of the suggested form. Hence solve the differential equations :

(a) $y^4 dx + (1 + 4xy^3) dy = 0$;

(b) $(3x + 2y^2) dx + (4xy + 3y^3) dy = 0$;

(c) $(2xy^2 + y^2 + 8) dx + 2xy\, dy = 0$,   (I.F. $= e^{kx}$);

(d) $(y + 1)^2 dx - (x(y + 1) + 2) dy = 0$,   (I.F. $= g(y)$);

(e) $(4xy + 3y^3) dx + (5x^2 + 7xy^2) dy = 0$,   (I.F. $= g(xy^2)$).

IX. VECTOR CALCULUS

---

121. SCALAR AND VECTOR FUNCTIONS

Let f be a scalar function and let v be a
vector function, both defined on domains which are subsets
of ordinary three dimensional space. This means that,
for each point (x,y,z) in their domains, f(x,y,z) is
a real number and v(x,y,z) is a point in three
dimensional space (or equivalently, v(x,y,z) can be
regarded as a vector with three real componenets). So,
for example, f and v could be given by

$$f(x,y,z) = (x^2 + y^2 + z^2)^{-1} \quad \text{(not defined at } (0,0,0)),$$

$$v(x,y,z) = (2x + y, y + z, z^2) \quad \text{(defined everywhere)}.$$

122. DIV, GRAD AND CURL

For a scalar function f and a vector function v
of the types mentioned in §121 we can produce associated
functions div v, grad f, curl v, which take values at
each point at which v or f is defined. Their
definitions and properties are discussed in §123 - §125
but the following table may be of some assistance:

	acts on	gives	notation
div	VECTOR	SCALAR	div v
grad	SCALAR	VECTOR	grad f
curl	VECTOR	VECTOR	curl v

123. THE DIVERGENCE OF A VECTOR FUNCTION (DIV)

Definition. Suppose v is a vector function defined on a
subset D of three dimensional space with component
functions v_1, v_2, v_3, i.e.

$$v(x,y,z) = (v_1(x,y,z), v_2(x,y,z), v_3(x,y,z)).$$

Then

$$\text{div } v = \frac{\partial v_1}{\partial x} + \frac{\partial v_2}{\partial y} + \frac{\partial v_3}{\partial z}.$$

(This gives a scalar value for div v at every point of
the domain D.)

The alternative notation for div v is $\nabla.v$, which
is suggestive of the definition if you think of
∇ as $(\partial/\partial x, \partial/\partial y, \partial/\partial z)$ and of . as scalar product.

A vector function v for which div v = 0 is
called solenoidal.

EXAMPLE.   Let $v(x,y,z) = (x + 2y, 3y - 3z, 2y + z^2)$, for all points (x,y,z).   Calculate   div v.

Solution.   div v = $\frac{\partial}{\partial x}(x + 2y) + \frac{\partial}{\partial y}(3y - 3z) + \frac{\partial}{\partial z}(2y + z^2)$

$$= 1 + 3 + 2z = 2z + 4.$$

124.   THE GRADIENT OF A SCALAR FUNCTION (GRAD)

Definition.   Suppose that f is a scalar function defined on a subset D of three dimensional space.   Then

$$\text{grad } f = \left(\frac{\partial f}{\partial x}, \frac{\partial f}{\partial y}, \frac{\partial f}{\partial z} \right).$$

(This gives a vector value for   grad f at each point of the domain D.)

The alternative notation for   grad f is ∇f,   which is suggestive of the definition if you think of ∇ as $(\partial/\partial x, \partial/\partial y, \partial/\partial z)$.

EXAMPLE.   Let $f(x,y,z) = z(x^2 + y^2)$ for each point (x,y,z).   Find   grad f.

Solution.   grad f = $\left(\frac{\partial f}{\partial x}, \frac{\partial f}{\partial y}, \frac{\partial f}{\partial z} \right)$ = $(2xz, 2yz, x^2 + y^2)$.

125.   THE CURL OF A VECTOR FUNCTION

Definition.   Suppose that v is a vector function defined on a subset D of three dimensional space with component functions v_1, v_2, v_3 (as in §123).   Then

$$\text{curl } v = \left(\frac{\partial v_3}{\partial y} - \frac{\partial v_2}{\partial z}, \frac{\partial v_1}{\partial z} - \frac{\partial v_3}{\partial x}, \frac{\partial v_2}{\partial x} - \frac{\partial v_1}{\partial y} \right).$$

(This gives a vector value for   curl v at each point of the domain D.)

The alternative notation for   curl v is $\nabla \times v$,   which is suggestive of the definition if you think of ∇ as $(\partial/\partial x, \partial/\partial y, \partial/\partial z)$ and of $\times$ as vector product.   The components of   curl v can be read off the scheme

$$\begin{vmatrix} \frac{\partial}{\partial x} & \frac{\partial}{\partial y} & \frac{\partial}{\partial z} \\ v_1 & v_2 & v_3 \end{vmatrix}$$

in a way similar to the components of a vector product.

A vector function v for which   curl $v = 0$ is called irrotational.

EXAMPLE.   Let $v(x,y,z) = (xy^3 z, 3y - 3z, 2y + z^2)$,   for all (x,y,z) in   three dimensional space.   Find   curl v.

Solution.   From the scheme

$$
\begin{vmatrix}
\dfrac{\partial}{\partial x} & \dfrac{\partial}{\partial y} & \dfrac{\partial}{\partial z} \\[2mm]
xy^3z & 3y - 3z & 2y + z^2
\end{vmatrix}
$$

we find that   curl v = $(5,\ xy^3,\ -3xy^2z)$ at (x,y,z).

EXAMPLES TO DO: Page 123: Ex. 1.

126.   DIRECTIONAL DERIVATIVES

Definition.   Let ϕ be a scalar function defined on a
subset of three dimensional space, let (x,y,z) be an
interior point of the subset and let n be a unit vector.
Then the directional derivative of ϕ at $(x,\overline{y,z)}$ in the
direction of n is defined to have the value $(n \cdot \operatorname{grad} \phi)$
and may be denoted by $\dfrac{\partial\phi}{\partial n}$.   So

$$
\frac{\partial\phi}{\partial n} = n \cdot \operatorname{grad} \phi ,
$$

where the dot denotes scalar product.

   The value of $\dfrac{\partial\phi}{\partial n}$ at a point (x,y,z) gives a measure
of how fast ϕ is changing in the direction of the vector
n at the point (x,y,z), in much the same way as the
partial derivative $\dfrac{\partial\phi}{\partial x}$ gives a measure of whether ϕ is
increasing or decreasing in the direction of the positive
x-axis.   If $\dfrac{\partial\phi}{\partial n}$ is positive then ϕ is increasing in the
direction of n,   while if it is negative then ϕ is
decreasing in the direction of n at the point (x,y,z).

EXAMPLE.   Find the directional derivative of x^2y^3z
at the point $(1,2,5)$ in the direction of the vector
$(1,-2,2)$.

Solution.   Here $\phi(x,y,z) = x^2y^3z$ and the unit vector n
in the required direction is $\frac{1}{3}(1,-2,2)$.   So

$$
\frac{\partial\phi}{\partial n} = \tfrac{1}{3}(1,-2,2) \cdot (2xy^3z,\ 3x^2y^2z,\ x^2y^3)
$$
$$
\text{where } (x,y,z) = (1,2,5),
$$
$$
= \tfrac{1}{3}(1,-2,2) \cdot (80,60,8)
$$
$$
= \frac{80 - 120 + 16}{3} = -8.
$$

EXAMPLES TO DO: Pages 123-124: Exs. 2, 3, 11.

127. IDENTITIES

RESULT. Let ϕ be a scalar function and let v be a vector function. Then

    (i) $\operatorname{curl}(\operatorname{grad}\phi) = 0$,

    (ii) $\operatorname{div}(\operatorname{curl} v) = 0$,

    (iii) $\operatorname{div}(\phi v) = \phi \operatorname{div} v + v \cdot \operatorname{grad}\phi$,

    (iv) $\operatorname{curl}(\phi v) = \phi \operatorname{curl} v - v \times \operatorname{grad}\phi$.

(Here we assume that ϕ and the components of v are functions for which the commutative property of partial differentiation (§88) holds.)

Proof. (i) $\operatorname{curl}(\operatorname{grad}\phi) = \operatorname{curl}\left(\dfrac{\partial\phi}{\partial x}, \dfrac{\partial\phi}{\partial y}, \dfrac{\partial\phi}{\partial z}\right)$.

So the first component of $\operatorname{curl}(\operatorname{grad}\phi) = \dfrac{\partial}{\partial y}\left(\dfrac{\partial\phi}{\partial z}\right) - \dfrac{\partial}{\partial z}\left(\dfrac{\partial\phi}{\partial y}\right)$

$$= \dfrac{\partial^2\phi}{\partial y \partial z} - \dfrac{\partial^2\phi}{\partial z \partial y} = 0 \quad \text{(by §88)}.$$

Similarly the other components are also zero.

(ii) $\operatorname{div}(\operatorname{curl} v) = \dfrac{\partial}{\partial x}\left(\dfrac{\partial v_3}{\partial y} - \dfrac{\partial v_2}{\partial z}\right) + \dfrac{\partial}{\partial y}\left(\dfrac{\partial v_1}{\partial z} - \dfrac{\partial v_3}{\partial x}\right)$

$$+ \dfrac{\partial}{\partial z}\left(\dfrac{\partial v_2}{\partial x} - \dfrac{\partial v_1}{\partial y}\right)$$

$= \dfrac{\partial^2 v_3}{\partial x \partial y} - \dfrac{\partial^2 v_2}{\partial x \partial z} + \dfrac{\partial^2 v_1}{\partial y \partial z} - \dfrac{\partial^2 v_3}{\partial y \partial x} + \dfrac{\partial^2 v_2}{\partial z \partial x} - \dfrac{\partial^2 v_1}{\partial z \partial y} = 0 \quad \text{(by §88)}.$

(iii) We have $\phi v = (\phi v_1, \phi v_2, \phi v_3)$. So

$$\operatorname{div}(\phi v) = \dfrac{\partial}{\partial x}\left(\phi v_1\right) + \dfrac{\partial}{\partial y}\left(\phi v_2\right) + \dfrac{\partial}{\partial z}\left(\phi v_3\right)$$

$$= \dfrac{\partial\phi}{\partial x} v_1 + \phi\dfrac{\partial v_1}{\partial x} + \dfrac{\partial\phi}{\partial y} v_2 + \phi\dfrac{\partial v_2}{\partial y} + \dfrac{\partial\phi}{\partial z} v_3 + \phi\dfrac{\partial v_3}{\partial z}$$

$$= \phi\left[\dfrac{\partial v_1}{\partial x} + \dfrac{\partial v_2}{\partial y} + \dfrac{\partial v_3}{\partial z}\right] + \left[v_1\dfrac{\partial\phi}{\partial x} + v_2\dfrac{\partial\phi}{\partial y} + v_3\dfrac{\partial\phi}{\partial z}\right]$$

$$= \phi \operatorname{div} v + v \cdot \operatorname{grad}\phi.$$

(iv) The first component on the left hand side

$$= \dfrac{\partial}{\partial y}\left(\phi v_3\right) - \dfrac{\partial}{\partial z}\left(\phi v_2\right)$$

$$= \phi\dfrac{\partial v_3}{\partial y} + v_3\dfrac{\partial\phi}{\partial y} - \phi\dfrac{\partial v_2}{\partial z} - v_2\dfrac{\partial\phi}{\partial z}.$$

The first component on the right hand side

$$= \phi\left(\dfrac{\partial v_3}{\partial y} - \dfrac{\partial v_2}{\partial z}\right) - \left(v_2\dfrac{\partial\phi}{\partial z} - v_3\dfrac{\partial\phi}{\partial y}\right)$$

$$= \phi \frac{\partial v_3}{\partial y} + v_3 \frac{\partial \phi}{\partial y} - \phi \frac{\partial v_2}{\partial z} - v_2 \frac{\partial \phi}{\partial z} .$$

So the first components are equal.   Similarly for the other components.

Notice: (i) Keeping in mind that (iii) is a <u>scalar</u> identity and that (iv) is a <u>vector</u> identity may assist in remembering the terms on the right hand sides.

(ii) Knowing these identities (or at least having access to them) can be a great help in doing examples, e.g. §128 and §130.

128.   In this book we use r to denote the position vector of the general point (x,y,z),   and we use r to denote its length.   So

$$r = (x,y,z) \quad \text{and} \quad r = \sqrt{(x^2 + y^2 + z^2)} .$$

Notice that $r.r = r^2$.

EXAMPLE.   Show that   div $r = 3$ and   curl $r = 0$ and find a simple expression for $\text{grad}(r^n)$.   Hence find expressions for

$$\text{div}(r^n r) \quad \text{and} \quad \text{curl}(r^n r) .$$

Solution.   div $r = \text{div}(x,y,z) = \frac{\partial}{\partial x}\left(x\right) + \frac{\partial}{\partial y}\left(y\right) + \frac{\partial}{\partial z}\left(z\right) = 3.$

$$\text{curl } r = \left(\frac{\partial}{\partial y}\left(z\right) - \frac{\partial}{\partial z}\left(y\right), \ldots , \ldots \right)$$

$$= (0 - 0, \ldots , \ldots) = 0.$$

Also, $\text{grad}(r^n) = \left(\frac{\partial}{\partial x}\left(r^n\right), \frac{\partial}{\partial y}\left(r^n\right), \frac{\partial}{\partial z}\left(r^n\right)\right)$

$$= \left(nr^{n-1}\frac{\partial r}{\partial x}, nr^{n-1}\frac{\partial r}{\partial y}, nr^{n-1}\frac{\partial r}{\partial z}\right) .$$

To find $\frac{\partial r}{\partial x}$, $\frac{\partial r}{\partial y}$, $\frac{\partial r}{\partial z}$ notice that $r^2 = x^2 + y^2 + z^2$,   so that $2r\frac{\partial r}{\partial x} = 2x$ which gives $\frac{\partial r}{\partial x} = \frac{x}{r}$ etc.

So $\text{grad}(r^n) = \left(nr^{n-1}.\frac{x}{r}, nr^{n-1}.\frac{y}{r}, nr^{n-1}.\frac{z}{r}\right)$

$$= \left(nr^{n-2}x, nr^{n-2}y, nr^{n-2}z\right)$$

$$= nr^{n-2}(x, y, z) = nr^{n-2} r .$$

To do the last two parts we use the identities (iii) and (iv) of §127 with $\phi = r^n$ and $v = r$ as follows:

$$\mathrm{div}(r^n r) = r^n \mathrm{div}\ r + r.\mathrm{grad}(r^n) = 3r^n + r.(nr^{n-2}r)$$

$$= 3r^n + nr^{n-2}r^2 = (n+3)r^n,$$

and

$$\mathrm{curl}(r^n r) = r^n \mathrm{curl}\ r - r \times \mathrm{grad}(r^n)$$

$$= 0 - r \times (nr^{n-2}r) = 0 \quad (\text{since}\quad r \times r = 0).$$

Notice: If the identities of §127 are not available then $\mathrm{div}(r^n r)$ could be calculated directly as follows:

$$\mathrm{div}(r^n r) = \frac{\partial}{\partial x}\left(r^n x\right) + \frac{\partial}{\partial y}\left(r^n y\right) + \frac{\partial}{\partial z}\left(r^n z\right)$$

$$= nr^{n-1}\frac{\partial r}{\partial x}.x + r^n + nr^{n-1}\frac{\partial r}{\partial y}.y + r^n + nr^{n-1}\frac{\partial r}{\partial z}.z + r^n$$

$$= nr^{n-1}\left(\frac{x^2}{r} + \frac{y^2}{r} + \frac{z^2}{r}\right) + 3r^n \quad (\text{using}\ \frac{\partial r}{\partial x}\ \text{from above})$$

$$= nr^{n-1}.\frac{r^2}{r} + 3r^n = (n+3)r^n.$$

We can also find $\mathrm{curl}(r^n r)$ from first principles:

$$\mathrm{curl}(r^n r) = \mathrm{curl}(r^n x,\ r^n y,\ r^n z)$$

$$= \left(\frac{\partial}{\partial y}\left(r^n z\right) - \frac{\partial}{\partial z}\left(r^n y\right),\ \dots,\ \dots\right)$$

$$= \left(nr^{n-1}\frac{\partial r}{\partial y}.z - nr^{n-1}\frac{\partial r}{\partial z}.y,\ \dots,\ \dots\right)$$

$$= \left(nr^{n-1}.\frac{y}{r}.z - nr^{n-1}.\frac{z}{r}.y,\ \dots,\ \dots\right)$$

$$= (0,\ 0,\ 0) = 0.$$

[Here once we have found the first component to be zero, we can conclude the other components are zero by symmetry.]

EXAMPLES TO DO: Page 123: Exs. 4, 5.

129.   EXAMPLE. Let a be a constant vector and let $r = (x,y,z)$ as usual. Find

$$\mathrm{grad}(a . r), \quad \mathrm{div}(a \times r), \quad \mathrm{curl}(a \times r).$$

Solution. Let $a = (a_1, a_2, a_3)$. Then

$$\mathrm{grad}(a . r) = \mathrm{grad}(a_1 x + a_2 y + a_3 z)$$

$$= \left(\frac{\partial}{\partial x}(a_1 x + a_2 y + a_3 z),\ \frac{\partial}{\partial y}(\dots),\ \frac{\partial}{\partial z}(\dots)\right)$$

$$= (a_1, a_2, a_3) = a.$$

$$\text{div}(a \times r) = \text{div}(a_2 z - a_3 y, \; a_3 x - a_1 z, \; a_1 y - a_2 x)$$

$$= \frac{\partial}{\partial x}\Big[a_2 z - a_3 y\Big] + \frac{\partial}{\partial y}\Big[a_3 x - a_1 z\Big] + \frac{\partial}{\partial z}\Big[a_1 y - a_2 x\Big]$$

$$= 0 + 0 + 0 = 0.$$

$$\text{curl}(a \times r) = \text{curl}(a_2 z - a_3 y, \; a_3 x - a_1 z, \; a_1 y - a_2 x)$$

$$= \left[\frac{\partial}{\partial y}\Big[a_1 y - a_2 x\Big] - \frac{\partial}{\partial z}\Big[a_3 x - a_1 z\Big], \; \ldots \; , \; \ldots \; \right]$$

$$= (2a_1, \; \ldots \; , \; \ldots \;)$$

$$= (2a_1, \; 2a_2, \; 2a_3) \qquad \text{[by symmetry]}$$

$$= 2a.$$

130. **EXAMPLE.** Let a be a constant vector and let $r = (x, y, z)$. Find

(i) $\text{grad}\left[\dfrac{a \cdot r}{r^n}\right]$,   (ii) $\text{div}\left[r^n(a \times r)\right]$,

(iii) $\text{curl}\left[r^n(a \times r)\right]$.

<u>Solution.</u> (i) $\text{grad}\left[\dfrac{a \cdot r}{r^n}\right] = \left[\dfrac{\partial}{\partial x}\left[\dfrac{a_1 x + a_2 y + a_3 z}{r^n}\right], \; \ldots \; , \; \ldots \; \right]$

$$= \left[\frac{a_1}{r^n} - \frac{n(a \cdot r)}{r^{n+1}} \frac{\partial r}{\partial x}, \; \ldots \; , \; \ldots \; \right]$$

$$= \left[\frac{a_1}{r^n} - \frac{n(a \cdot r)}{r^{n+1}} \cdot \frac{x}{r}, \; \ldots \; , \; \ldots \; \right] \qquad \text{(as in §128)}$$

$$= \left[\frac{a_1}{r^n} - \frac{n(a \cdot r)}{r^{n+2}} \cdot x, \; \ldots \; , \; \ldots \; \right]$$

$$= \frac{1}{r^n}a - \frac{n(a \cdot r)}{r^{n+2}}r \qquad \begin{array}{l}\text{[the other components} \\ \text{coming by symmetry].}\end{array}$$

(ii) Use the identity of §127(iii) with $\phi = r^n$ and $v = a \times r$. So

$$\text{div}\left[r^n(a \times r)\right] = r^n \text{div}(a \times r) + (a \times r) \cdot \text{grad}(r^n)$$

$$= r^n \cdot 0 + (a \times r) \cdot nr^{n-2}r \qquad \begin{array}{l}\text{(using facts} \\ \text{from §128,129)}\end{array}$$

$$= 0 + nr^{n-2}[a, r, r] \qquad \begin{array}{l}\text{(where [ ] is the} \\ \text{triple scalar product)}\end{array}$$

$$= 0 + 0 = 0.$$

(iii) Use the identity of §127(iv) with $\phi = r^n$ and $v = a \times r$. So the result is

$$\text{curl}\left[r^n(a \times r)\right] = r^n \text{curl}(a \times r) \ - \ (a \times r) \times \text{grad}(r^n)$$

$$= r^n(2a) \ - \ (a \times r) \times nr^{n-2}r \quad \text{(by §128,129)}$$

$$= 2r^n a \ + \ nr^{n-2}r \times (a \times r)$$

$$= 2r^n a \ + \ nr^{n-2}(r^2 a \ - \ (r \cdot a)r)$$

$$[\text{using} \quad a \times (b \times c) = (a \cdot c)b - (a \cdot b)c]$$

$$= (n+2)r^n a \ - \ n(r \cdot a)r^{n-2}r.$$

Notice in this example the value of the identities of §127. If these are not available it may be good policy to work out only the first component of the answer if it is a vector, and then deduce the other components by symmetry.

EXAMPLES TO DO: Pages 123-124: Exs. 6 - 10, 12.

131.   Notice that if ϕ is a scalar function then

$$\text{div}(\text{grad }\phi) = \text{div}\left(\frac{\partial \phi}{\partial x}, \frac{\partial \phi}{\partial y}, \frac{\partial \phi}{\partial z}\right)$$

$$= \frac{\partial^2 \phi}{\partial x^2} + \frac{\partial^2 \phi}{\partial y^2} + \frac{\partial^2 \phi}{\partial z^2} = \nabla^2 \phi,$$

in the usual notation for the Laplacian mentioned in §104.

An extension of this notation is $\nabla^2 v$ where v is a vector function. The meaning is

$$\nabla^2 v = (\nabla^2 v_1, \nabla^2 v_2, \nabla^2 v_3),$$

where v_1, v_2, v_3 being the components of v are scalar functions. This appears in the identity given in the following example.

EXAMPLE.   Prove that

$$\text{curlcurl } v = \text{grad div } v \ - \ \nabla^2 v.$$

Solution.   Let $v = (v_1, v_2, v_3)$.   Then

$$\text{curl } v = \left(\frac{\partial v_3}{\partial y} - \frac{\partial v_2}{\partial z}, \frac{\partial v_1}{\partial z} - \frac{\partial v_3}{\partial x}, \frac{\partial v_2}{\partial x} - \frac{\partial v_1}{\partial y}\right)$$

So the first component of curlcurl v

$$= \frac{\partial}{\partial y}\left(\frac{\partial v_2}{\partial x} - \frac{\partial v_1}{\partial y}\right) - \frac{\partial}{\partial z}\left(\frac{\partial v_1}{\partial z} - \frac{\partial v_3}{\partial x}\right)$$

$$= \frac{\partial^2 v_2}{\partial x \partial y} - \frac{\partial^2 v_1}{\partial y^2} - \frac{\partial^2 v_1}{\partial z^2} + \frac{\partial^2 v_3}{\partial x \partial z}$$

$$= \frac{\partial^2 v_1}{\partial x^2} + \frac{\partial^2 v_2}{\partial x \partial y} + \frac{\partial^2 v_3}{\partial x \partial z} - \frac{\partial^2 v_1}{\partial x^2} - \frac{\partial^2 v_1}{\partial y^2} - \frac{\partial^2 v_1}{\partial z^2}$$

(on introducing two cancelling terms)

$$= \frac{\partial}{\partial x}\left(\frac{\partial v_1}{\partial x} + \frac{\partial v_2}{\partial y} + \frac{\partial v_3}{\partial z}\right) - \nabla^2 v_1$$

$$= \frac{\partial}{\partial x}\left(\text{div } v\right) - \nabla^2 v_1$$

$$= \text{first component of } \text{grad div } v - \nabla^2 v.$$

Similarly for the other components.

EXAMPLES 9

1. Let a scalar function ϕ and a vector function v be defined by

$$\phi(x,y,z) = x^2 yz^3, \qquad v(x,y,z) = (x^2 y, \ x + 2yz, \ x + yz).$$

Find grad ϕ, div v, curl v and divgrad ϕ. Verify that curlgrad $\phi = 0$.

2. Find the directional derivative of xyz^2 at the point $(1,5,1)$ in the direction of the vector $(1,-1,2)$.

3. Find the directional derivative of $(xy + 3yz)$ at the point $(0,3,-2)$ in the direction of the vectors

   (a) $(2,2,-1)$, (b) $(1,0,1)$, (c) $(4,-7,-4)$.

What are the maximum and minimum values of the directional derivative at $(0,3,-2)$ and in which directions do they occur?

4. Let a be a constant vector and let $r = (x, y, z)$. Show that $\text{div}(r^n a) = nr^{n-2}(a \cdot r)$.

5. Show that, for scalar functions f and g,

$$\text{grad}(fg) = f \text{ grad } g + g \text{ grad } f.$$

6. Prove that, for vector functions u and v,

$$\text{div}(u \times v) = v \cdot \text{curl } u - u \cdot \text{curl } v.$$

Deduce that, for every scalar function ϕ,

$$\text{div}(r \times \text{grad } \phi) = 0,$$

where as usual $r = (x, y, z)$.

7. Let $r = (x, y, z)$ and let a be a constant vector. Prove that

(a) $\text{div}((a \cdot r)a) = a^2$,   (b) $\text{curl}((a \cdot r)a) = 0$,

(c) $\text{div}((a \cdot r)r) = 4(a \cdot r)$,   (d) $\text{curl}((a \cdot r)r) = a \times r$,

(e) $\text{div}((a \cdot r)(a \times r)) = 0$,

(f) $\text{curl}((a \cdot r)(a \times r)) = 3(a \cdot r)a - a^2 r$,

(g) $\text{curl}\left(\dfrac{a \times r}{r^2}\right) = \dfrac{2(r \cdot a)}{r^4} r$,

(h) $\text{curl}(r \times (a \times r)) = 3(r \times a)$,

(i) $\text{div}((a \cdot r)^n r) = (n + 3)(a \cdot r)^n$.

8.   Let $r = (x, y, z)$ and let a, b be constant vectors.   Prove, using suitable identities, that

$$\text{div}(a \times (b \times r)) = -2(a \cdot b) \quad \text{and} \quad \text{curl}(a \times (b \times r)) = (a \times b).$$

9.   Do the examples in §128-131 again.

10.   Let $u = \log r$, where $r = \sqrt{(x^2 + y^2 + z^2)}$.   Show that $\text{grad } u = \dfrac{1}{r^2} r$ and that $\nabla^2 u = \dfrac{1}{r^2}$.

11.   The temperature at the point (x, y, z) is given by
$$T(x, y, z) = (x + 3y)z^2.$$
Find the direction in which one should move from the point $(2, 2, 1)$ in order to achieve (a) the most rapid increase in temperature, (b) the most rapid decrease in temperature. [One wonders if such calculations are done aboard heat-seeking missiles.]

12.   A vector field F is called <u>conservative</u> if $F = \text{grad } \phi$, for some scalar function ϕ.   Prove that if F is conservative then F is irrotational, i.e. $\text{curl } F = 0$.   The converse is also true for suitably well behaved functions.   So we shall assume that if $\text{curl } F = 0$ then there exists a scalar function ϕ such that $F = \text{grad } \phi$.

Determine which of the following vector fields F are irrotational and for each such case determine a corresponding scalar function ϕ:

(a) $F = (2x + 8y - z, \; 8x + 4y - 6z, \; -x - 6y)$,

(b) $F = (3x^2 + y^2, \; 6xy, \; 2x^2 + 2z)$,

(c) $F = (y, \; x + 4z^2, \; 8yz)$.

(Compare the situation for exact differentials in §115-116. Look also at §154-155.)

X.   LINE AND SURFACE INTEGRALS

132.   TO EVALUATE A LINE INTEGRAL IN TWO DIMENSIONS

The following example illustrates the idea of a line integral.   In such an integral the integration is done along a curve in the xy-plane.

EXAMPLE.   Evaluate I given by

$$I = \int_K xy \, dx + 2y^2 \, dy,$$

where K is the curve which runs first from (2,0) to (0,2)   anticlockwise along the circle $x^2 + y^2 = 4$ and then from (0,2) to (0,0) along the y-axis.

Solution.   (First method)

In the diagram parametrise the curve
AB by $x = 2 \cos t$, $y = 2 \sin t$,
where t runs from 0 to $\tfrac{1}{2}\pi$.
Also parametrise BO by
$x = 0$, $y = t$, where t runs from
2 to 0.

Then $I = \int_{AB} + \int_{BO} = I_1 + I_2$.

$I_1 = \int_0^{\frac{1}{2}\pi} xy \frac{dx}{dt} \, dt + \int_0^{\frac{1}{2}\pi} 2y^2 \frac{dy}{dt} \, dt$

$= \int_0^{\frac{1}{2}\pi} (2 \cos t)(2 \sin t)(-2 \sin t) \, dt + \int_0^{\frac{1}{2}\pi} (8 \sin^2 t)(2 \cos t) \, dt$

$= \int_0^{\frac{1}{2}\pi} -8 \cos t \sin^2 t \, dt + \int_0^{\frac{1}{2}\pi} 16 \sin^2 t \cos t \, dt$

$= 8 \int_0^{\frac{1}{2}\pi} \sin^2 t \cos t \, dt = \frac{8}{3}$ (on putting $u = \sin t$).

$I_2 = \int_2^0 0 \cdot t \frac{dx}{dt} \, dt + \int_2^0 2t^2 \frac{dy}{dt} \, dt$

$= \int_2^0 0 \cdot t \cdot 0 \, dt + \int_2^0 2t^2 \cdot 1 \, dt = \int_2^0 2t^2 \, dt = -\frac{16}{3}$.

So $I = I_1 + I_2 = \frac{8}{3} - \frac{16}{3} = -\frac{8}{3}$.

(Second method)   As before $I = I_1 + I_2$.

$I_1 = \int_2^0 x \sqrt{(4 - x^2)} \, dx + \int_0^2 2y^2 \, dy = [-\frac{1}{3}(4 - x^2)^{\frac{3}{2}}]_2^0 + [\frac{2y^3}{3}]_0^2$

$= -\frac{8}{3} + \frac{16}{3} = \frac{8}{3}$.

$I_2 = \int_0^0 \ldots dx + \int_2^0 2y^2 \, dy = [\frac{2y^3}{3}]_2^0 = -\frac{16}{3}$.

So $I = I_1 + I_2 = 8/3 - 16/3 = -8/3$ as before.

<u>Notice</u>: The order of the limits must reflect the direction along the curve: the integral in one direction along a curve is minus the integral in the other direction along the same curve.

<u>EXAMPLES TO DO</u>:   Page 146:   Ex. 1.

133.   THE INTERPRETATION OF A LINE INTEGRAL

Suppose that a particle moves against a resistance in the xy-plane and that the resistance varies from point to point.   (Think for example of a person trying to cut his way through a jungle.)   Suppose that when the particle is at the point (x,y) the force needed to move it in the x-direction is P(x,y) and that the force needed to move it in the y-direction is Q(x,y).

Let C be a suitably well behaved curve joining two points A and B.   Then the line integral

$$\int_C P(x,y)\, dx + Q(x,y)\, dy$$

represents the <u>work done</u> in moving the particle from A to B along the curve C.

As justification of this interpretation consider a small segment of C of length δs corresponding to steps δx and δy in the x and y directions at the point (x,y).   Assuming that the curve C is sufficiently well behaved, we can think of the the segment as approximately the diagonal of the small rectangle shown.

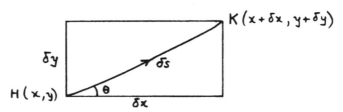

If we resolve the x and y resistances along the diagonal HK we have the total resistance force along this diagonal as

P cos θ + Q cos(90° − θ) = P cos θ + Q sin θ.

So the work done in moving along HK

        = Force required × Distance moved

        = (P cos θ + Q sin θ)δs

        = P cos θ δs + Q sin θ δs

        = P δx + Q δy (since $\delta x = \delta s$ cos θ etc).

This represents a typical contribution to the work done

from a small element of the curve C.   Summation of these
small contributions along the whole curve corresponds to
performing the line integral

$$\int_C P\ dx + Q\ dy$$

and so this line integral gives a measure of the total work
done in moving along C from A to B.

134.   GREEN'S THEOREM IN TWO DIMENSIONS

This relates a line integral round a closed curve in
the xy-plane to a double integral over the two dimensional
region which the curve encloses.   So, faced with a line
integral round a closed curve, we may prefer to calculate
the relevant double integral over the enclosed region
rather than work out the line integral directly.

It lies beyond the scope of this book to specify
in full which types of closed curve (and corresponding
enclosed region) permit the application of Green's theorem:
there are difficult topological questions involved.   In
this book the regions which we allow in this context are
simply connected (i.e. without holes) and the corresponding
boundary curves can be split into a finite number of
pieces, each piece being given by parametric equations
x = x(t), y = y(t)   (a $\leq$ t $\leq$ b), where x and y are
differentiable functions of t.   (Many important special
cases, e.g. circle, ellipse, rectangle, etc, fall into this
category.)

For such a closed curve K with corresponding
enclosed region A, Green's theorem gives the following
result:

Let P(x,y) and Q(x,y) denote functions of x and y
such that $\partial Q/\partial x$ and $\partial P/\partial y$ are continuous throughout A
and on the boundary curve K.   Then

$$\int_K P\ dx + Q\ dy = \iint_A \left(\frac{\partial Q}{\partial x} - \frac{\partial P}{\partial y}\right) dxdy,$$

where the integral round K is taken in the positive
direction, (i.e. we move round K keeping the enclosed
region on our left).

We do not prove this result, but §135-137 give
examples of its use.   More advanced books give indications
of the proof.

135.   EXAMPLE.   Using Green's theorem, evaluate the line integral

$$\int x^2\ dx + x^3 y\ dy,$$

round the curve K in the positive direction, where K is
the closed curve made up of the straight line segment from
(0,0) to (2,0), followed by the arc of the circle

$x^2 + y^2 = 4$ in the first quadrant from (2,0) to (0,2), followed by the straight line segment from (0,2) to (0,0).

Solution. Green's theorem applies because the curve is closed and $\partial Q/\partial x$ and $\partial P/\partial y$ are continuous. So, by Green's theorem,

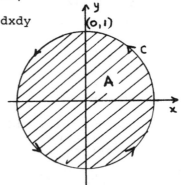

$$\int_K x^2\ dx + x^3y\ dy$$

$$= \iint_A \frac{\partial}{\partial x}\left(x^3y\right) - \frac{\partial}{\partial y}\left(x^2\right)\ dxdy = \iint_A 3x^2y\ dxdy$$

$$= \int_0^{\frac{1}{2}\pi} d\theta \int_0^2 3r^2\cos^2\theta\ r\sin\theta\ r\ dr \quad \text{(changing to polars)}$$

$$= 3\int_0^{\frac{1}{2}\pi} \cos^2\theta\ \sin\theta\ d\theta \int_0^2 r^4\ dr$$

$$= 3[-\cos^3\theta/3]_0^{\frac{1}{2}\pi}\ [r^5/5]_0^2 = 32/5 .$$

Notice: Evaluating this line integral <u>directly</u> would involve splitting the given integral into three parts corresponding to the three parts of the curve. These would then be evaluated directly as in the example in §132.

136. EXAMPLE. Evaluate the line integral

$$\int x^3y^2\ dy$$

round the circle $x^2 + y^2 = 1$ in the anti-clockwise direction (a) using Green's theorem, (b) directly.

Solution. (a) Using Green's theorem,

$$\int_C 0\ dx + x^3y^2\ dy = \iint_A (3x^2y^2 - 0)dxdy$$

$$= \int_0^{2\pi} d\theta \int_0^1 3r^2\cos^2\theta\ r^2\sin^2\theta\ r\ dr$$

$$= 3 \int_0^{2\pi} \cos^2\theta\ \sin^2\theta\ d\theta \int_0^1 r^5\ dr$$

$$= 3.4 \int_0^{\frac{1}{2}\pi} \cos^2\theta\ \sin^2\theta\ d\theta\ [r^6/6]_0^1$$

$$= \frac{12}{6}\cdot\frac{1\cdot 1}{4\cdot 2}\cdot\tfrac{1}{2}\pi \quad \text{(by §39)}$$

$$= \pi/8 .$$

(b) Parametrise C by $x = \cos t$, $y = \sin t$, where $0 \le t \le 2\pi$. Then $\int x^3y^2\ dy = \int_0^{2\pi} \cos^3 t\ \sin^2 t\ \frac{dy}{dt}\ dt$

$$= \int_0^{2\pi} \cos^3 t \, \sin^2 t \, \cos t \, dt = \int_0^{2\pi} \cos^4 t \, \sin^2 t \, dt$$

$$= \int_0^{2\pi} \cos^4 t \, \sin^2 t \, dt = 4 \cdot \frac{1 \cdot 3}{6 \cdot 4 \cdot 2} \cdot \tfrac{1}{2}\pi \quad \text{(by §39)}$$

$$= \pi/8 \, , \quad \text{(which agrees with (a)).}$$

Notice: Here there is little difference in the amount of work involved in the evaluation by the two methods. There is no doubt however that in some cases the evaluation of a line integral using Green's theorem demands less effort than the direct approach.

EXAMPLES TO DO: Pages 146-147: Exs. 2 - 6.

137. LINE INTEGRALS WHICH ARE INDEPENDENT OF THE PATH BETWEEN THE ENDPOINTS

If the line integral $\int P \, dx + Q \, dy$ is taken along _different_ admissible curves joining the same two points in the xy-plane, the resulting values are in general different. The work done interpretation of §133 would suggest this: one path through a jungle may require less effort than another.

If however P and Q have continuous partial derivatives and

$$\frac{\partial Q}{\partial x} = \frac{\partial P}{\partial y} \quad \text{at all points of the xy-plane,}$$

then the value of the line integral $\int P \, dx + Q \, dy$ is the _same_ for all admissible curves joining any given pair of endpoints, i.e. the value of the line integral is independent of the choice of path between these endpoints.

We can give justification of this assertion using Green's theorem as follows:

Take the points A and B and the curves C_1 and C_2 joining them and let the region enclosed be R as shown in the diagram. Consider the closed curve formed by running on C_1 from A to B and then on C_2 reversed from B to A. Green's theorem then tells us that

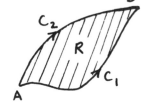

$$\left[\int_{C_1} P \, dx + Q \, dy \right] + \left[\int_{-C_2} P \, dx + Q \, dy \right] = \iint_R \left(\frac{\partial Q}{\partial x} - \frac{\partial P}{\partial y} \right) dx \, dy.$$

Now introduce the assumption that $\partial Q / \partial x = \partial P / \partial y$ at all points of the xy-plane. The double integral on the right is then zero. So the left side is zero too. So

$$\int_{C_1} P \, dx + Q \, dy = -\int_{-C_2} P \, dx + Q \, dy = \int_{C_2} P \, dx + Q \, dy,$$

because the value of the line integral in one direction is the negative of its value along the same curve in the opposite direction. The integrals along C_1 and C_2 are thus proved to be equal as required.

Notice: (i) From §115 we know that $\partial P/\partial y = \partial Q/\partial x$ if and only if P dx + Q dy is an exact differential. This can also be regarded as a criterion for the line integral $\int$ P dx + Q dy to be independent of the path.

(ii) Suppose that we are to find I, where

$$I = \int_C P \, dx + Q \, dy,$$

where P dx + Q dy is an exact differential dF and C is a suitably well-behaved curve joining the points (a,b) and (c,d). From above the value of this integral is independent of the path taken. The fact is that

$$I = F(c,d) - F(a,b).$$

To see why this is reasonable, consider the curve C to have parametric equations x = x(t), y = y(t) for $\alpha \le t \le \beta$, where x and y are differentiable functions of t. Then

$$I = \int_C \frac{\partial F}{\partial x} \, dx + \frac{\partial F}{\partial y} \, dy$$

$$= \int_\alpha^\beta \frac{\partial F}{\partial x} \frac{dx}{dt} \, dt + \frac{\partial F}{\partial y} \frac{dy}{dt} \, dt$$

$$= \int_\alpha^\beta \frac{d}{dt} F(x,y) \, dt$$

$$= [F(x,y)]_{t=\alpha}^{t=\beta} = F(c,d) - F(a,b).$$

EXAMPLES TO DO: Page 147: Exs. 7, 8.

138. SOME STANDARD SURFACES IN THREE DIMENSIONS

In the following list a, b, c, d, L, M, N are constants:

1. $ax + by + cz + d = 0$ (PLANE)

2. $\dfrac{x-a}{L} = \dfrac{y-b}{M} = \dfrac{z-c}{N}$ (STRAIGHT LINE)

3. $x^2 + y^2 + z^2 = a^2$ (a > 0)   (SPHERE)

4. $\dfrac{x^2}{a^2} + \dfrac{y^2}{b^2} + \dfrac{z^2}{c^2} = 1$ (a,b,c positive) (ELLIPSOID)

5A. $\dfrac{x^2}{a^2} + \dfrac{y^2}{b^2} - \dfrac{z^2}{c^2} = 1$ (a,b,c positive) (HYPERBOLOID)

5B. $-\dfrac{x^2}{a^2} - \dfrac{y^2}{b^2} + \dfrac{z^2}{c^2} = 1$ (a,b,c positive)   (HYPERBOLOID)

6A. $x^2 + y^2 = az$ (a > 0)   (PARABOLOID)

6B. $x^2 + y^2 = az$ (a < 0)   (PARABOLOID)

7. $x^2 + y^2 = az^2$ (a > 0)   (CONE)

8. $x^2 + y^2 = a^2$ (a > 0)   (CIRCULAR CYLINDER)

In attempting to draw these and similar surfaces it is often helpful to put particular values of z into the given equation: this shows which type of curve is cut by the surface on the resulting plane section.   For example try setting z = 2, 1, 0, -1 in turn in equation (6A) above and compare with the surface in the diagram below.

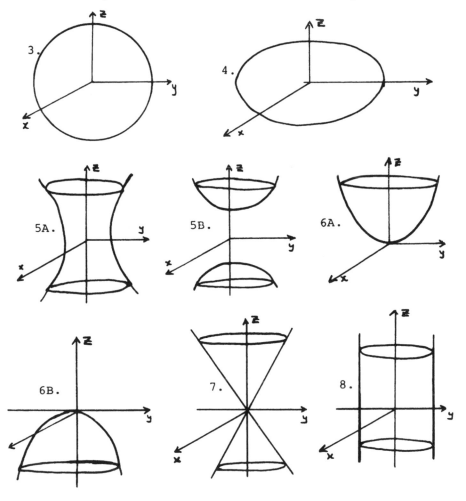

139. FINDING THE NORMAL TO A SURFACE

Suppose that a well behaved surface in three dimensions has the equation $F(x,y,z) = 0$. Then a set of direction numbers for the normal vector to the surface at (x,y,z) is given by

$$\left(\frac{\partial F}{\partial x}, \frac{\partial F}{\partial y}, \frac{\partial F}{\partial z} \right),$$

where the partial derivatives are evaluated at the point (x,y,z). We do not justify this rule, but as evidence of its correctness notice that it <u>does</u> give (a, b, c) as a set of direction numbers for the normal to the plane $ax + by + cz + d = 0$. The following example provides further evidence.

EXAMPLE. Find a set of direction numbers for the normal to the sphere $x^2 + y^2 + z^2 = a^2$ at the point (x,y,z).

Solution. According to the above rule, if we take $F(x,y,z) = x^2 + y^2 + z^2 - a^2$, we have $(2x, 2y, 2z)$, i.e. (x, y, z) as a set of direction numbers for the normal. [This agrees with what you would expect from the geometry of the sphere, because the normal does lie along the radius vector from $(0,0,0)$ to (x,y,z).]

EXAMPLE. Find a set of direction numbers for the normal to the paraboloid $z = 4 - x^2 - y^2$ at the point (x,y,z).

Solution. Let $F(x,y,z) = 4 - x^2 - y^2 - z$. Then the above rule gives direction numbers for the normal at the point (x,y,z) as $(-2x, -2y, -1)$, i.e. $(2x, 2y, 1)$.

For a surface the equation of which can be taken in the form $z = z(x,y)$ the above rule can be simplified to give the normal direction as $(\partial z/\partial x, \partial z/\partial y, -1)$, or in a common notation $(p, q, -1)$, where p and q denote $\partial z/\partial x$ and $\partial z/\partial y$ respectively. [The example of §105 shows the connection between the two forms of the rule.] In §141 we will find it convenient to take our surface in the form $z = z(x,y)$. For such a surface it follows that <u>unit</u> normal vectors are

$$\frac{1}{\sqrt{(1 + p^2 + q^2)}} (p, q, -1) \quad \text{and} \quad \frac{-1}{\sqrt{(1 + p^2 + q^2)}} (p, q, -1),$$

i.e. plus or minus the above vector divided by its length.

So for the sphere $x^2 + y^2 + z^2 = a^2$, a unit normal is

$$n = \frac{(x, y, z)}{\sqrt{(x^2 + y^2 + z^2)}}, \quad \text{i.e.} \quad n = \left(\frac{x}{a}, \frac{y}{a}, \frac{z}{a} \right).$$

Also, for $z = 4 - x^2 - y^2$ a unit normal at (x,y,z) is

$$n = \frac{(2x, 2y, 1)}{\sqrt{(4x^2 + 4y^2 + 1)}} \; .$$

140. THE IDEA OF A SURFACE INTEGRAL

Think of crops growing on a hillside S. Suppose that the crop yield per unit of surface area varies across the surface of the surface of the hillside and that it has the value $f(x,y,z)$ at the point (x,y,z). We may then ask what is the total yield of crops over the whole surface of the hillside. This is where surface integrals have something to say.

For, consider a small element of surface δS containing the point (x,y,z). Then (assuming that f is suitably well behaved) the contribution to the total crop from this small element of surface is

$$f(x,y,z) \; \delta S,$$

and summing all such contribution gives the total crop over the hillside as

$$\Sigma \; f(x,y,z) \; \delta S \; ,$$

where the summation is done over all small elements of surface. Taking the limit of this sum as $\delta S \to 0$, we obtain the <u>surface integral</u>

$$\iint_S f(x,y,z) \; dS,$$

which measures the total crop over the whole surface S. This gives an interpretation of surface integrals. §141 explains how to evaluate them.

141. HOW TO EVALUATE A SURFACE INTEGRAL

We wish to evaluate

$$\iint_S f(x,y,z) \; dS.$$

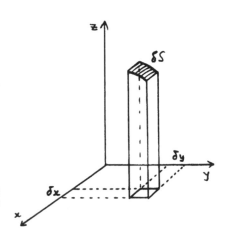

We deal here with the case of a surface S the equation of which can be put into the form $z = z(x,y)$. (A word is said about other cases at the end of this section.)

We look at a small element δS of the surface at (x,y,z) corresponding to a small rectangle of sides δx and δy in the xy-plane as shown.

We can consider δS as approximately a plane rectangle with a unit normal vector

$$n = \frac{-1}{\sqrt{1 + p^2 + q^2}}(p, q, -1).$$

In the diagram it is easy to see by comparing the areas of the rectangles ABCD and BCEF that

$$\delta S \, |\cos \gamma| = \delta x \delta y,$$

i.e. $\quad \delta S = \dfrac{\delta x \delta y}{|\cos \gamma|}, \quad \ldots (*)$

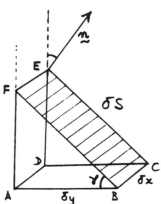

where γ is the angle shown. Notice however that γ is also the angle that the unit normal n makes with the z-axis. It follows that since $n = (n_1, n_2, n_3)$ has length 1, we have from the definition of scalar product that

$$(n_1, n_2, n_3).(0, 0, 1) = 1 \times 1 \times \cos \gamma,$$

i.e. $\quad n_3 = \cos \gamma.$

But from above $n_3 = 1/\sqrt{1 + p^2 + q^2}$. So we conclude that

$$|\cos \gamma| = \frac{1}{\sqrt{1 + p^2 + q^2}}.$$

Together with (*) this then gives

$$\delta S = \sqrt{1 + p^2 + q^2} \; \delta x \delta y \qquad \ldots (**)$$

This is the key to the evaluation of the surface integral.

Recall from §140 that the surface integral arises as the limiting case of the sum

$$\Sigma \; f(x,y,z) \; \delta S,$$

where the summation ranges over all small elements of surface δS. It follows then from (**) that this can be calculated as the limiting case of

$$\Sigma \; f(x,y,z) \sqrt{1 + p^2 + q^2} \; \delta x \delta y,$$

where the summation ranges over all the small corresponding areas $\delta x \delta y$ in the xy-plane.

· So the rule is

$$\iint_S f(x,y,z) \; dS = \iint_A f(x,y,z) \; \sqrt{1 + p^2 + q^2} \; dxdy \, ,$$

where A is the projection of the surface S on the xy-plane. This means that a surface integral over S can be calculated from the corresponding double integral over A. This is illustrated in §142 and §143.

[The above treatment of surface integrals assumes that the equation of the surface can be put into the form $z = z(x,y)$: this assumption effectively allows the surface to be projected down on to the xy-plane using (*). For a surface integral over a surface like the plane $x + y = 1$, which <u>cannot</u> be put into the form $z = z(x,y)$, you could <u>either</u> give a similar treatment in which the projection is done on to the xz-plane <u>or</u> alternatively permute the coordinates in both the equation of the surface and the integrand to make it amenable to the method given above. We shall not be much concerned with such cases in this book however.]

142. <u>EXAMPLE</u>. Evaluate

$$\iint_S z \, dS,$$

where S is the triangle with vertices at $(1,0,0)$, $(0,1,0)$ and $(0,0,1)$.

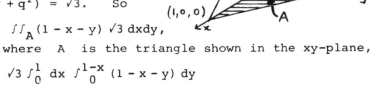

<u>Solution</u>. The triangle is part of the plane $x + y + z = 1$, and so this is the equation of S. It follows that $p = \frac{\partial z}{\partial x} = -1$, $q = \frac{\partial z}{\partial y} = -1$.

So $\sqrt{(1 + p^2 + q^2)} = \sqrt{3}$. So

$$\iint_S z \, dS = \iint_A (1 - x - y) \sqrt{3} \, dxdy,$$

where A is the triangle shown in the xy-plane,

$$= \sqrt{3} \int_0^1 dx \int_0^{1-x} (1 - x - y) \, dy$$

$$= \sqrt{3} \int_0^1 [(1 - x)y - \tfrac{1}{2}y^2]_0^{1-x} \, dx$$

$$= \tfrac{1}{2}\sqrt{3} \int_0^1 (1 - x)^2 \, dx = \sqrt{3}/6.$$

143. <u>EXAMPLE</u>. Evaluate

$$\iint_S z^2 \, dS,$$

where S is the part of the surface of the sphere $x^2 + y^2 + z^2 = a^2$ with $z \geq 0$.

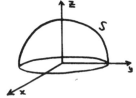

<u>Solution</u>. We calculate p, q by partially differentiating $x^2 + y^2 + z^2 = a^2$ w.r.t. x and y:

$2x + 2z \frac{\partial z}{\partial x} = 0$ and $2y + 2z \frac{\partial z}{\partial y} = 0$.

So p = -x/z and q = -y/z with the result that

$$\sqrt{(1 + p^2 + q^2)} = \sqrt{(1 + \frac{x^2}{z^2} + \frac{y^2}{z^2})}$$

$$= \sqrt{\left(\frac{x^2 + y^2 + z^2}{z^2}\right)}$$

$$= \frac{a}{\sqrt{(a^2 - x^2 - y^2)}} \quad \text{on} \quad S.$$

So the rule in §141 gives

$$\iint_S z^2 \, dS = \iint_A (a^2 - x^2 - y^2) \frac{a}{\sqrt{(a^2 - x^2 - y^2)}} \, dxdy,$$

where A is the disc $x^2 + y^2 \leq a^2$,

$$= \iint_A a \sqrt{(a^2 - x^2 - y^2)} \, dxdy$$

$$= \int_0^{2\pi} d\theta \int_0^a ar \sqrt{(a^2 - r^2)} \, dr$$

$$= 2\pi a \left[-\frac{1}{3}(a^2 - r^2)^{3/2}\right]_0^a = 2\pi a^4/3.$$

EXAMPLE. Show that $\iint z^2 \, dS$, where the integration is done over the whole surface of the sphere $x^2 + y^2 + z^2 = a^2$, has the value $4\pi a^4/3$, (i.e. twice the value in the example above).

Solution. The contribution from the upper half of the sphere is given by the previous example. On the lower half (i.e. for $z \leq 0$), $\sqrt{(1 + p^2 + q^2)}$ is unaltered because the √ sign means the positive root. Also the integrand z^2 still translates as $a^2 - x^2 - y^2$. So the contribution from the lower half is equal to that from the upper half. So the value of this surface integral is twice the value in the previous example, i.e. $4\pi a^4/3$.

EXAMPLE. Show that $\iint z \, dS$, where the integration is done over the whole surface of the sphere $x^2 + y^2 + z^2 = a^2$, has the value 0.

Solution. Denote the integrals over the upper and lower hemispheres (i.e. the parts with $z \geq 0$ and $z \leq 0$) by U and L. Then as in the previous two examples

$$U = \iint_A +\sqrt{(a^2 - x^2 - y^2)} \frac{a}{\sqrt{(a^2 - x^2 - y^2)}} \, dxdy$$

while $L = \iint_A -\sqrt{(a^2 - x^2 - y^2)} \frac{a}{\sqrt{(a^2 - x^2 - y^2)}} \, dxdy.$

So $\iint z \, dS = U + L = 0$, as required.

[Notice that the $-$ sign arises in L because on the lower hemisphere $z = -\sqrt{(a^2 - x^2 - y^2)}$.]

EXAMPLES TO DO: Pages 147-148: Exs. 9 - 11, 18 - 21.

144. FINDING THE AREA OF A SURFACE

Evaluating $\iint_S 1 \, dS$ gives the area of the surface S. This is consistent with the interpretation given in §140: if the crop yield is 1 unit per unit of surface area then the total yield of crops will be numerically equal to the area of the surface. §145 gives an example on calculation of a surface area.

145. EXAMPLE. Find the area of the ellipse cut on the plane $2x + 3y + 6z = 60$ by the circular cylinder $x^2 + y^2 = 2x.$

Solution. In the diagram the area sought is marked as S.

For S, we have

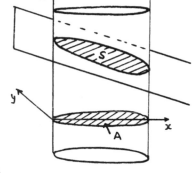

$$2 + 6\frac{\partial z}{\partial x} = 0, \quad 3 + 6\frac{\partial z}{\partial y} = 0,$$

so that $p = -\frac{1}{3}$, $q = -\frac{1}{2}$

and $\sqrt{(1 + p^2 + q^2)} = \frac{7}{6}$.

So the required area $= \iint_S 1 \, dS$

$= \iint_A 7/6 \, dxdy$, where A is the interior of the circle shown,

$= \frac{7}{6} \iint_A 1 \, dxdy \quad = \frac{7}{6} \times$ (area of circle $x^2 + y^2 = 2x$)

$= \frac{7\pi}{6}$.

EXAMPLES TO DO: Pages 147-148: Exs. 12 - 17, 22.

146. GAUSS'S DIVERGENCE THEOREM

This is an analogue for three dimensions of Green's theorem in two dimensions. In two dimensional space, Green's theorem relates a line integral round the boundary curve of a two dimensional region to a double integral over the interior of the region. Likewise in three dimensional space, Gauss's Divergence Theorem relates a surface integral over the boundary surface of a three dimensional region to a triple integral over the interior of the region.

Notice that the surface in Gauss's Divergence Theorem must be a <u>closed</u> surface, just as the curve in Green's theorem must be a <u>closed</u> curve.

It lies beyond the scope of this book to discuss the types of closed surface to which Gauss's Divergence Theorem applies. We shall limit ourselves to simple surfaces, e.g. spheres, ellipsoids, cuboids etc and we shall not allow holes inside them. (These conditions can be relaxed somewhat: see more advanced books for details.) For such a <u>closed</u> surface S enclosing a three dimensional region K, <u>Gauss's Divergence Theorem</u> gives the following result:

Let $v = (v_1, v_2, v_3)$ be a vector function such that $\partial v_1/\partial x$, $\partial v_2/\partial y$, $\partial v_3/\partial z$ are continuous throughout K and on the surface S. Then

$$\iint_S (v \cdot n)\, dS = \iiint_K \operatorname{div} v\, dxdydz\,,$$

where n denotes the outward drawn unit normal to the surface at each point.

We do not prove the result but §147-148 give examples of its use. From these examples it can be seen that, for some surface integrals over closed surfaces, evaluation by using the Divergence Theorem to produce a triple integral may be shorter and easier than a direct assault on the given surface integral.

Notice in passing that many books write $v.dS$ for $v \cdot n\, dS$. So the Divergence Theorem may appear as

$$\iint_S v.dS = \iiint_K \operatorname{div} v\, dxdydz\,.$$

147. EXAMPLE. <u>(The second example in §143 solved using the Divergence Theorem)</u> Evaluate

$$\iint_S z^2\, dS,$$

where S is the whole surface of the sphere $x^2 + y^2 + z^2 = a^2$ (a > 0).

<u>Solution.</u> For this sphere the unit outward normal at the point (x,y,z) is, by §139,

$$n = \left(\frac{x}{a}, \frac{y}{a}, \frac{z}{a}\right).$$

We need to express the given integrand as $(v \cdot n)$ for some vector v. We can take

$$z^2 = (0, 0, az).\left(\frac{x}{a}, \frac{y}{a}, \frac{z}{a}\right) \text{ so that } v = (0, 0, az).$$

Gauss's Divergence Theorem then gives

$$\iint_S z^2 \, dS = \iint_S v \cdot n \, dS$$

$$= \iiint_K \text{div}(0, \, 0, \, az) \, dxdydz, \quad \text{where} \quad K \quad \text{is the interior of the sphere,}$$

$$= \iiint_K a \, dxdydz$$

$$= a \iiint_K 1 \, dxdydz$$

$$= a \times \text{(volume of the sphere)} \quad = \quad a \cdot \frac{4}{3} \pi a^3$$

$$= 4\pi a^4 / 3 \quad \text{(as in §143).}$$

148. <u>EXAMPLE</u>. Evaluate

$$\iint_S x^2 y^2 + y^2 z^2 + z^2 x^2 \quad dS,$$

where S is the whole surface of the sphere $x^2 + y^2 + z^2 = 1$.

<u>Solution</u>. For this sphere, the unit outward normal at the point (x,y,z) is, by §139, $n = (x, \, y, \, z)$. We need to express the given integrand as $v \cdot n$. So

$$x^2 y^2 + y^2 z^2 + z^2 x^2 \quad = \quad (xy^2, \, yz^2, \, zx^2) \cdot (x, \, y, \, z)$$

$$= \quad v \cdot n,$$

where $v = (xy^2, \, yz^2, \, zx^2)$.
Gauss's Divergence Theorem then gives

$$\iint_S v \cdot n \, dS = \iiint_K \text{div}(xy^2, \, yz^2, \, zx^2) \, dxdydz$$

$$= \iiint_K (y^2 + z^2 + x^2) \, dxdydz$$

$$= \iiint_K (x^2 + y^2 + z^2) \, dxdydz$$

$$= \int_0^{2\pi} d\phi \int_0^{\pi} d\theta \int_0^1 r^2 \cdot r^2 \sin \theta \, dr$$

$$= 2\pi \int_0^{\pi} \sin \theta \, d\theta \int_0^1 r^4 \, dr$$

$$= 2\pi \cdot 2 \cdot \frac{1}{5} = 4\pi / 5.$$

<u>EXAMPLES TO DO</u>: Pages 149-150: Exs. 23 - 25, 31 - 33.

149. CURVILINEAR LINE INTEGRALS IN THREE DIMENSIONS

These are similar to line integrals in two dimensional space, but the curves involved need not be plane curves. Often such integrals can be evaluated by parametrising the curve as in the following example.

EXAMPLE.   Evaluate

$$I = \int_C xz \, dx + y^2 \, dy + x \, dz,$$

where C is the curve in which the plane $y = z$ cuts the sphere $x^2 + y^2 + z^2 = 2$, the direction being given by starting at $(\sqrt{2}, 0, 0)$ and moving into the first octant.

Solution.   The curve is the circle cut on the sphere by the plane.   We parametrise this curve by taking

$$x^2 + y^2 + z^2 = 2 \quad \text{and} \quad y = z,$$

i.e. $x^2 + 2y^2 = 2$,

i.e. $\dfrac{x^2}{2} + y^2 = 1$.

So we can take $x = \sqrt{2}\cos t$, $y = \sin t$, $z = \sin t$,   where t runs from 0 to 2π.   (This does take the direction indicated in the question.)

So $I = \int_0^{2\pi} \sqrt{2}\cos t \sin t \dfrac{dx}{dt} \, dt + \int_0^{2\pi} \sin^2 t \dfrac{dy}{dt} \, dt$

$$+ \int_0^{2\pi} \sqrt{2}\cos t \dfrac{dz}{dt} \, dt$$

$= \int_0^{2\pi} -\sin^2 t \cos t + \sqrt{2}\cos^2 t \, dt$

$= 0 \ + \ 4\sqrt{2}.\tfrac{1}{2}.\tfrac{1}{2}\pi \ = \ \pi\sqrt{2}.$

EXAMPLES TO DO: Page 149: Ex. 26 (first part).

150. THE THEOREM OF STOKES

This relates a curvilinear line integral round a closed curve in three dimensional space to a surface integral over a well behaved piece of surface whose edges make up the closed curve.   For example, you could think of the surface as a circus tent and the closed curve as the curve bounding the base of the tent.

As with Green's theorem and the Divergence Theorem we shall not specify in full the surfaces or corresponding boundary curves for which the result of Stokes holds.

The statement of the <u>theorem of Stokes</u> (for admissible curves and surfaces) is:

Let S be an admissible piece of surface in three dimensional space and let C be its closed boundary curve. Let $v = (v_1, v_2, v_3)$ be a vector function the components of which have continuous partial derivatives on an open set containing S and C.   Then

$$\int_C v_1\ dx + v_2\ dy + v_3\ dz \ = \ \iint_S (\text{curl } v).n\ dS$$

where n is the outward drawn unit normal to one of S and the line integral is taken round C anti-clockwise direction viewed from that same s

Notice the alternative statements in other notat

> (a) $\int_C v\ .\ dr = \iint_S (\text{curl } v).n\ dS$,
>
> (b) $\int_C v\ .\ dr = \iint_S (\text{curl } v).dS$.

Here dr denotes (dx, dy, dz) and dS deno

We do not prove the result but §151-153 illustrate its use.

151. EXAMPLE.

A circle C is cut on the surface of the sphere $x^2 + y^2 + z^2 = 25$ by the plane z = 3. Evaluate

$$I = \int_C z\ dx + x\ dy - x\ dz,$$

(a) directly,   (b) using the result of Stokes.   (The diection round C is to be anticlockwise when viewed from (0,0,5).)

Solution. (a) For z = 3, we have $x^2 + y^2 = 16$ on C, so that the projection of C on the xy-plane is the circle $x^2 + y^2 = 16$.   We can therefore parametrise C as

x = 4 cos t, y = 4 sin t, z = 3

for $0 \le t \le 2\pi$.   So,

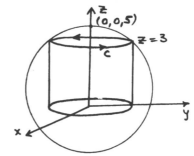

$$I = \int_0^{2\pi} \left(3\frac{dx}{dt} + 4\cos t\ \frac{dy}{dt} - 4\cos t\ \frac{dz}{dt} \right) dt$$

$$= \int_0^{2\pi} (-12\sin t + 16\cos^2 t - 0)\ dt$$

$$= 0\ +\ 64\int_0^{\frac{1}{2}\pi} \cos^2 t\ dt\ =\ 16\pi.$$

(b)   In using Stokes we can choose to take the surface
S   as the disc enclosed by   C, i.e. a disc on the plane
surface $z = 3$.   For this choice of   S   we have the unit
normal $n = (0, 0, 1)$.   So Stokes gives

$$I = \iint_S \text{curl}(z, x, -x) \cdot (0, 0, 1) \ dS$$

$$= \iint_S (0, 2, 1) \cdot (0, 0, 1) \ dS$$

$$= \iint_S 1 \ dS = \text{area of the disc surface} \ S$$

$$= 16\pi \qquad \text{(since the radius is} \ 4).$$

<u>Notice</u>:   (i) The answers from the two methods agree as you
would expect.

(ii) There is an element of choice about the surface
in using the result of Stokes. We could have taken the
surface as the spherical cap above the plane $z = 3$.
This is the subject of Ex. 10.30.

152.   <u>EXAMPLE</u>.   Use the theorem of Stokes to evaluate

$$I = \int_K y^2 \ dx + 0 \ dy + 2xz \ dz,$$

where   K   is the closed curve made up of the sides of the
triangle   ABC   (in that order), where   A, B, C   are the
points in which the plane $4x + y + z = 4$ meets the
x, y   and   z   axes respectively.

<u>Solution</u>.   Setting $y = z = 0$,
$x = z = 0$, $y = z = 0$ in the
equation of the plane gives
$A = (1,0,0)$, $B = (0,4,0)$ and
$C = (0,0,4)$.   By Stokes the
given line integral round the
triangle   ABC   is related to
a surface integral over any
surface with triangle   ABC   as

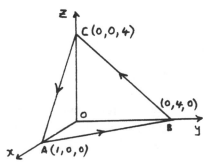

its boundary.   The simplest choice of surface is the plane
triangular surface   ABC.   For this surface   S,   which has
the equation $4x + y + z = 4$,   the unit outward normal is

$$n = \frac{1}{\sqrt{18}} (4, 1, 1) .$$

So, using the result of Stokes,
$$I = \iint_S \text{curl}(y^2, 0, 2xz) \cdot \frac{1}{\sqrt{18}} (4, 1, 1) \ dS$$

$$= \iint_S (0, -2z, -2y) \cdot \frac{1}{\sqrt{18}} (4, 1, 1) \ dS$$

$$= \iint \frac{(-2z - 2y)}{\sqrt{18}} \sqrt{(1 + p^2 + q^2)} \ dxdy \quad \text{over triangle OAB}$$

$$= \iint_{\triangle OAB} \frac{(-2(4 - 4x - y) - 2y)}{\sqrt{18}} \cdot \sqrt{18} \ dxdy$$

$$\text{(on using} \quad 4x + y + z = 4)$$

$$= \iint_{\triangle OAB} 8x - 8 \ dxdy = \int_0^1 dx \int_0^{4-4x} (8x - 8) \ dy$$

$$= -32/3 \quad \text{(on evaluation)}.$$

<u>Notice</u>: Stokes's theorem allows us to choose any surface with the given curve as boundary. In this problem (as in §151) the surface chosen is part of a plane: this has obvious advantages.

153. EXAMPLE. A curve C is cut on the hemisphere $x^2 + y^2 + z^2 = 1$, $z \geq 0$ by the circular cylinder $x^2 + y^2 = y$. Use Stokes's theorem to evaluate

$$I = \int_C -y^2 \ dx + y^2 \ dy + z^2 \ dz,$$

where the direction of integration is given by starting at $(0,0,1)$ and moving into the first octant.

<u>Solution.</u> We shall take the surface S to be the part of the hemisphere inside the circular cylinder $x^2 + y^2 = y$. The normal to S in the correct direction is $n = (x, y, z)$. So, by Stokes, we have

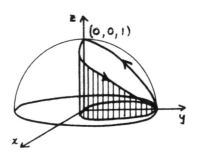

$$I = \iint_S \text{curl}(-y^2, \ y^2, \ z^2) \cdot (x, \ y, \ z) \ dS$$

$$= \iint_S (0, \ 0, \ 2y) \cdot (x, \ y, \ z) \ dS$$

$$= \iint_S 2yz \ dS$$

$$= \iint_A 2yz \sqrt{(1 + p^2 + q^2)} \ dxdy, \quad \text{where A is the interior of the circle } x^2 + y^2 = y,$$

$$= \iint_A 2yz \cdot \frac{1}{z} \ dxdy \quad \text{(because} \quad \sqrt{(1 + p^2 + q^2)} = \frac{1}{z} \text{ as in §143)}$$

$$= \iint_A 2y \ dxdy = \int_0^\pi d\theta \int_0^{\sin \theta} 2r^2 \sin \theta \ dr = \tfrac{2}{3} \int_0^\pi \sin^4\theta \ d\theta$$

$$= \tfrac{4}{3} \int_0^{\frac{1}{2}\pi} \sin^4\theta \ d\theta \ = \pi/4 \ , \ \text{on using} \quad \S39.$$

EXAMPLES TO DO: Page 149:   Exs. 26 - 30.

154. CURVILINEAR INTEGRALS WHICH ARE INDEPENDENT OF THE PATH BETWEEN THE ENDPOINTS

In §134 we saw that the value of a line integral along a curve in two dimensions can be interpreted as the work done in moving along the curve against a force, the force being given by the integrand.   The matter was taken further in §137 where we saw that the value of the integral was independent of the path taken between the endpoints if P dx + Q dy is an exact differential, i.e. if there exists a function ϕ such that $P = \partial\phi/\partial x$ and $Q = \partial\phi/\partial y$.

Similar considerations apply in the case of curvilinear integrals in three dimensions.   The integral

$$\int_C F.dr \qquad \text{or} \qquad \int_C F_1 \ dx + F_2 \ dy + F_3 \ dz,$$

where $F = (F_1, F_2, F_3)$, can again be interpreted as the work done in moving along C against the force F.   Also, this integral is independent of the path between the endpoints if there exists a function ϕ of three variables such that $F_1 = \partial\phi/\partial x$, $F_2 = \partial\phi/\partial y$, $F_3 = \partial\phi/\partial z$,   i.e. if there exists a scalar function ϕ such that $F = \text{grad } \phi$, i.e. if the vector field F is <u>conservative</u>, as defined in Ex.9.12 on page 124.

To see that this is reasonable, suppose that F is conservative in an open set U in three dimensional space.   Let A and B be points in U joined by an admissible curve C in U.   Suppose also that C can be parametrised by parametric equations $x = x(t)$, $y = y(t)$, $z = z(t)$ with $\alpha \leq t \leq \beta$, and that A and B correspond to the parameter values α and β respectively.   Then, since F is conservative there exists a scalar function ϕ such that $F = \text{grad } \phi$.   Then

$$\int_C F . dr = \int_C F_1 \ dx + F_2 \ dy + F_3 \ dz$$

$$= \int_C \frac{\partial\phi}{\partial x} \ dx + \frac{\partial\phi}{\partial y} \ dy + \frac{\partial\phi}{\partial z} \ dz$$

$$= \int_\alpha^\beta \frac{\partial\phi}{\partial x}\frac{dx}{dt} \ dt + \frac{\partial\phi}{\partial y}\frac{dy}{dt} \ dt + \frac{\partial\phi}{\partial z}\frac{dz}{dt} \ dt$$

$$= \int_\alpha^\beta \frac{d\phi}{dt} \ dt \ = \ [\phi]_\alpha^\beta \ = \ \phi_{(at \ B)} \ - \ \phi_{(at \ A)} .$$

So, if F is conservative then the value of the integral depends only on the values at the endpoints.   §155 gives an example.

Notice: (i) Not all vector fields are conservative.

  (ii) If F is conservative, so that F = grad ϕ, then the function ϕ is called a <u>potential function</u> for F.   Electrical potential arises in this way.

155,   <u>EXAMPLE</u>.   Vector fields v and w are defined by

$$v = (2x - 3y + z, \ -3x - y + 4z, \ 4y + z),$$

$$w = (2x - 4y - 5z, \ -4x + 2y, \ -5x + 6z).$$

One of these is conservative while the other is not. Determine which is conservative and denote it by F.   Find a potential function ϕ for F and evaluate

$$\int_C F \cdot dr \ ,$$

where C is the curve from A (1,0,0) to B (0,0,1) in which the plane $x + z = 1$ cuts the hemisphere given by $x^2 + y^2 + z^2 = 1$, $y \geq 0$.

<u>Solution</u>.   From Ex.9.12 we can take it that the field x is conservative if and only if curl x = 0.   Now,

$$\text{curl } v = (0, \ 1, \ 0) \quad \text{and} \quad \text{curl } w = (0, \ 0, \ 0).$$

So w is conservative and v is not.

  Let a potential function for w be ϕ.   Then

$$w = \text{grad } \phi = \left(\frac{\partial \phi}{\partial x}, \ \frac{\partial \phi}{\partial y}, \ \frac{\partial \phi}{\partial z} \right) \ .$$

So
$$\frac{\partial \phi}{\partial x} = 2x - 4y - 5z \quad \ldots (1),$$

$$\frac{\partial \phi}{\partial y} = -4x + 2y \quad \ldots (2), \qquad \frac{\partial \phi}{\partial z} = -5x + 6z \quad \ldots (3).$$

Integrate (1) to find that

$$\phi(x,y,z) = x^2 - 4xy - 5xz + g(y,z).$$

Differentiate this partially with respect to y and equate it to (2) to obtain

$$-4x + \frac{\partial g}{\partial y} = -4x + 2y.$$

So $\frac{\partial g}{\partial y} = 2y$, which gives $g(y,z) = y^2 + h(z)$.   So

$$\phi(x,y,z) = x^2 - 4xy - 5xz + y^2 + h(z).$$

Differentiate this partially with respect to z and equate with (3) to obtain

$$-5x + h'(z) = -5x + 6z,$$

$$\text{i.e.} \quad h'(z) = 6z.$$

So $h(z) = 3z^2 + C$, where C is an arbitrary constant. This gives

$$\phi(x,y,z) = x^2 - 4xy - 5xz + y^2 + 3z^2$$

as a potential function.

Since w is conservative the required line integral $\int_C w \cdot dr$ is independent of the path taken between the endpoints and its value by §154 is

$$\phi(0,0,1) - \phi(1,0,0) = 3 - 1 = 2.$$

EXAMPLES TO DO: Pages 150 – 151:   Exs. 34 – 36.

EXAMPLES 10

1.   The curve C consists of the part of the circle $x^2 + y^2 = 1$ in the first quadrant starting at $(1,0)$ and ending at $(0,1)$.   Evaluate

$$\int_C 3xy^2 \, dx + x^2y \, dy,$$

(a) by parametrising the curve, (b) using x,y coordinates.

2.   Evaluate

$$\int_C y^3 \, dx + 4xy^2 \, dy,$$

where C consists of the circle $x^2 + y^2 = a^2$ described in the anticlockwise direction , (a) by Green's theorem, (b) directly.

3.   Evaluate

$$\int_C 2xy^3 \, dx + 3x^2 \, dy,$$

where C consists of the perimeter of the square with vertices at $(0,0)$, $(1,0)$, $(1,1)$ and $(0,1)$ described in the anticlockwise direction.

4. C is the curve consisting of the perimeter of the triangle with vertices at $(0,0)$, $(1,0)$ and $(0,1)$ described in the anticlockwise direction.   Evaluate

$$\int_C xy \, dx + 6(1 + x) \, dy$$

(a) by Green's theorem, (b) directly.

5. Use Green's theorem to evaluate

$$\int_C y(1 - xy)\, dx + x(3xy + 1)\, dy$$

along the three sided curve which starts at $(1,1)$ and moves to $(\sqrt{2},2)$ along the parabola $y = x^2$, then moves from $(\sqrt{2},2)$ to $(\frac{1}{2},2)$ along the line $y = 2$ and then returns to $(1,1)$ along the hyperbola $xy = 1$.

6. C is the circle $x^2 + y^2 = 1$ described in the anticlockwise direction. Show that Green's theorem cannot be used to evaluate

$$\int_C \log(2(x^2 + y^2))\, dx + 0\, dy,$$

and explain why. Evaluate this integral.

7. Show that

$$(2xy^3 + 4y^2)\, dx + (3x^2y^2 + 8xy)\, dy$$

is an exact differential. Hence evaluate

$$\int_C (2xy^3 + 4y^2)\, dx + (3x^2y^2 + 8xy)\, dy,$$

where C is the arc of the parabola $y = 5x^2 - 3x$ from $(0,0)$ to $(1,2)$.

8. Let A, B be two points in the xy-plane and let C be a curve joining them. Show that the line integral

$$\int_C (2x + 3y)\, dx + (3x - 4y)\, dy$$

is independent of the path taken by C between A and B. Evaluate the integral when C starts at $(1,0)$ and ends at $(0,3)$.

9. Evaluate

$$\iint_S y\, dS,$$

where S is the plane surface given by the equations $x \geq 0$, $y \geq 0$, $z \geq 0$, $x + y + z = 1$.

10. Evaluate

$$\iint_S z\, dS,$$

where S is the hemispherical surface given by $x^2 + y^2 + z^2 = a^2$, $z \geq 0$.

11. Evaluate $\iint z^3\, dS$ over the hemisphere in Ex.10 above. What is the value of this integral taken over the whole surface of the sphere $x^2 + y^2 + z^2 = a^2$?

12. Show that the surface area of the hemisphere $x^2 + y^2 + z^2 = a^2$, $z \geq 0$ is $2\pi a^2$.

13. In three dimensional space an infinite cylinder with triangular cross section is determined by the planes $y = 0$, $x = 1$ and $y = 3x$. Using a surface integral determine the area of the triangle in which the plane $2x + y + 6z = 55$ meets this cylinder.

14. A tent is in the form of the paraboloid $z = 6 - x^2 - y^2$ for $z > 0$. Find its surface area.

15. Show that the surface area of the part of the hemisphere $x^2 + y^2 + z^2 = a^2$, $z \geq 0$ which lies inside the cylinder $x^2 + y^2 = b^2$, where $0 < b < a$, is $2\pi a[a - \sqrt{(a^2 - b^2)}]$.

16. Show that the area of the ellipse cut on the plane $ax + by + cz + d = 0$ (with $c \neq 0$) by the cylinder $x^2 + y^2 = k^2$ is $[\pi k^2 \sqrt{(a^2 + b^2 + c^2)}]/|c|$. What is the significance of the restriction that $c \neq 0$?

17. In three dimensional space the equation $4x^2 + 9y^2 = 36$ represents a cylinder with elliptical cross section. Find the area of the part of the plane $5x + y + 3z = 0$ that lies inside this cylinder.

18. Find the mean value of z at all points on the surface of the hemisphere $x^2 + y^2 + z^2 = a^2$, $z \geq 0$.

19. Evaluate $\iint z^2 \, dS$ where the surface is the part of the cone $x^2 + y^2 = 2z^2$ which lies between the planes $z = 1$ and $z = 3$.

20. Evaluate

$$\iint_S (ax^2 + by^2 + cz^2) \, dS,$$

where S is the part of the surface of the sphere $x^2 + y^2 + z^2 = 1$ with $x \geq 0$, $y \geq 0$, $z \geq 0$. (Here a, b, c are constants.)

21. Evaluate

$$\iint_S (ax + by + cz)^2 \, dS,$$

where S is the surface of the sphere $x^2 + y^2 + z^2 = 1$. [Hint. The length of the perpendicular from the point (x,y,z) on the surface of the sphere on to the plane $ax + by + cz = 0$, which incidentally passes through the origin, is $|(ax + by + cz)| /\sqrt{(a^2 + b^2 + c^2)}$. Consider the effect on the given integral of rotating the axes to make the plane $ax + by + cz = 0$ into the plane $Z = 0$ in the new X, Y, Z coordinates.]

22. The roof of a dome shaped sports centre is in the shape of the paraboloid $z = 36 - x^2 - y^2$, $z \geq 0$. It is made of material of mass k units per unit of surface area. Find the mass of (a) the entire roof, (b) the part of the roof outside the cylinder $x^2 + y^2 = 25$.

23.   Evaluate $\iint x^2 z^2 \, dS$ over the entire surface of the sphere $x^2 + y^2 + z^2 = a^2$ (a) by Gauss's Divergence Theorem, (b) directly.

24.   Evaluate $\iint (x^2 + y^2 + z^2) \, dS$ over the entire surface of the sphere $x^2 + y^2 + z^2 = a^2$.   Deduce the value of $\iint x^2 \, dS$ over the same surface.

25.   A closed surface is made up of S_1, the part of the paraboloid $z = 1 - x^2 - y^2$ with $z \geq 0$, together with S_2, the circular disc $\{(x,y,z): \; x^2 + y^2 \leq 1 \; \text{and} \; z = 0\}$. Verify the Divergence Theorem for this closed surface in the case when the vector $v = (2x, \; 2y, \; 1)$ in the notation of §146.

26.   Let S be the semicircular region given by $S = \{(x,y,z): \; x^2 + y^2 \leq 1, \quad z = 2, \quad y \geq 0\}$.   Let C denote the boundary curve of S (so that C consists of a line segment C_1 and a semicircular arc C_2).   Draw a good diagram and find parametric equations for C_1 and C_2. Evaluate $\int_C 3x^2 z \, dx + x \, dy + y \, dz$,   (a) directly,   (b) using the result of Stokes.   [The direction round C is to be taken as anticlockwise when seen from $(0,0,3)$.]

27.   Let $v = (-4y, \; z, \; -2x)$.   Let S be the part of the plane $x + y + z = 1$ in the first octant, and let C be the curve made up of the straight lines joining $(1,0,0)$, $(0,1,0)$ and $(0,0,1)$ in a triangle.   Verify the theorem of Stokes for this choice of v, S and C.

28.   Verify the theorem of Stokes for the curve cut on the plane $2x + y + z = 0$ by the cylinder $x^2 + y^2 = 1$ and the vector function $v = (2y, \; -z, \; y)$.   (You will need to parametrise the curve and choose a surface.)

29.   Verify Stokes's theorem where the curve is the curve of intersection of the sphere $x^2 + y^2 + z^2 = 4$ and the plane $x = z$,   and the vector $v = (y, \; -x, \; z^2)$. (For the surface take the plane section.)

30.   Look at (ii) in §151.   Verify that if as suggested there we take the surface to be the spherical cap instead of the plane section the value of the surface integral is still 16π.

31.   Show that for a well behaved closed surface S enclosing a three dimensional region R

$$\frac{1}{3} \iint_S r \cdot n \, dS$$

measures the volume of R.   (As usual $r = (x, \; y, \; z)$ and n denotes the outward drawn normal.)

32.   Let ϕ and ψ be scalar functions which along with their derivatives are continuous on an open set U containing a region R enclosed by a closed surface S.

Use Gauss's Divergence Theorem to show that

$$\iint_S \phi(\text{grad }\psi).n \; dS$$

$$= \iiint_R (\phi \, \nabla^2\psi + (\text{grad }\phi).(\text{grad }\psi))dxdydz \quad \dots (1)$$

Deduce that

$$\iint_S \left(\phi \frac{\partial\psi}{\partial n} - \psi \frac{\partial\phi}{\partial n}\right) dS = \iiint_R (\phi \, \nabla^2\psi - \psi \, \nabla^2\phi) \; dxdydz, \quad \dots (2)$$

where $\partial\phi/\partial n$ is as defined in §126.

A scalar function V is called <u>harmonic</u> in a region if $\nabla^2 V = 0$ in that region. Show that if in addition to the above conditions it is given that ϕ and ψ are harmonic in U then

$$\iint_S \phi \frac{\partial\psi}{\partial n} \; dS = \iint_S \psi \frac{\partial\phi}{\partial n} \; dS.$$

[<u>Note</u>. The formulae (1) and (2) are associated with the name of Green.]

33. Let ϕ, R and S be as in the first sentence of Ex. 32 above. Let $v = \text{grad } \phi$, where $\nabla^2 \phi = 0$ throughout the region R. Prove that

$$\iiint_R v^2 \; dxdydz = \iint_S \phi \, v.n \; dS.$$

Deduce that if it is further given that $\phi = 0$ on S then $\phi = 0$ throughout R.

Deduce that if ϕ_1 and ϕ_2 are well behaved functions such that $\nabla^2 \phi_1 = \nabla^2 \phi_2 = 0$ throughout R and such that $\phi_1 = \phi_2$ on the boundary surface S, then $\phi_1 = \phi_2$ throughout the three dimensional region R. (In other words there is a unique solution of Laplace's equation in R with prescribed behaviour on the boundary surface S.)

34. Verify that the vector function

$$F = (2x + 3yz^2, \; 3xz^2, \; 6xyz)$$

is irrotational and find a potential function for it, i.e. find ϕ such that $F = \text{grad } \phi$. Evaluate

$$\int_C F . dr$$

where C is the straight line segment joining $(1,2,5)$ to $(0,6,6)$.

35. Show that the vector function F defined by

$$F = (3x^2 + 2y^2, \; 4xy + z^2 - 2z, \; 2y(z - 1))$$

is conservative. Find a potential function for F and find the work done when F moves along any curve between the points (1,0,9) and (2,2,0).

36. Find the general form of the function g such that the vector function

$$F = (2xz, 6yz, g(x,y,z))$$

is irrotational. Find the particular function g for which g is independent of z and such that $g(0,0,0) = 0$. For this particular choice of g find a potential function ϕ such that $F = \text{grad } \phi$ and evaluate

$$\int_C F \cdot dr$$

where C is the straight line segment joining (0,0,1) to (1,-4,3). Is this value independent of the path taken between the endpoints?

XI. FOURIER SERIES

156. Many functions have power series expansions, e.g.

$$e^x = 1 + \frac{x}{1!} + \frac{x^2}{2!} + \frac{x^3}{3!} + \dots \qquad (x \in R),$$

$$\cosh x = 1 + \frac{x^2}{2!} + \frac{x^4}{4!} + \dots \qquad (x \in R),$$

$$\frac{1}{1-x} = 1 + x + x^2 + x^3 + \dots \qquad (-1 < x < 1).$$

These are <u>Maclaurin series</u> (or <u>Taylor series</u>): each attempts to represent some given function as a series of multiples of building bricks – the building bricks being the functions 1, x, x^2, x^3, ...   The resulting expansions are then valid for certain values of x.

Fourier Series (often shortened to F.S.) are in some respects similar to the above: they also attempt to represent certain given functions as a series of multiples of building bricks, but the building bricks for Fourier Series are the functions

1, cos x, cos 2x, cos 3x, ... , sin x, sin 2x, sin 3x, ...

instead of 1, x, x^2, x^3, ...   The resulting Fourier Series then represents the function for certain values of x.

157. THE RULES FOR FINDING THE COEFFICIENTS

Let f be a bounded function defined on $[-\pi, \pi]$ with at most a finite number of maxima and minima and at most a finite number of discontinuities in the interval $[-\pi, \pi]$.   Then the <u>Fourier Series</u> of f is the series

$$\tfrac{1}{2}a_0 + \sum_{n=1}^{\infty} (a_n \cos nx + b_n \sin nx), \qquad \dots (*)$$

where the coefficients a_n and b_n are given by the formulae

$$a_n = \frac{1}{\pi} \int_{-\pi}^{\pi} f(x) \cos nx \, dx,$$

$$b_n = \frac{1}{\pi} \int_{-\pi}^{\pi} f(x) \sin nx \, dx.$$

When n = 0, notice that this means that

$$a_0 = \frac{1}{\pi} \int_{-\pi}^{\pi} f(x) \, dx.$$

158. WHY THE COEFFICIENTS ARE FOUND AS THEY ARE

To illustrate the idea we simplify the situation by taking a function f all of whose b_n coefficients are zero. (Many such functions do exist, e.g. x^2.) So the Fourier Series of f is

$$\tfrac{1}{2}a_0 + \sum_{n=1}^{\infty} a_n \cos nx .$$

Suppose that the sum of the Fourier Series is $f(x)$ for all $x \in [-\pi,\pi]$. This means that

$$f(x) = \tfrac{1}{2}a_0 + a_1 \cos x + a_2 \cos 2x + a_3 \cos 3x + \ldots \qquad \ldots (*)$$

for all x in the interval $[-\pi,\pi]$.

Now multiply through in (*) by $\cos 2x$ (a particular choice for illustration) and integrate term by term on the interval $[-\pi,\pi]$. This gives

$$\int_{-\pi}^{\pi} f(x) \cos 2x\, dx = \tfrac{1}{2}a_0 \int_{-\pi}^{\pi} \cos 2x\, dx + a_1 \int_{-\pi}^{\pi} \cos x \cos 2x\, dx$$

$$+ a_2 \int_{-\pi}^{\pi} \cos^2 2x\, dx + a_3 \int_{-\pi}^{\pi} \cos 3x \cos 2x\, dx$$

$$+ a_4 \int_{-\pi}^{\pi} \cos 4x \cos 2x\, dx + \ldots \qquad \ldots (\dagger)$$

On the right hand side, the first term integrates at once to 0. Also the second, fourth, fifth and all subsequent terms succumb to the identity

$$\cos mx \cos nx = \tfrac{1}{2}(\cos((m+n)x) + \cos((m-n)x)) \quad (m \neq n).$$

So once we do the integration on these terms the results are of the form

$$\frac{1}{2}\left[\frac{\sin((m+n)x)}{m+n} + \frac{\sin((m-n)x)}{m-n} \right]_{-\pi}^{\pi}$$

which on evaluation gives the value 0 for all these terms. The only remaining term on the right hand side is

$$a_2 \int_{-\pi}^{\pi} \cos^2 2x\, dx = a_2 \int_{-\pi}^{\pi} \tfrac{1}{2}(1 + \cos 4x)\, dx$$

$$= a_2 [\tfrac{1}{2}x + \tfrac{1}{8} \sin 4x]_{-\pi}^{\pi} = \pi a_2 .$$

It then follows from ($\dagger$) above that

$$\pi a_2 = \int_{-\pi}^{\pi} f(x) \cos 2x\, dx, \quad \text{i.e.} \quad a_2 = \frac{1}{\pi} \int_{-\pi}^{\pi} f(x) \cos 2x\, dx .$$

Notice how this confirms the formula for a_n (for $n = 2$)

stated in §157. The b_n coefficients can be treated
similarly.

159. THE RANGE OF VALIDITY OF A FOURIER SERIES

For some <u>Maclaurin series</u> the <u>sum of the series</u> keeps
pace with the <u>value of the function</u> for <u>all</u> real values
of x : a case in point is the exponential function, for
which the agreement given by

$$e^x = 1 + x + \frac{x^2}{2!} + \frac{x^3}{3!} + \ldots$$

occurs for <u>all</u> real values of x.

In contrast, the <u>sum of a Fourier Series</u> <u>cannot</u> in
general keep pace with the <u>value of the function</u> from which
it is calculated for <u>all</u> real values of x : as a general
rule we can <u>at best</u> hope to make the sum of the series
keep pace with the value of the function on the interval
$[-\pi,\pi]$ or on some other interval of length 2π. We
illustrate this below with the Fourier Series of the
function x^2 on $[-\pi,\pi]$, which we will work out in §163.
In this argument be careful to distinguish between the
<u>value of the function</u> and the <u>sum of the series</u>.

The Fourier Series of x^2 on the interval $[-\pi,\pi]$
is actually

$$\frac{\pi^2}{3} - 4\left(\frac{\cos x}{1^2} - \frac{\cos 2x}{2^2} + \frac{\cos 3x}{3^2} - \frac{\cos 4x}{4^2} + \ldots\right)$$

and it is true that

$$x^2 = \frac{\pi^2}{3} - 4\left(\frac{\cos x}{1^2} - \frac{\cos 2x}{2^2} + \frac{\cos 3x}{3^2} - \frac{\cos 4x}{4^2} + \ldots\right)$$

for all x in the interval $[-\pi,\pi]$.

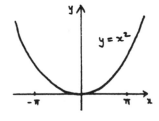

Outside the interval $[-\pi,\pi]$ the
graph of the <u>function</u> x^2 climbs
rapidly but the <u>sum of the Fourier</u>
<u>Series</u> cannot match this behaviour.
To get some idea of how badly it
falls behind we look
at the point $x = 2\pi$.   For $x = 2\pi$
the <u>sum of the series</u> is

$$\frac{\pi^2}{3} - 4\left(\frac{\cos 2\pi}{1^2} - \frac{\cos 4\pi}{2^2} + \frac{\cos 6\pi}{3^2} - \frac{\cos 8\pi}{4^2} + \ldots\right)$$

i.e. $\frac{\pi^2}{3} - 4\left(\frac{1}{1^2} - \frac{1}{2^2} + \frac{1}{3^2} - \frac{1}{4^2} + \ldots\right)$,

and this is exactly the <u>same</u> <u>sum</u> as we get from the series
when $x = 0$.   This sum is x^2 when $x = 0$, i.e. 0.
So the <u>sum of the series</u> when $x = 2\pi$ is actually 0 and
<u>NOT</u> the <u>value of the function</u> (which is $(2\pi)^2 = 4\pi^2$).

In fact we can say more: since $\cos(n(x+2\pi)) = \cos nx$

and $\sin(n(x + 2\pi)) = \sin nx$, the <u>sum</u> of a Fourier Series
is the <u>same</u> at $(x + 2\pi)$ as it is <u>at</u> x. So, in other
words, the sum of the Fourier Series repeats itself in
intervals of length 2π. So the graph of the <u>sum</u> of
the above Fourier Series is

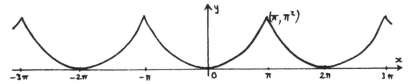

so that agreement between the <u>sum of the series</u> and the
<u>value of the function</u> x^2 occurs only on the interval
$[-\pi,\pi]$.

160. THE SUM FUNCTION OF THE FOURIER SERIES COMPARED WITH THE GIVEN FUNCTION ON $[-\pi,\pi]$

As a general statement about the situation for a
Fourier Series on $[-\pi,\pi]$ for the type of function
specified in §157, notice that:

1. Special care is needed at any point where the given
function has a jump discontinuity. At such a point b
with $-\pi < b < \pi$, the sum of the series at b is

$$\tfrac{1}{2}(f(b-) + f(b+)),$$

i.e. the average of the limit values of $f(x)$ as x
approaches b on the left and on the right.

2. Special care is also needed at $\pm\pi$. At both $\pm\pi$,
the sum of the series is

$$\tfrac{1}{2}(f(-\pi+) + f(\pi-)),$$

i.e. the average of the limit values of $f(x)$ as x
approaches $-\pi$ on the right and π on the left.

3. Otherwise, the sum of the Fourier Series agrees
with the given function. In other words, at all points
b with $-\pi < b < \pi$ and such that f is continuous
at b, the sum of the Fourier Series is $f(b)$.

<u>EXAMPLE.</u> The function f is defined on $[-\pi,\pi]$ by

$$f(x) = 1 \quad (-\pi \leq x < 0), \qquad f(0) = 5,$$
$$f(x) = 3 \quad (0 < x < \pi), \qquad f(\pi) = 4.$$

Let $s(x)$ denote the sum of the Fourier Series of f at
the point x. Sketch the graphs of f and s on
the interval $[-\pi,\pi]$.

<u>Solution</u>.   The graphs of f and s are respectively:

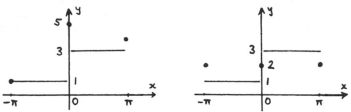

Notice that by the rules 1, 2, 3 above s agrees with f
on [-π,π] except at -π, 0 and π, where s takes the
value 2.

161.   EVEN AND ODD FUNCTIONS AND THEIR FOURIER SERIES

If $f(-x) = f(x)$ for all real x then f is
an <u>even function</u>.   If $f(-x) = -f(x)$ for all real x
then f is called an <u>odd function</u>.   So, for example,

x^2, $x^2 + 1$, x^4, x^6, cos x, $|x|$, cos 2x, $x^4 - 5x^2$ are

all <u>even</u>, while

x, x^3, x^5, $x^3 - 12x$, sin x, sin 2x, tan x are all

<u>odd</u>.

Some functions like e^x and $x^2 + x$ are neither even
nor odd.

<u>Notice</u>: The Fourier Series of an <u>even</u> function consists
only of terms which are <u>even</u> functions, i.e. of constant
and cosine terms only.   So in such a case all the b_n
coefficients are 0.   Likewise, the Fourier Series of
an <u>odd</u> function consists only of terms which are <u>odd</u>
functions themselves, i.e. of sine terms only.   So for
an odd function all the a_n coefficients are 0.

If therefore you are asked to calculate the Fourier
Series of a given function it is well worth checking <u>at
the outset</u> whether the given function is even or odd.
If it is even you need only calculate the coefficients a_n
(because the coefficients b_n are all automatically 0).
Likewise, if the given function is odd you need only
calculate the coefficients b_n (because the coefficients
a_n are automatically 0).   This is illustrated in §162
and §163.

162.   <u>EXAMPLE</u>.   Let $f(x) = x$ for $-\pi \leq x \leq \pi$.   Find

the Fourier Series of f.   Sketch the graph of
the sum of this series on [-3π,3π]. Deduce that

$$1 - \tfrac{1}{3} + \tfrac{1}{5} - \tfrac{1}{7} + \ldots = \pi/4.$$

<u>Solution.</u>   x is an <u>odd</u> function so that by §161 all the a_n coefficients are automatically 0 and need not be calculated by integration.   For the others we have

$$b_n = \frac{1}{\pi}\int_{-\pi}^{\pi} x \sin nx \ dx = \frac{1}{\pi}\left[-\frac{x \cos nx}{n} + \frac{\sin nx}{n^2} \right]_{-\pi}^{\pi}$$

(on integration by parts)

$$= \frac{1}{\pi}\left(-\frac{\pi \cos n\pi}{n} - \frac{\pi \cos(-n\pi)}{n} \right) = \frac{1}{\pi}\left(\frac{-\pi . 2\cos n\pi}{n} \right)$$

$$= \frac{-2(-1)^n}{n} = \frac{2(-1)^{n+1}}{n} \quad \text{(on using} \quad \cos n\pi = (-1)^n$$

and $\sin n\pi = 0$)

$$= \begin{cases} 2/n & (n \quad \text{odd}) \\ -2/n & (n \quad \text{even}). \end{cases}$$

So the required Fourier Series is

$$2\left(\frac{\sin x}{1} - \frac{\sin 2x}{2} + \frac{\sin 3x}{3} - \frac{\sin 4x}{4} + \frac{\sin 5x}{5} - \cdots \right).$$

From §159 and §160 the graph of the <u>sum</u> of the series on $[-3\pi, 3\pi]$ is

For the last part we would like to lose the terms with the denominators 2, 4, 6 etc.   Putting $\sin 2x = 0$ would seem reasonable - this means $2x = \pi$,   i.e. $x = \frac{1}{2}\pi$. So put $x = \frac{1}{2}\pi$.   Then the sum of the corresponding series is $\frac{1}{2}\pi$ (from the graph).   So

$$\tfrac{1}{2}\pi = 2\left(\frac{1}{1} - \frac{0}{2} + \frac{-1}{3} - \frac{0}{4} + \frac{1}{5} - \cdots \right),$$

which gives $1 - \frac{1}{3} + \frac{1}{5} - \frac{1}{7} + \cdots = \frac{\pi}{4}$.

<u>Notice:</u> (i) $\cos n\pi = (-1)^n$ and $\sin n\pi = 0$ for all integers n.

(ii) Writing out the first few terms of the series explicitly (as above) can sometimes be more illuminating than giving only a general nth term.

(iii) In the last part of the question the choice $x = \frac{1}{2}\pi$ is made after comparing the series

$$1 - \frac{1}{3} + \frac{1}{5} - \frac{1}{7} + \cdots$$

with the Fourier Series of the function.

163. **EXAMPLE.** Let $f(x) = x^2$ for $-\pi \leq x \leq \pi$. Find the Fourier Series of f. Sketch the graph of the sum of the series on $[-3\pi, 3\pi]$. Find the sum of

$$1 - \frac{1}{2^2} + \frac{1}{3^2} - \frac{1}{4^2} + \frac{1}{5^2} - \cdots ,$$

$$1 + \frac{1}{2^2} + \frac{1}{3^2} + \frac{1}{4^2} + \frac{1}{5^2} + \cdots .$$

Solution. x^2 is an <u>even</u> function so that by §161 all the b_n coefficients are 0 automatically. We then have

$$a_0 = \frac{1}{\pi} \int_{-\pi}^{\pi} x^2 \, dx = \frac{1}{\pi} [x^3/3]_{-\pi}^{\pi} = 2\pi^2/3,$$

and for $n \geq 1$,

$$a_n = \frac{1}{\pi} \int_{-\pi}^{\pi} x^2 \cos nx \, dx$$

$$= \frac{1}{\pi} \left[\frac{x^2 \sin nx}{n} + \frac{2x \cos nx}{n^2} - \frac{2 \sin nx}{n^3} \right]_{-\pi}^{\pi}$$

$$= \frac{4 \cos n\pi}{n^2} = \frac{4(-1)^n}{n^2} = \begin{cases} -4/n^2 & (n \text{ odd}), \\ 4/n^2 & (n \text{ even}). \end{cases}$$

So the Fourier Series is

$$\frac{\pi^2}{3} - 4 \left(\frac{\cos x}{1^2} - \frac{\cos 2x}{2^2} + \frac{\cos 3x}{3^2} - \frac{\cos 4x}{4^2} + \cdots \right). \cdots (*)$$

For the graph of the sum of this series see §159.

Put $x = 0$ in the series $(*)$ and on the graph to find

$$\frac{\pi^2}{3} - 4 \left(\frac{\cos 0}{1^2} - \frac{\cos 0}{2^2} + \frac{\cos 0}{3^2} - \frac{\cos 0}{4^2} + \cdots \right) = 0,$$

i.e. $1 - \frac{1}{2^2} + \frac{1}{3^2} - \frac{1}{4^2} + \cdots = \frac{\pi^2}{12}.$

Now put $x = \pi$ in the series $(*)$ and on the graph to find

$$\frac{\pi^2}{3} - 4 \left(\frac{\cos \pi}{1^2} - \frac{\cos 2\pi}{2^2} + \frac{\cos 3\pi}{3^2} - \frac{\cos 4\pi}{4^2} + \cdots \right) = \pi^2,$$

i.e. $-4 \left(-1 - \frac{1}{2^2} - \frac{1}{3^2} - \frac{1}{4^2} - \cdots \right) = \frac{2\pi^2}{3},$

i.e. $1 + \frac{1}{2^2} + \frac{1}{3^2} + \frac{1}{4^2} + \cdots = \frac{\pi^2}{6}.$

164. **EXAMPLE.** Let f be defined on $[-\pi, \pi]$ by

$$f(x) = \begin{cases} 0 & (-\pi \leq x < 0), \\ 2x - \pi & (0 \leq x \leq \pi). \end{cases}$$

Find the Fourier Series of f. Sketch the graph of the sum of this series on $[-3\pi, 3\pi]$. Deduce that

$$\frac{1}{1^2} + \frac{1}{3^2} + \frac{1}{5^2} + \frac{1}{7^2} + \cdots = \frac{\pi^2}{8}.$$

<u>Solution</u>.   The given function is neither even nor odd.   So

$$a_0 = \frac{1}{\pi}\int_{-\pi}^{\pi} f(x)\ dx = \frac{1}{\pi}\left(\int_{-\pi}^{0} 0\ dx + \int_{0}^{\pi} 2x - \pi\ dx \right)$$

$$= \frac{1}{\pi}\left[x^2 - \pi x \right]_0^{\pi} = 0,$$

and, for $n \geq 1$,

$$a_n = \frac{1}{\pi}\int_{-\pi}^{\pi} f(x)\cos nx\ dx = \frac{1}{\pi}\int_{0}^{\pi} (2x - \pi)\cos nx\ dx$$

$$= \frac{1}{\pi}\left[(2x - \pi)\frac{\sin nx}{n} + \frac{2\cos nx}{n^2} \right]_0^{\pi} \quad \text{(on integration by parts)}$$

$$= \frac{1}{\pi}\left(\frac{2\cos n\pi}{n^2} - \frac{2}{n^2} \right) = \frac{2}{n^2\pi}\left((-1)^n - 1 \right)$$

$$= \begin{cases} -4/(n^2\pi) & (n\ \text{odd}), \\ 0 & (n\ \text{even}). \end{cases}$$

Also, for $n \geq 1$,

$$b_n = \frac{1}{\pi}\int_{-\pi}^{\pi} f(x)\sin nx\ dx = \frac{1}{\pi}\int_{0}^{\pi} (2x - \pi)\sin nx\ dx$$

$$= \frac{1}{\pi}\left[-(2x - \pi)\frac{\cos nx}{n} + \frac{2\sin nx}{n^2} \right]_0^{\pi} = \frac{1}{\pi}\left(-\frac{\pi\cos n\pi}{n} - \frac{\pi}{n} \right)$$

$$= -\frac{1}{n}\left((-1)^n + 1 \right) = \begin{cases} 0 & (n\ \text{odd}), \\ -2/n & (n\ \text{even}). \end{cases}$$

It follows that the Fourier Series of f is

$$-\frac{4}{\pi}\left(\cos x + \frac{\cos 3x}{3^2} + \frac{\cos 5x}{5^2} + \ldots \right)$$

$$-2\left(\frac{\sin 2x}{2} + \frac{\sin 4x}{4} + \frac{\sin 6x}{6} + \ldots \right).$$

The graph of the sum of this series is

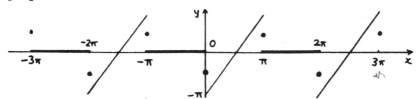

For the last part put $x = 0$ in the series and equate it with the value given by the graph for $x = 0$, i.e. $-\frac{1}{2}\pi$.

This gives $1 + \frac{1}{3^2} + \frac{1}{5^2} + \ldots = \frac{\pi^2}{8}$.

<u>EXAMPLES TO DO</u> (on §162-164):   Pages 167-169: Exs. 1 - 5, 13.

165. **EXAMPLE.** Let $s(x)$ denote the value of the sum function of the Fourier Series in the example in §164 at the point x. By considering $s(x) + s(-x)$ and $s(x) - s(-x)$, find the sums of the series

(a) $\cos x + \dfrac{\cos 3x}{3^2} + \dfrac{\cos 5x}{5^2} + \ldots$

and (b) $\sin 2x + \dfrac{\sin 4x}{2} + \dfrac{\sin 6x}{3} + \ldots$

for $0 < x < \pi$.

Solution. From §164,

$$s(x) = -\frac{4}{\pi}\left(\cos x + \frac{\cos 3x}{3^2} + \ldots\right) - \left(\frac{\sin 2x}{1} + \frac{\sin 4x}{2} + \ldots\right),$$

$$s(-x) = -\frac{4}{\pi}\left(\cos(-x) + \frac{\cos(-3x)}{3^2} + \ldots\right) - \left(\frac{\sin(-2x)}{1} + \frac{\sin(-4x)}{2} + \ldots\right)$$

$$= -\frac{4}{\pi}\left(\cos x + \frac{\cos 3x}{3^2} + \ldots\right) + \left(\frac{\sin 2x}{1} + \frac{\sin 4x}{2} + \ldots\right).$$

So, on addition, we have

$$s(x) + s(-x) = -\frac{8}{\pi}\left(\cos x + \frac{\cos 3x}{3^2} + \frac{\cos 5x}{5^2} + \ldots\right),$$

i.e. $\cos x + \dfrac{\cos 3x}{3^2} + \dfrac{\cos 5x}{5^2} + \ldots = -\dfrac{\pi}{8}\Big[s(x) + s(-x)\Big]$.

Similarly, on subtraction, we can obtain

$$\sin 2x + \frac{\sin 4x}{2} + \frac{\sin 6x}{3} + \ldots = -\frac{1}{2}\Big[s(x) - s(-x)\Big].$$

Now, for $0 < x < \pi$, we have from the graph in §164 that $s(x) = 2x - \pi$ and $s(-x) = 0$ (since $-x$ lies in the range $-\pi < -x < 0$ and $s = 0$ at such points). So putting in these values gives that, for $0 < x < \pi$,

$$\cos x + \frac{\cos 3x}{3^2} + \frac{\cos 5x}{5^2} + \ldots = -\frac{\pi}{8}\Big(2x - \pi\Big)$$

and $\sin 2x + \dfrac{\sin 4x}{2} + \dfrac{\sin 6x}{3} + \ldots = -\dfrac{1}{2}\Big(2x - \pi\Big)$.

EXAMPLES TO DO: Page 169: Ex. 14.

166. THE IDEA OF HALF RANGE FOURIER SERIES

A Fourier Series expresses a given function in terms of building bricks, the building bricks being drawn from the sets C and S given by

$$C = \{1, \cos x, \cos 2x, \cos 3x, \ldots\}$$

and $S = \{\sin x, \sin 2x, \sin 3x, \ldots\}$.

In general, as in the example in §164, we need to draw both from C and from S to construct the required series and the series then agrees† with the given function on $[-\pi, \pi]$.

If however we are willing to cut our demands and ask only for a series agreeing† with the given function on $[0, \pi]$ (i.e. on half the interval) then correspondingly we require only half the building bricks in the sense that a series agreeing† with the given function on $[0, \pi]$ can be constructed using <u>only</u> functions from C, and another such series can be constructed using <u>only</u> functions from S. These two series, one using only cosine terms, the other using only sine terms, but both agreeing† with the given function on $[0, \pi]$, are the <u>Fourier half range cosine series</u> and the <u>Fourier half range sine series</u> of the given function.

† <u>Note</u>: The "agreement" is in the sense of §160.

167. HOW TO FIND THE COEFFICIENTS FOR HALF RANGE SERIES

Let f be a bounded function defined on $[0, \pi]$ with at most a finite number of maxima and minima and at most a finite number of discontinuities on $[0, \pi]$.

Then let a_n $(n \geq 0)$ and b_n $(n \geq 1)$ be defined by

$$a_n = \frac{2}{\pi} \int_0^\pi f(x) \cos nx \, dx, \qquad b_n = \frac{2}{\pi} \int_0^\pi f(x) \sin nx \, dx.$$

Notice in particular that this means

$$a_0 = \frac{2}{\pi} \int_0^\pi f(x) \, dx .$$

The series

$$\tfrac{1}{2}a_0 + \sum_{n=1}^{\infty} a_n \cos nx \qquad \text{and} \qquad \sum_{n=1}^{\infty} b_n \sin nx$$

are then the <u>Fourier half range cosine series</u> and the <u>Fourier half range sine series</u> of the function f on the interval $[0, \pi]$.

168. EXAMPLE. Find the Fourier half range cosine and the Fourier half range sine series of the function x on the interval $[0, \pi]$.

<u>Solution</u>.   For the half range cosine series we have

$$a_0 = \frac{2}{\pi} \int_0^\pi x \, dx = \frac{2}{\pi} [\tfrac{1}{2}x^2]_0^\pi = \pi ,$$

and for $n \geq 1$,

$$a_n = \frac{2}{\pi} \int_0^{\pi} x \cos nx \, dx = \frac{2}{\pi} \left[\frac{x \sin nx}{n} + \frac{\cos nx}{n^2} \right]_0^{\pi}$$

$$= \frac{2}{\pi} \left(\frac{\cos n\pi - 1}{n^2} \right) = \frac{2}{\pi} \left(\frac{(-1)^n - 1}{n^2} \right)$$

$$= \begin{cases} 0 & (n \quad \text{even}), \\ -4/(\pi n^2) & (n \quad \text{odd}). \end{cases}$$

So the Fourier half range <u>cosine</u> series of x on $[0,\pi]$ is

$$\tfrac{1}{2}\pi - \frac{4}{\pi} \left(\frac{\cos x}{1^2} + \frac{\cos 3x}{3^2} + \frac{\cos 5x}{5^2} + \cdots \right).$$

For the half range sine series we have, for $n \geq 1$,

$$b_n = \frac{2}{\pi} \int_0^{\pi} x \sin nx \, dx = \frac{2}{\pi} \left[\frac{-x \cos nx}{n} + \frac{\sin nx}{n^2} \right]_0^{\pi}$$

$$= \frac{2}{\pi} \left(\frac{-\pi(-1)^n}{n} \right) = \frac{2(-1)^{n+1}}{n}.$$

So the Fourier half range <u>sine</u> series of x on $[0,\pi]$ is

$$2 \left(\sin x - \frac{\sin 2x}{2} + \frac{\sin 3x}{3} - \frac{\sin 4x}{4} + \cdots \right).$$

169. THE RELATIONSHIP BETWEEN HALF RANGE SERIES AND FULL RANGE SERIES

From §168 we see that the function x on $[0,\pi]$ has the half range series

$$(1) \qquad \tfrac{1}{2}\pi - \frac{4}{\pi} \left(\frac{\cos x}{1^2} + \frac{\cos 3x}{3^2} + \frac{\cos 5x}{5^2} + \cdots \right)$$

and $(2) \qquad 2 \left(\sin x - \frac{\sin 2x}{2} + \frac{\sin 3x}{3} - \frac{\sin 4x}{4} + \cdots \right).$

These series however make sense for <u>all</u> values of x not just on $[0,\pi]$. It turns out that (1) is the full range Fourier Series of the function $|x|$ on $[-\pi,\pi]$, while (2) is the full range Fourier Series of the function x on $[-\pi,\pi]$. The graphs of these two functions are shown.

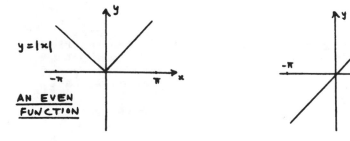

$y = |x|$

AN EVEN FUNCTION

$y = x$

AN ODD FUNCTION

Notice that <u>both</u> these functions agree with the function   x
on the interval [0,π] but that their behaviour between
−π   and   0   is very different.   Notice also that |x|
on   [−π,π]   is an <u>even</u> function (corresponding to the
<u>cosine</u> series) while x on   [−π,π]   is an <u>odd</u> function
(corresponding to the <u>sine</u> series).

These series illustrate the following rules:−

A.   The Fourier half range <u>cosine</u> series for the
function f   on   [0,π]   is the <u>full</u> range Fourier Series
for that <u>even</u> function on   [−π,π]   which agrees with   f
on   [0,π].

B.   The Fourier half range <u>sine</u> series for the
function f   on   [0,π]   is the <u>full</u> range Fourier Series
for that <u>odd</u> function on   [−π,π]   which agrees with   f
on   (0,π].

170.   THE SUM FUNCTION OF A HALF RANGE SERIES

To find the sum on [−π,π] of a half range series
calculated on [0,π] proceed as follows.   Extend the given
function (from which the half range series was calculated)
to [−π,π] as an <u>even</u> function for a half range <u>cosine</u>
series, as an <u>odd</u> function for a half range <u>sine</u> series.
The sum of the half range series on [−π,π] is then the
sum of the Fourier Series of the <u>extended function</u> on
[−π,π].   (Recall how to find the sum of a full range
Fourier Series from §160.)

§171 and §172 illustrate the process.

171.   <u>EXAMPLE</u>.   Let   f   be defined on   [0,π]   by

$$f(x) = \begin{cases} 2 & (0 \leq x \leq \tfrac{1}{2}\pi), \\ 1 & (\tfrac{1}{2}\pi < x \leq \pi). \end{cases}$$

Find the half range cosine series of f.   Draw the graph
of the sum function of this series on   [−2π,2π].   Hence
find

(a) $1 - \frac{1}{3} + \frac{1}{5} - \frac{1}{7} + \dots$,

(b) $1 + \frac{1}{3} - \frac{1}{5} - \frac{1}{7} + \frac{1}{9} + \frac{1}{11} - \dots$.

<u>Solution</u>.   It is fairly routine to show that the half
range series required is

$$\frac{3}{2} + \frac{2}{\pi}\left(\cos x - \frac{\cos 3x}{3} + \frac{\cos 5x}{5} - \dots \right).$$

The graph of the sum function is drawn overleaf.   For (a)
set x = 0   so that all the cosine terms become 1 and

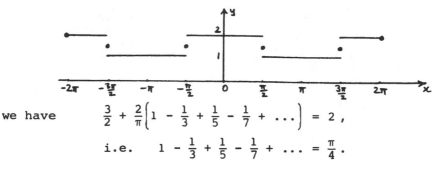

we have $\quad \frac{3}{2} + \frac{2}{\pi}\left(1 - \frac{1}{3} + \frac{1}{5} - \frac{1}{7} + \ldots\right) = 2$,

i.e. $\quad 1 - \frac{1}{3} + \frac{1}{5} - \frac{1}{7} + \ldots = \frac{\pi}{4}$.

For (b) set $x = \pi/4$ so that

$$\frac{3}{2} + \frac{2}{\pi}\left(\frac{1}{\sqrt 2} + \frac{1}{3\sqrt 2} - \frac{1}{5\sqrt 2} - \frac{1}{7\sqrt 2} + \ldots\right) = 2,$$

i.e. $\quad 1 + \frac{1}{3} - \frac{1}{5} - \frac{1}{7} + \ldots = \frac{\pi\sqrt 2}{4}$.

172. **EXAMPLE.** Let f be defined on $[0,\pi]$ by

$$f(x) = \begin{cases} \sin x & (0 \le x < \tfrac{1}{2}\pi), \\ 0 & (\tfrac{1}{2}\pi \le x \le \pi). \end{cases}$$

Find the half range sine series of f on $[0,\pi]$ and sketch the graph of its sum function on $[-\pi,\pi]$.

<u>Solution.</u> We have $b_n = \frac{2}{\pi}\int_0^{\frac{1}{2}\pi} \sin x \sin nx\, dx$

$$= \frac{1}{\pi}\int_0^{\frac{1}{2}\pi} \cos((n-1)x) - \cos((n+1)x)\, dx$$

$$= \frac{1}{\pi}\left[\frac{\sin((n-1)x)}{(n-1)} - \frac{\sin((n+1)x)}{(n+1)}\right]_0^{\frac{1}{2}\pi} \quad \left(\begin{matrix} \text{N.B.} \\ n \ne 1 \end{matrix}\right)$$

$$= \frac{1}{\pi}\left(\frac{\sin(\frac{1}{2}(n-1)\pi)}{(n-1)} - \frac{\sin(\frac{1}{2}(n+1)\pi)}{(n+1)}\right) \quad (n \ne 1)$$

So, from this, if n is odd and not equal to 1 then both terms are 0 and therefore $b_n = 0$.
Also, from this, if n is of the form $(4k+2)$ for k an integer then

$$b_n = \frac{1}{\pi}\left(\frac{1}{n-1} + \frac{1}{n+1}\right) = \frac{2n}{(n-1)(n+1)}.$$

Also, if n is of the form $4k$ for an integer k then

$$b_n = \frac{1}{\pi}\left(\frac{-1}{n-1} - \frac{1}{n+1}\right) = \frac{-2n}{(n-1)(n+1)}$$

For b_1 which cannot be found above because of a zero denominator we do a direct calculation as follows:

$$b_1 = \frac{2}{\pi} \int_0^{\frac{1}{2}\pi} \sin^2 x \, dx = \frac{2}{\pi} \int_0^{\frac{1}{2}\pi} \frac{1}{2}(1 - \cos 2x) \, dx = \frac{1}{2}.$$

The required series is therefore

$$\frac{1}{2} \sin x + \frac{2}{\pi} \left(\frac{2}{1.3} \sin 2x - \frac{4}{3.5} \sin 4x + \frac{6}{5.7} \sin 6x - \dots \right).$$

The required graph is

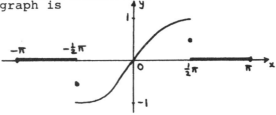

EXAMPLES TO DO: Pages 168-169:   Exs. 6 - 9.

173.   PARSEVAL'S RESULT

The following result can be used to find the sum of certain series from calculated Fourier Series.

RESULT.   Let   f   be a function of the type described in §157 with the Fourier Series

$$\frac{1}{2}a_0 + \sum_{n=1}^{\infty} (a_n \cos nx + b_n \sin nx).$$

Then

$$\frac{1}{2}a_0^2 + \sum_{n=1}^{\infty} (a_n^2 + b_n^2) = \frac{1}{\pi} \int_{-\pi}^{\pi} (f(x))^2 \, dx.$$

We do not give a formal proof but to see why the result is reasonable consider the equation

$$f(x) \left[\frac{1}{2}a_0 + \sum(a_n \cos nx + b_n \sin nx) \right] = (f(x))^2$$

i.e. $\frac{1}{2}a_0 f(x) + \sum(a_n f(x) \cos nx + b_n f(x) \sin nx) = (f(x))^2.$

Dividing this by π and integrating term by term on the interval $[-\pi, \pi]$ gives

$$\frac{1}{2}a_0 \left(\frac{1}{\pi} \int_{-\pi}^{\pi} f(x) \, dx \right) + \sum a_n \left(\frac{1}{\pi} \int_{-\pi}^{\pi} f(x) \cos nx \, dx \right)$$

$$+ \sum b_n \left(\frac{1}{\pi} \int_{-\pi}^{\pi} f(x) \sin nx \, dx \right) = \frac{1}{\pi} \int_{-\pi}^{\pi} (f(x))^2 \, dx,$$

i.e. $\frac{1}{2}a_0^2 + \sum(a_n^2 + b_n^2) = \frac{1}{\pi} \int_{-\pi}^{\pi} (f(x))^2 \, dx,$

which is the required result.

EXAMPLE.   Use Parseval's result on the Fourier Series of x^2 (calculated in §163) to prove that

$$1 + \frac{1}{2^4} + \frac{1}{3^4} + \frac{1}{4^4} + \ldots = \frac{\pi^4}{90}.$$

Solution.   The series for x^2 is

$$\frac{\pi^2}{3} - 4\left(\cos x - \frac{\cos 2x}{2^2} + \frac{\cos 3x}{3^2} - \frac{\cos 4x}{4^2} + \ldots\right).$$

Parseval's result then gives

$$\frac{1}{2}\cdot\frac{4\pi^4}{9} + 16\left(1 + \frac{1}{2^4} + \frac{1}{3^4} + \frac{1}{4^4} + \ldots\right) = \frac{1}{\pi}\int_{-\pi}^{\pi} x^4\,dx = \frac{2\pi^4}{5}.$$

On rearrangement this gives

$$1 + \frac{1}{2^4} + \frac{1}{3^4} + \frac{1}{4^4} + \ldots = \frac{\pi^4}{90}.$$

WARNING.   Notice that in this example that it is $\frac{1}{2}a_0$ not a_0 that is $\pi^2/3$.   Failure to observe this is a common source of trouble.

EXAMPLES TO DO: Page 169: Exs. 10 - 12.

174.   FOURIER SERIES ON OTHER INTERVALS

The foregoing treatment of Fourier Series is based on the interval $[-\pi,\pi]$.   It is however equally possible to take the basic interval as $[0,2\pi]$, the coefficients then being calculated as

$$a_n = \frac{1}{\pi}\int_0^{2\pi} f(x)\cos nx\,dx \quad \text{and} \quad b_n = \frac{1}{\pi}\int_0^{2\pi} f(x)\sin nx\,dx.$$

The resulting series then agrees (in a sense similar to that in §160) with the given function f on the interval $[0,2\pi]$.

It is also possible to alter the <u>length</u> of the interval.   For example, on the interval $[-a,a]$ we can find a Fourier Series of the form

$$\frac{1}{2}a_0 + \sum_{n=1}^{\infty}\left(a_n\cos\left(\frac{n\pi x}{a}\right) + b_n\sin\left(\frac{n\pi x}{a}\right)\right),$$

where

$$a_n = \frac{1}{a}\int_{-a}^{a} f(x)\cos\left(\frac{n\pi x}{a}\right)dx, \quad b_n = \frac{1}{a}\int_{-a}^{a} f(x)\sin\left(\frac{n\pi x}{a}\right)dx.$$

EXAMPLE. Find the Fourier Series on [-a,a] of the function f defined by

$$f(x) = \frac{h}{a}\Big(|x| - a\Big) \qquad (-a \le x \le a).$$

Solution. The given function is even so that the Fourier Series contains only cosine terms. So

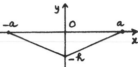

$$a_0 = \frac{1}{a}\int_{-a}^{a} f(x)\,dx = \frac{2}{a}\int_{0}^{a} f(x)\,dx \quad \text{(by symmetry)}$$

$$= \frac{2}{a}\int_{0}^{a} \frac{h}{a}(x - a)\,dx = -h.$$

Also, for n ≥ 1,

$$a_n = \frac{2}{a}\int_{0}^{a} \frac{h}{a}(x - a)\cos\left(\frac{n\pi x}{a}\right)dx = \begin{cases} -4h/(n^2\pi^2) & (n \text{ odd}), \\ 0 & (n \text{ even}). \end{cases}$$

So the required series is

$$-\tfrac{1}{2}h - \frac{4h}{\pi^2}\left(\cos\left(\frac{\pi x}{a}\right) + \frac{1}{3^2}\cos\left(\frac{3\pi x}{a}\right) + \frac{1}{5^2}\cos\left(\frac{5\pi x}{a}\right) + \ldots\right).$$

EXAMPLES 11

1. A function f is defined on [-π,π] by

$$f(x) = 3 \quad (-\pi \le x < 0), \quad f(0) = 0, \quad f(x) = -1 \quad (0 < x \le \pi).$$

Let s(x) denote the sum of the Fourier Series of f at the point x. Sketch the graphs of f and s on [-π,π].

2. Let f and g be defined for -π ≤ x ≤ π by

$$f(x) = x \quad \text{and} \quad g(x) = x^2.$$

Without looking at §162 and §163, determine the Fourier Series of f and g on the interval [-π,π].

3. Show that the Fourier Series of f defined on [-π,π] by

$$f(x) = \begin{cases} 0 & (-\pi \le x < 0), \\ 1 & (0 \le x \le \pi). \end{cases}$$

is

$$\frac{1}{2} + \frac{2}{\pi}\left(\sin x + \frac{\sin 3x}{3} + \frac{\sin 5x}{5} + \ldots\right).$$

Sketch the graph of the sum function of this series on [-3π,3π]. By giving x particular values find the values of

(a) $1 - \frac{1}{3} + \frac{1}{5} - \frac{1}{7} + \ldots$, (b) $1 - \frac{1}{5} + \frac{1}{7} - \frac{1}{11} + \frac{1}{13} - \frac{1}{17} + \ldots$.

4. Show that the Fourier Series of f defined on $[-\pi,\pi]$ by

$$f(x) = \begin{cases} 0 & (-\pi \leq x < 0), \\ \pi - x & (0 \leq x \leq \pi), \end{cases}$$

is $\dfrac{\pi}{4} + \dfrac{2}{\pi}\left(\dfrac{\cos x}{1^2} + \dfrac{\cos 3x}{3^2} + \dfrac{\cos 5x}{5^2} + \cdots\right)$

$$+ \left(\sin x + \frac{\sin 2x}{2} + \frac{\sin 3x}{3} + \cdots\right).$$

Deduce that $1 + \dfrac{1}{3^2} + \dfrac{1}{5^2} + \dfrac{1}{7^2} + \cdots = \dfrac{\pi^2}{8}$.

5. Noting that the function $\sin \tfrac{1}{2}x$ is an odd function, find its Fourier Series on $[-\pi,\pi]$. Sketch the graph of the sum function of this series on the interval $[-3\pi,3\pi]$. Deduce that

$$\frac{1}{1.3} - \frac{3}{5.7} + \frac{5}{9.11} - \cdots = \frac{\pi\sqrt{2}}{16}.$$

6. Let f be defined on $[0,\pi]$ by $f(x) = 1$ for $0 \leq x \leq \pi$. Show that the half range cosine and half range sine series of f are

$$1 \quad \text{and} \quad \frac{4}{\pi}\left(\sin x + \frac{\sin 3x}{3} + \frac{\sin 5x}{5} + \cdots\right)$$

respectively. By giving x particular values, show that

(a) $1 - \dfrac{1}{3} + \dfrac{1}{5} - \dfrac{1}{7} + \cdots = \dfrac{\pi}{4}$,

(b) $1 + \dfrac{1}{3} - \dfrac{1}{5} - \dfrac{1}{7} + \dfrac{1}{9} + \dfrac{1}{11} - \cdots = \dfrac{\pi\sqrt{2}}{4}$.

7. Let f be defined on $[0,\pi]$ by

$$f(x) = \begin{cases} 1 & (0 \leq x \leq \tfrac{1}{2}\pi), \\ 0 & (\tfrac{1}{2}\pi < x \leq \pi). \end{cases}$$

Show that its half range cosine series is

$$\frac{1}{2} + \frac{2}{\pi}\left(\frac{\cos x}{1} - \frac{\cos 3x}{3} + \frac{\cos 5x}{5} - \cdots\right).$$

Sketch the sum function of this series on $[-\pi,\pi]$.

8. Show that the half range sine series of f in Ex.7 above is

$$\frac{2}{\pi}\left(\sin x + \frac{2\sin 2x}{2} + \frac{\sin 3x}{3}\right.$$

$$\left. + \frac{\sin 5x}{5} + \frac{2\sin 6x}{6} + \frac{\sin 7x}{7} + \cdots\right).$$

Sketch the sum function of this series on $[-\pi,\pi]$ and deduce the values of

(a) $1 - \frac{1}{3} + \frac{1}{5} - \frac{1}{7} + \ldots$,   (b) $1 + \frac{1}{3} - \frac{1}{5} - \frac{1}{7} + \ldots$.

9.   Show that the function $\cos x$ has the Fourier half range sine series

$$\frac{4}{\pi}\left\{\frac{2 \sin 2x}{1.3} + \frac{4 \sin 4x}{3.5} + \frac{6 \sin 6x}{5.7} + \ldots\right\}$$

on $[0,\pi]$.   Sketch the graph of the sum of this series on $[-2\pi,2\pi]$.

10.   Find the half range cosine series of the function x on $[0,\pi]$.   Of which function is this the Fourier Series on $[-\pi,\pi]$?   By choosing a suitable value of x show that

$$1 + \frac{1}{3^2} + \frac{1}{5^2} + \frac{1}{7^2} + \ldots = \frac{\pi^2}{8} .$$

Use Parseval's result to show that

$$1 + \frac{1}{3^4} + \frac{1}{5^4} + \ldots = \frac{\pi^4}{96} .$$

11.   Use Parseval's result with the series in §171 to show that

$$1 + \frac{1}{3^2} + \frac{1}{5^2} + \frac{1}{7^2} + \ldots = \frac{\pi^2}{8} .$$

12.   In §165 the sums of two series (a) and (b) are found for $0 < x < \pi$.   Deduce their sums for $-\pi < x < 0$ from their sums for $0 < x < \pi$.
Use Parseval's result with these series to show that

$$1 + \frac{1}{3^4} + \frac{1}{5^4} + \frac{1}{7^4} + \ldots = \frac{\pi^4}{96} ,$$

$$1 + \frac{1}{2^2} + \frac{1}{3^2} + \frac{1}{4^2} + \ldots = \frac{\pi^2}{6} .$$

13.   Notice that the function $(x^2 + x)$ is neither even nor odd.   If you were asked to calculate its Fourier Series on $[-\pi,\pi]$ would you make a direct assault on a_n and b_n with the formulae of §157?   Answer YES or NO. Find the Fourier Series.

14.   Let $s(x)$ denote the sum at $x \in [-\pi,\pi]$ of the Fourier Series calculated in Ex.4 above.   By considering $s(x) + s(-x)$ and $s(x) - s(-x)$ find, for $0 < x < \pi$, the sums of the series

$$\frac{\cos x}{1^2} + \frac{\cos 3x}{3^2} + \frac{\cos 5x}{5^2} + \ldots ,$$

$$\sin x + \frac{\sin 2x}{2} + \frac{\sin 3x}{3} + \dots \ .$$

Deduce that

$$1 + \frac{1}{2} - \frac{1}{4} - \frac{1}{5} + \frac{1}{7} + \frac{1}{8} - \dots = \frac{2\pi\sqrt{3}}{9} \ .$$

XII. MAXIMA AND MINIMA OF FUNCTIONS OF SEVERAL VARIABLES

175. A RECAP ON STATIONARY POINTS FOR FUNCTIONS OF ONE VARIABLE

Recall that ordinary differentiation gives a method for finding local maxima and minima of functions of one real variable. For example, the local maxima and minima of f given by $f(x) = x^3 - 3x - 8$ can be found by looking at its stationary points, i.e. those points a for which $f'(a) = 0$.

The sign of the derivative near such a point settles whether the point is a local maximum, a local minimum or a horizontal point of inflexion. The sign of the second derivative (provided it is non-zero) gives an alternative method for settling the nature of the stationary point.

176. LOCAL MAXIMA AND MINIMA OF FUNCTIONS OF TWO VARIABLES

Recall from §2 that a function f of two variables x and y can be thought of as a surface $z = f(x,y)$ in three dimensional space.
For example, the function
f given by

$$f(x,y) = x^2 + y^2 + 3$$

can be thought of as the paraboloid $z = x^2 + y^2 + 3$ shown in the diagram. Clearly f has a minimum value 3 when $(x,y) = (0,0)$.

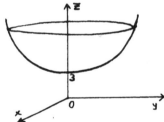

With this example in mind we say that such a function has a <u>local minimum</u> when $(x,y) = (a,b)$ if there is a neighbourhood U of (a,b) in the xy-plane such that

$$f(x,y) > f(a,b)$$

for all (x,y) in U except for the point (a,b).
(<u>Local maximum</u> is defined similarly.)

177. STATIONARY POINTS FOR FUNCTIONS OF TWO VARIABLES

For a function f of two variables x and y, the point (a,b) is a <u>stationary point</u> if

$$\frac{\partial f}{\partial x} = 0 \quad \text{and} \quad \frac{\partial f}{\partial y} = 0$$

when $(x,y) = (a,b)$. This definition is similar to the corresponding definition for functions of one variable (i.e. $f'(a) = 0$) in §175. Also similar to the situation for one variable is the following result.

RESULT. The local maxima and local minima of a function
f of two variables (on an open set on which the first
partial derivatives of f exist) are to be found at points
which are stationary points, i.e. at points for which

$$\frac{\partial f}{\partial x} = 0 \quad \text{and} \quad \frac{\partial f}{\partial y} = 0.$$

As justification of this result, think for example of
a function f of two variables x and y which has a
local minimum at (x,y) = (a,b). Now define a function ϕ
of one variable by $\phi(x) = f(x,b)$. (This effectively holds
y constant and the graph of ϕ is a section of the
surface z = f(x,y) along the plane y = b.) Since f
has a local minimum at (a,b), it follows that ϕ has a
local minimum at x = a, (i.e. the section has a minimum
where the whole surface has a minimum). But then, from
the theory for functions of one variable, the point a
must be a stationary point for ϕ,

i.e. $\phi'(x) = 0$ at x = a,

i.e. $\frac{\partial f}{\partial x} = 0$ at (x,y) = (a,b).

Likewise by considering the function ψ defined by
$\psi(y) = f(a,y)$ we can show that

$$\frac{\partial f}{\partial y} = 0 \quad \text{at} \quad (x,y) = (a,b).$$

So the conclusion is that if f(x,y) has a local
minimum or local maximum at (a,b) then (a,b) is a
stationary point of f.

EXAMPLE. Find the stationary points of the function f
defined on R (i.e. the whole xy-plane) by
$f(x,y) = x^2 + y^2 + 3$.

Solution. Here $\frac{\partial f}{\partial x} = 2x$ and $\frac{\partial f}{\partial y} = 2y$.

For a stationary point we need therefore

2x = 0 and 2y = 0, i.e. x = y = 0.

So the only stationary point is (0,0).

Notice: This stationary point does actually give a local
minimum of the function $x^2 + y^2 + 3$ as is clear from the
sketch of the surface $z = x^2 + y^2 + 3$ in §176. In
general however, we may be unable to draw the surface
z = f(x,y) easily and other methods (e.g. §179) are
needed to settle whether a given stationary point gives
a maximum, a minimum or neither.

178. SADDLE POINTS

Not all stationary points give maxima or minima, e.g. take f defined by

$$f(x, y) = x^2 - y^2.$$

Here the stationary points are given by

$$\frac{\partial f}{\partial x} = 2x = 0 \quad \text{and} \quad \frac{\partial f}{\partial y} = -2y = 0,$$

i.e. $(x,y) = (0,0)$. This point is however neither a local maximum nor a local minimum, as the sketch of the surface illustrates. A point which is a stationary point but which is neither a local minimum nor a local maximum is called a <u>saddle point</u> or a <u>non-turning value</u>. So $(0,0)$ in the above example is a saddle point. (Compare horizontal points of inflexion in the one variable situation.)

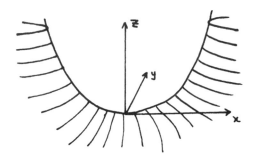

In the above example notice that $f(0,0) = 0$, but

$$f(c,0) = c^2 > 0 \quad \text{while} \quad f(0,d) = -d^2 < 0$$

for non-zero c and d. This makes clear that $(0,0)$ is neither a local minimum nor a local maximum without appeal to the diagram.

Try to think of a crossroads in your area at which the road surface has a non-turning value.

179. THE HESSIAN AND ITS USE IN SETTLING THE NATURE OF A STATIONARY POINT

Recall that the second derivative of a function of <u>one</u> variable can in some cases be used to determine the nature of a stationary point as mentioned in §175. The following gives the corresponding method for functions of <u>two</u> variables.

Let f be a function of two variables x, y which has continuous second partial derivatives on an open set U. Suppose that f has a stationary point at (a,b) in U. To settle the nature of this stationary point, evaluate the <u>Hessian</u> matrix H of f at (a,b), where H is the matrix given by:-

$$H = \begin{bmatrix} f_{xx} & f_{xy} \\ f_{xy} & f_{yy} \end{bmatrix}.$$

In the matrix H the notation f_{xx} is used for $\frac{\partial^2 f}{\partial x^2}$ etc as in §88 and these partial derivatives are evaluated at (a,b). We then evaluate $\det H$, the <u>determinant of the matrix</u> H with the formula

$$\det H = f_{xx} f_{yy} - (f_{xy})^2.$$

<u>The following can then be said about the stationary point (a,b)</u> :

    1. If $\det H > 0$ and $f_{xx} > 0$ then (a,b) gives a local minimum of f.

    2. If $\det H > 0$ and $f_{xx} < 0$ then (a,b) gives a local maximum of f.

    3. If $\det H < 0$ then (a,b) gives a saddle point for f.

    4. If $\det H = 0$ then more powerful methods (§182) are required.

    For examples on the use of these rules see §180, §181. For justification and the insight that comes from seeing the whole picture see §185 and §186.

180.   EXAMPLE. Discuss the nature of the stationary points of the function f given by
$$f(x,y) = x^2 - 2x - y^3 + y^2 + 8y.$$

<u>Solution</u>. We have $f_x = 2x - 2$ and $f_y = -3y^2 + 2y + 8$.

For a stationary point we need $f_x = 0$ <u>and</u> $f_y = 0$,

    i.e. $2(x - 1) = 0$ <u>and</u> $-(3y^2 - 2y - 8) = 0$,

    i.e. $x = 1$ <u>and</u> $(3y + 4)(y - 2) = 0$,

    i.e. $x = 1$ <u>and</u> $\{y = -4/3$ <u>or</u> $y = 2\}$,

    i.e. $\{x = 1$ <u>and</u> $y = -4/3\}$ <u>or</u> $\{x = 1$ <u>and</u> $y = 2\}$.

So the stationary points are $(1,-4/3)$, $(1,2)$.

    For the Hessian, $f_{xx} = 2$, $f_{xy} = 0$, $f_{yy} = -6y + 2$.

So $H = \begin{bmatrix} 2 & 0 \\ 0 & -6y + 2 \end{bmatrix}$. So <u>at $(1,-4/3)$</u>, $H = \begin{bmatrix} 2 & 0 \\ 0 & 10 \end{bmatrix}$,

for which $\det H = 20 > 0$ and $f_{xx} = 2 > 0$. So we

can conclude from §179 that (1,-4/3) gives a local minimum of f.

At (1,2), $H = \begin{bmatrix} 2 & 0 \\ 0 & -10 \end{bmatrix}$, for which det H = -20.   So we conclude that (1,2) gives a saddle point for f.

[Notice carefully the use of the words and and or in the above solution.]

181. EXAMPLE.   Determine the nature of the stationary points of f defined by

$$f(x,y) = 4x^2y - y^2 - 8x^2 - 2x^4.$$

Solution.   Here $f_x = 8xy - 16x - 8x^3$, $f_y = 4x^2 - 2y$.

The stationary points are therefore given by

$$8x(y - 2 - x^2) = 0 \quad \text{and} \quad 2(2x^2 - y) = 0,$$

i.e. $x(y - 2 - x^2) = 0 \quad \text{and} \quad y = 2x^2,$

i.e. $\{x = 0 \ \text{and} \ y = 2x^2\} \ \text{or} \ \{y - 2 - x^2 = 0 \ \text{and} \ y = 2x^2\},$

i.e. (0,0) or $\{2x^2 - 2 - x^2 = 0 \ \text{and} \ y = 2x^2\}$,

i.e. (0,0) or $\{x^2 = 2 \ \text{and} \ y = 2x^2\},$

i.e. (0,0), ($\sqrt{2}$,4), ($-\sqrt{2}$,4).

So the stationary points are (0,0), ($\sqrt{2}$,4), ($-\sqrt{2}$,4).

Then $f_{xx} = 8y - 16 - 24x^2$, $f_{xy} = 8x$, $f_{yy} = -2$.   So

$$H = \begin{bmatrix} 8y - 16 - 24x^2 & 8x \\ 8x & -2 \end{bmatrix}.$$

At (0,0), $H = \begin{bmatrix} -16 & 0 \\ 0 & -2 \end{bmatrix}$ with det H = 32 and $f_{xx} < 0$.

So (0,0) gives a local maximum.

At ($\sqrt{2}$,4) and ($-\sqrt{2}$,4),   we have

$$H = \begin{bmatrix} -32 & 8\sqrt{2} \\ 8\sqrt{2} & -2 \end{bmatrix} \quad \text{and} \quad \begin{bmatrix} -32 & -8\sqrt{2} \\ -8\sqrt{2} & -2 \end{bmatrix},$$

which both have det H < 0 and so ($\sqrt{2}$,4) and ($-\sqrt{2}$,4) both give saddle points.

EXAMPLES TO DO (on §180-181):   Page 185: Exs. 1(a)-(o).

182. WHAT TO DO IF THE DETERMINANT OF THE HESSIAN IS ZERO

The examples in §180 and §181 fall into Cases 1, 2 and 3 in §179, det H being non-zero at the stationary points in question. If det H $\underline{is}$ zero at a stationary point (a,b) then the Hessian method fails (Case 4 in §179): failure in this context means that being shown the Hessian matrix on its own does $\underline{not}$ allow us to say with certainty whether the stationary point is maximum, minimum or saddle. As evidence of this take the two cases in §183: the same Hessian matrix (with determinant zero) occurs both for a minimum and a saddle. We then proceed by examining the difference (f(a+h,b+k) - f(a,b)) for small values of h and k. The examples of §183 and §184 illustrate this.

183. (i) EXAMPLE. Discuss the stationary points of f defined by

$$f(x,y) = x^2 + y^4 + 1.$$

$\underline{\text{Solution.}}$ Here $f_x = 2x$, $f_y = 4y^3$ and the only stationary point occurs at (0,0). Now, $f_{xx} = 2$, $f_{xy} = 0$ and $f_{yy} = 12y^2$. So

$$H = \begin{bmatrix} 2 & 0 \\ 0 & 12y^2 \end{bmatrix} \quad \text{which is} \quad \begin{bmatrix} 2 & 0 \\ 0 & 0 \end{bmatrix} \quad \text{at} \quad (0,0).$$

So det H = 0 and the method of §179 fails. Then

$$f(h,k) - f(0,0) = h^2 + k^4 > 0$$

for all h, k not both zero. So we conclude that

$$f(h,k) > f(0,0)$$

on a neighbourhood of (0,0). So $\underline{(0,0) \text{ is a local minimum}}$ $\underline{\text{of} \quad f.}$

(ii) EXAMPLE. Discuss the stationary points of f defined by

$$f(x,y) = x^2 - y^4 + 1.$$

$\underline{\text{Solution.}}$ Proceeding as in (i) we find the same stationary point (0,0) and the same Hessian matrix

$$H = \begin{bmatrix} 2 & 0 \\ 0 & 0 \end{bmatrix} \quad \text{at} \quad (0,0).$$

So det H = 0 and the method of §179 fails again. Now

$$f(h,k) - f(0,0) = h^2 - k^4. \qquad \ldots(*)$$

If we then take $h \neq 0$ and $k = 0$, we find that

$f(h,k) - f(0,0) = h^2 > 0$, i.e. $f(h,0) > f(0,0)$.

If we then take $h = 0$ and $k \neq 0$,

$f(h,k) - f(0,0) = -k^4 < 0$, i.e. $f(0,k) < f(0,0)$.

It follows that on all neighbourhoods of $(0,0)$ there are some points at which $f(h,k) > f(0,0)$ and other points at which $f(h,k) < f(0,0)$. It follows that $(0,0)$ <u>gives a saddle point.</u>

184. <u>EXAMPLE</u>. Show that $(0,0)$ is a stationary point of the function f defined by

$$f(x,y) = xy^2 - x^2y^2 - x^4 + 3$$

and determine its nature.

<u>Solution</u>. Here $f_x = y^2 - 2xy^2 - 4x^3$, $f_y = 2xy - 2x^2y$,

$f_{xx} = -2y^2 - 12x^2$, $f_{xy} = 2y - 4xy$, $f_{yy} = 2x - 2x^2$.

At $(0,0)$, $f_x = f_y = 0$ confirming $(0,0)$ as a stationary point. The Hessian matrix at $(0,0)$ is however

$$H = \begin{bmatrix} 0 & 0 \\ 0 & 0 \end{bmatrix}$$

so that the method of §179 gives no result. However

$$f(h,k) - f(0,0) = hk^2 - h^2k^2 - h^4.$$

If we take $h = k$ in this (i.e. consider points along the line $y = x$ near $(0,0)$), we have

$$f(h,h) - f(0,0) = h^3 - 2h^4.$$

For small values of h, h^3 is the dominant term here and since h^3 can be of either sign according as h is positive or negative we conclude that $(f(h,k) - f(0,0))$ can vary in sign near $(0,0)$. So <u>$(0,0)$ is a saddle point.</u>

<u>EXAMPLES TO DO</u>: Page 185: Ex. 1(p).

185. THE BACKGROUND TO THE HESSIAN METHOD

Under suitable conditions involving existence of partial derivatives, a function of two variables can be expanded using Taylor's theorem (§111) as

$$f(a+h,b+k) = f(a,b) + (h\,f_x + k\,f_y)$$
$$+ \tfrac{1}{2}(h^2\,f_{xx} + 2hk\,f_{xy} + k^2\,f_{yy})$$

+ terms of higher degree

in a neighbourhood of (a,b), the partial derivatives being evaluated at (a,b).

Suppose further that (a,b) is a stationary point of f so that f_x and f_y are both zero at (a,b). Then we can rewrite the above as

$$f(a+h,b+k) - f(a,b) = \tfrac{1}{2}\phi(h,k) + \text{higher terms}, \quad \dots (*)$$

where $\phi(h,k) = h^2\,f_{xx} + 2hk\,f_{xy} + k^2\,f_{yy}$.

In fact, in terms of matrices,

$$\phi(h,k) = \begin{bmatrix} h & k \end{bmatrix} \begin{bmatrix} f_{xx} & f_{xy} \\ f_{xy} & f_{yy} \end{bmatrix} \begin{bmatrix} h \\ k \end{bmatrix}$$

$$= u^T H u,$$

where H is the Hessian and u^T denotes the transpose of the column vector u. So (*) becomes

$$f(a+h,b+k) - f(a,b) = \tfrac{1}{2}u^T H u + \text{higher terms.} \quad \dots (\dagger)$$

It follows that near (a,b) the sign of the difference $(f(a+h,b+k) - f(a,b))$ is determined by the sign of the quadratic form $u^T H u$. A short summary of the properties of quadratic forms is given in the Appendix (§216). The rules given in §179 concerning the sign of det H etc are derived from these properties.

In this context these rules in §179 can be seen as deciding on a local minimum, local maximum, saddle point or no conclusion according as the Hessian matrix is positive definite, negative definite, indefinite or none of these respectively. This characterisation has the advantage of applying to functions of more than two variables (§186).

186. STATIONARY POINTS FOR FUNCTION OF THREE OR MORE VARIABLES

The situation for three or more variables is similar to that for two variables (§177) though a graphical representation as a surface is no longer available. For a function f of n variables (n ≥ 2) whose value at $x = (x_1, x_2, \dots, x_n)$ is $f(x_1, x_2, \dots, x_n)$, the point $a = (a_1, a_2, \ldots, a_n)$ is a <u>stationary point</u> if

$$\frac{\partial f}{\partial x_1} = \frac{\partial f}{\partial x_2} = \ldots = \frac{\partial f}{\partial x_n} = 0$$

for $x = a$. The local maxima and local minima of such a function are to be found among its stationary points. The <u>Hessian matrix</u> is the $n \times n$ matrix

$$\left[\frac{\partial^2 f}{\partial x_i \partial x_j}\right] \qquad (i = 1, 2, \ldots, n; \quad j = 1, 2, \ldots, n).$$

In particular for a function of three variables x, y, z, the Hessian is given by

$$H = \begin{bmatrix} f_{xx} & f_{xy} & f_{xz} \\ f_{xy} & f_{yy} & f_{yz} \\ f_{xz} & f_{yz} & f_{zz} \end{bmatrix}.$$

(We are assuming throughout this chapter of course that the functions we are dealing with possess the commutative property of partial differentiation (§88).)

The nature of the stationary point given by $x = a$ is determined by the Hessian matrix H with the partial derivatives evaluated at a as follows:

1. If H is positive definite then a gives a local minimum.

2. If H is negative definite then a gives a local maximum.

3. If H is indefinite then a gives a saddle point.

4. Otherwise this method gives no conclusion and you must resort to methods similar to those exemplified in the examples of §183 and §184.

Methods of deciding whether a given matrix is positive definite are suggested in the Appendix (§216). §187 gives an example.

187. EXAMPLE. Show that the function f defined by

$$f(x, y, z) = (x + y + z)^2 - 6xyz$$

has a stationary point at $(1, 1, 1)$ and determine its nature.

<u>Solution</u>. We have $f_x = 2(x + y + z) - 6yz$,

$$f_y = 2(x + y + z) - 6xz, \quad f_z = 2(x + y + z) - 6xy.$$

These partial derivatives are all zero at (1,1,1), which is therefore a stationary point.   Also,

$f_{xx} = f_{yy} = f_{zz} = 2$, $f_{xy} = 2 - 6z$, $f_{xz} = 2 - 6y$, $f_{yz} = 2 - 6x$,   so that at (1,1,1) we have

$$H = \begin{bmatrix} 2 & -4 & -4 \\ -4 & 2 & -4 \\ -4 & -4 & 2 \end{bmatrix}.$$

Here, in the notation of §216, $\Delta_1 = 2$, $\Delta_2 = -12$ and $\Delta_3 = -216$.   So from §216 we conclude that H is indefinite.   So (1,1,1) is a saddle point.

EXAMPLE TO DO: Page 185: Ex. 2.

188.   THE SIGNIFICANCE OF THE WORD LOCAL

Be warned that the maxima and minima found by the preceding methods are only local, i.e. a local maximum at (a,b) is only a maximum in a neighbourhood of (a,b):   it is still possible that the function takes larger values elsewhere.   For example, the function f given by

$$f(x,y) = x^3 - 3x + y^2$$

is easily checked to have a local maximum value of 2   at (-1,0) and a local minimum value of -2   at (1,0). Notice however that there are many points at which f takes values larger than 2   or less than -2 , e.g.

$$f(4,0) = 52 \quad \text{and} \quad f(-5,2) = -106.$$

189.   MAXIMA AND MINIMA OF FUNCTIONS SUBJECT TO RESTRICTIONS

Consider the following problem.   Suppose that we wish to find the minimum value of the function f defined by

$$f(x,y,z) = x^2 + y^2 + z^2$$

at points (x,y,z) for which $2x + 3y + 6z = 98$.   This effectively asks for the minimum value of the function $x^2 + y^2 + z^2$ at points on the plane $2x + 3y + 6z = 98$ in three dimensional space.   In fact, the function $x^2 + y^2 + z^2$ represents the square of the distance from (0,0,0) to the point (x,y,z).   So really the problem asks us to find the point (x,y,z) on the plane $2x + 3y + 6z = 98$ which is nearest to the origin (i.e. for which $x^2 + y^2 + z^2$ has a minimum value).   Such a

minimum clearly exists from
geometrical considerations.
(See the diagram.)

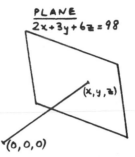

PLANE
$2x + 3y + 6z = 98$

(x,y,z)

$(0,0,0)$

The method of Lagrange
Multipliers deals with problems
of this type, in which one
function of several variables
is to be maximised or minimised
subject to a restriction or
restrictions specified by an
equation or equations.
Sometimes a geometrical interpretation is available as in
the above example.   §190 gives the method while its use
is illustrated by the examples in §191-193.

Notice: The minimum value of the above function f on the
whole of three dimensional space is clearly 0 and this
value is taken at the point (0,0,0).   (This could be
found as in §187.)   This is not what is wanted in the
above problem because we are interested only in points
(x,y,z) lying on the plane 2x + 3y + 6z = 98.
Incidentally, the point on the plane which gives the
minimum value of $x^2 + y^2 + z^2$ is (4,6,12) - the minimum
value being $4^2 + 6^2 + 12^2 = 196$.

190.   THE METHOD OF LAGRANGE MULTIPLIERS

Suppose that f is a function of n variables
$x_1, x_2, \ldots , x_n$.   (In §189, n = 3.)   Suppose that
we are restricted to considering points $x = (x_1, \ldots , x_n)$
satisfying m conditions given by the equations

$$g_1(x) = 0, \quad g_2(x) = 0, \quad \ldots , \quad g_m(x) = 0.$$

(In §189, m = 1.)   Suppose that we want to find the
local maxima and local minima of f for all values of
$x = (x_1, \ldots , x_n)$ satisfying these conditions.   The
method of Lagrange Multipliers then tells us that, for each
point c which gives such a local maximum or local minimum,
there exist scalars (i.e. numbers) $\lambda_1, \lambda_2, \ldots , \lambda_m$
such that c is a stationary point of the function

$$f + \lambda_1 g_1 + \lambda_2 g_2 + \ldots + \lambda_m g_m .$$

(In other words, the local maxima/local minima of f
subject to the conditions are to be found among the
stationary points of

$$f + \lambda_1 g_1 + \lambda_2 g_2 + \ldots + \lambda_m g_m ,$$

where $\lambda_1, \lambda_2, \ldots , \lambda_m$ are constants.)

Notice: (i) We do not spell out all the details of the types of functions f and g_i ($i = 1, \ldots, m$) for which the method works. Certainly these functions should have well behaved partial derivatives and the m conditions on the functions g_i should be independent in a certain sense. This is however a delicate area and more advanced books must be consulted for a complete treatment.

(ii) The numbers $\lambda_1, \lambda_2, \ldots, \lambda_m$ are the Lagrange Multipliers.

(iii) In many of the examples done in this book the nature of the stationary point found is clear from geometrical considerations, e.g. the minimum distance in the example in §189. §191-193 give examples of the method in practice.

191. EXAMPLE. Use Lagrange Multipliers to find the maximum and minimum values of the function $(x + y)$ at points on the ellipse $4x^2 + y^2 = 80$.

Solution. We look for stationary points of

$$x + y + \lambda(4x^2 + y^2 - 80) .$$

These occur where the partial derivatives of this function with respect to x and y are zero, i.e.

$$1 + 8\lambda x = 0 \quad \text{and} \quad 1 + 2\lambda y = 0,$$

$$\text{i.e.} \quad x = \frac{-1}{8\lambda} \text{ and } y = \frac{-1}{2\lambda} ,$$

$$\text{i.e.} \quad x = t \text{ and } y = 4t, \quad \text{say.}$$

So the required points are given by $(t, 4t)$, where $4x^2 + y^2 = 80$, i.e. $4t^2 + 16t^2 = 80$, i.e. $t = \pm 2$. So the points of interest are $(2,8)$ and $(-2,-8)$. So the maximum and minimum values of $(x + y)$ on the ellipse are 10 and -10. Confirmation of how the maximum and minimum values arise is given by the geometrical insight into the situation provided by the diagram. It shows the ellipse together with various lines of the family $x + y = c$. The lines $x + y = \pm 10$ are tangents.

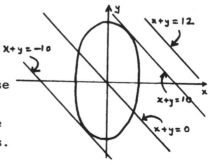

192. **EXAMPLE.** Find the points on the circle cut on the sphere $x^2 + y^2 + z^2 = 50$ by the plane $2x - y - z = -6$ at which the function $(x - 4y)$ takes its maximum and minimum values on this circle.

Solution. (Here there are two conditions which together determine the circle. So $m = 2$ in §190.) Using Lagrange's method we seek stationary points of

$$(x - 4y) + \lambda(x^2 + y^2 + z^2 - 50) + \mu(2x - y - z + 6).$$

These occur where

$$1 + 2\lambda x + 2\mu = 0$$

and $\quad -4 + 2\lambda y - \mu = 0 \qquad (\dagger)$

and $\quad 2\lambda z - \mu = 0.$

We can write these in matrix notation as

$$\begin{bmatrix} 1 & x & 2 \\ -4 & y & -1 \\ 0 & z & -1 \end{bmatrix} \begin{bmatrix} 1 \\ 2\lambda \\ \mu \end{bmatrix} = \begin{bmatrix} 0 \\ 0 \\ 0 \end{bmatrix},$$

i.e. $\quad A u = 0$, where $u \neq 0$.

It follows from Linear Algebra that the matrix A has no inverse so that $\det A = 0$, i.e.

$$4x + y + 7z = 0 \quad \text{(on simplification)}.$$

Together with the equation $2x - y - z = -6$ above this gives

$$z = -(x + 1), \quad y = (3x + 7). \qquad \ldots (*)$$

Putting these in the equation of the sphere gives

$$x^2 + (3x + 7)^2 + (x + 1)^2 = 50,$$

i.e. $\quad 11x^2 + 44x = 0$, i.e. $x(x + 4) = 0$,

i.e. $\quad x = 0$ or $x = -4$.

Together with (*) these give the points of interest as $(0,7,-1)$ and $(-4,-5,3)$. The values of $(x - 4y)$ at these points are -28 and 16. So the maximum on the circle is 16 at $(-4,-5,3)$ and the minimum is -28 at $(0,7,-1)$. [There are alternative ways of solving the equations ($\dagger$) to give $4x + y + 7z = 0$.]

EXAMPLES TO DO: Page 186: Exs. 3 - 11.

193.　LAGRANGE MULTIPLIERS APPLIED TO LEAST SQUARES ESTIMATION

　　In experimental situations measured values are usually subject to error.　So, if for example we measure the angles of a triangle it is possible that the resulting values may not add up to 180° as they should.　If the measured values are　a, b　and　c　then we can think of (a,b,c)　as a point in three dimensional space.　The least squares estimates of the angles are then given by that point　(x*,y*,z*) on the plane　x + y + z = 180 that is nearest to the point (a,b,c).　This means finding the minimum value of

$$(x - a)^2 + (y - b)^2 + (z - c)^2 \;..(\dagger)$$

subject to the condition that　x + y + z = 180.　This problem is　a clear candidate for Lagrange Multipliers. The phrase 'least squares' refers to the attempt to minimise the sum of squares in the expression (†).

　　The following example illustrates the same idea in a four dimensional situation.

EXAMPLE.　In the quadrilateral　XYZT　it is known that angle X = angle Y.　The angles　X, Y, Z, T　are measured (with errors) as　a, b, c, d.　Find the least squares estimates of the true values of these angles.　Give these estimates also in the particular case when　a = 82, b = 80, c = 91, d = 110.

Solution.　Denote the angles by　x, y, z, t.　Then from the given geometrical information we have

　　x + y + z + t = 360　...(1)　and　x - y = 0.　...(2)

So, by analogy with the three dimensional case described above, we wish to find the point　(x*,y*,z*,t*)　which gives a minimum value to the distance function

$$(x - a)^2 + (y - b)^2 + (z - c)^2 + (t - d)^2$$

subject to conditions　(1)　and　(2).　Using Lagrange's method we therefore look for stationary points of

$$(x - a)^2 + (y - b)^2 + (z - c)^2 + (t - d)^2 + \lambda(x + y + z + t - 360) + \mu(x - y).$$

These stationary points occur where

$$2(x - a) + \lambda + \mu = 0,$$
$$2(y - b) + \lambda - \mu = 0,$$
$$2(z - c) + \lambda \quad\;\; = 0,$$
$$2(t - d) + \lambda \quad\;\; = 0.$$

Eliminating λ and μ gives

$$x + y - z - t = a + b - c - d, \qquad\qquad \ldots (3)$$
$$z - t = c - d. \qquad\qquad \ldots (4)$$

Solving (1), (2), (3) and (4) gives

$$x = (360 + a + b - c - d)/4 ,$$
$$y = (360 + a + b - c - d)/4 ,$$
$$z = (360 - a - b + 3c - d)/4 ,$$
$$t = (360 - a - b - c + 3d)/4 .$$

These are the least squares estimates.

For the particular data given these estimates are $(80.25, 80.25, 90.25, 109.25)$.

EXAMPLES TO DO: Page 186: Exs. 12 – 14.

EXAMPLES 12

1. Determine the natures of the stationary points of the following functions:

(a) $xy - 5x - 3y$,   (b) $3x^2 - 4xy + 4y^2$,

(c) $2x + 2y - 2xy - x^2 - 3y^2$,   (d) $y^2 + 2xy + 2x - 1$,

(e) $xy^2 - 4x - 3y^2$,   (f) $x^3 - 2x^2 - 4x - y^2 + 6y$,

(g) $5x^2 - 4xy + y^2 - 10x$,   (h) $x^4 + 4x^2 - 8x + 8y - 2x^2y$,

(i) $xy^2 - 2y - x$,   (j) $x^4 + 2x^2 - 12x - 4x^2y + 4y^2$,

(k) $32x^2 - 32xy + y^4$,   (l) $x^2y^2 - 2xy - x^2 + 4x + 1$,

(m) $x^2y + y - 5x^2$,   (n) $x^4 - 2x^2 + y^3 - 3y$,

(o) $\sin^2 x + \sinh^2 y$,   (p) $x^4 - y^3 - 2x^2$.

2. Show that $x^3 + y^3 + z^3 - (x + y + z)^2$ has a stationary point at $(2,2,2)$ and determine its nature.

3. Use Lagrange Multipliers to find the point on the line $x + 3y = 27$ that is nearest to the point $(1,2)$. [HINT: Minimise the <u>square</u> of the distance rather than the distance, which involves a square root sign.]

4. Find the maximum value of xy^3 at points on the circle $x^2 + y^2 = a^2$, where $a > 0$.

5. Find the maximum value of xy subject to the condition $9x^2 + 4y^2 = 144$. Deduce the area of the rectangle of largest area that can be drawn inside the ellipse $9x^2 + 4y^2 = 144$ and with sides parallel to the coordinate axes.

6. Find the lengths of the sides of the rectangular box of largest volume that can be inscribed inside the ellipsoid $\frac{x^2}{a^2} + \frac{y^2}{b^2} + \frac{z^2}{c^2} = 1$ and with edges parallel to the x, y and z axes.   (a,b,c are positive.)

7. Find the maximum and minimum values of $(x^2 + y^2)$ at points on the ellipse $5x^2 + 4xy + 2y^2 = 30$. Give a geometrical interpretation.

8. Find the points which give the maximum and minimum values of $(x + z)$ at points on the ellipse which is cut on the plane $4x + y + z = 34$ by the cylinder $x^2 + y^2 = 40$.

9. Find the points which give the maximum and minimum values of $(2y + z)$ subject to the conditions $x^2 + y^2 + z^2 = 41$ and $x + z = 1$.

10. Find the points on the curve cut on the plane $x - y + 2z = 6$ by the ellipsoid $x^2 + y^2 + 2z^2 = 34$ at which z takes its maximum and minimum values.

11. Find the points on the curve cut on the cylinder $x^2 + y^2 = 90$ by the plane $3x + y + z = 40$ which are nearest to and furthest from $(0,0,0)$. [HINT: Work with $x^2 + y^2 + z^2$ <u>not</u> with $\sqrt{(x^2 + y^2 + z^2)}$.]

12. In the triangle XYZ, the angles are measured (with possible error) as a, b, c. Find the least squares estimates of the angles and give the particular solution when $(a,b,c) = (40,60,77)$.

13. In the quadrilateral XYZT, it is given that the sum of the angles X and Z is $180°$. The angles X, Y, Z, T are measured (with possible error) as a, b, c, d. Find the least squares estimates of the angles in terms of a, b, c, d. Give the particular solution when $(a,b,c,d) = (51,100,131,81)$.

14. XYZT is known to be a parallelogram. The angles X, Y, Z, T are measured as a, b, c, d. Find the least squares estimates of the angles.

XIII. FURTHER SECOND ORDER DIFFERENTIAL EQUATIONS

---

194. In Chapter 5 we looked at the solution of the differential equation

$$py'' + qy' + ry = s(x), \qquad \ldots \text{ (A)}$$

where p, q, r are constants and s(x) is of certain forms. The problem of finding a particular integral of (A) was considered when s(x) was:

(a) a polynomial in x,

or (b) $Me^{\alpha x}$ (M, α constants),

or (c) $K \cos \beta x + L \sin \beta x$ (K, L, β constants).

The case of a <u>sum</u> of any of these forms was easily dealt with in §65.

This chapter gives a method for dealing with the case where s(x) is a <u>product</u> of any or all of the functions (a), (b) and (c). So for example it allows treatment of cases like

$$s(x) = 5x^2 e^x \quad \text{and} \quad s(x) = 6xe^x \cos 2x.$$

195. COMPLEX POWERS

The basic properties of complex numbers a + ib, where a,b are real and $i^2 = -1$ are taken as known. The following important result may not be known.

<u>RESULT</u>. For every real number y,

$$e^{iy} = \cos y + i \sin y.$$

<u>Notice</u>: (i) We do not attempt a full justification of this result, but as evidence of its correctness notice the following argument using the power series for exponential, cosine and sine.

$$e^{iy} = 1 + iy + \frac{(iy)^2}{2!} + \frac{(iy)^3}{3!} + \frac{(iy)^4}{4!} + \ldots$$

$$= 1 + iy - \frac{y^2}{2!} - \frac{iy^3}{3!} + \frac{y^4}{4!} + \ldots$$

$$= (1 - \frac{y^2}{2!} + \frac{y^4}{4!} - \ldots) + i(y - \frac{y^3}{3!} + \ldots)$$

$$= \cos y + i \sin y.$$

(ii) The above result provides the following definition of e^z for a general complex number z.

188

__Definition.__ Let z = x + iy, where x, y are real.

Then $e^z = e^{x+iy} = e^x.e^{iy} = e^x(\cos y + i \sin y)$.

__EXAMPLE.__ Find the real and imaginary parts of

$$Q = (x^2 + 2ix)e^{(3 + 5i)x} , \text{ where } x \text{ is real.}$$

__Solution.__ $Q = e^{3x}(x^2 + 2ix)(\cos 5x + i \sin 5x)$

$$= e^{3x}\Big[(x^2\cos 5x - 2x\sin 5x) + i(2x\cos 5x + x^2 \sin 5x)\Big].$$

So $\text{Re}(Q) = e^{3x}(x^2\cos 5x - 2x\sin 5x)$

and $\text{Im}(Q) = e^{3x}(2x\cos 5x + x^2\sin 5x)$.

196. FINDING THE PARTICULAR INTEGRAL

For the differential equation

$$py" + qy' + ry = s(x), \qquad \ldots (A)$$

where p, q, r are constants and s(x) is a product of any two or all three of the functions (a), (b), (c) in §194, we find a particular integral by the following steps. For examples showing how to proceed in individual cases see §197 - §199.

__STEP 1.__ If s(x) involves sine or cosine leave equation (A) aside and consider instead the complexified equation in which s(x) involves e^{ikx} rather than cos kx or sin kx. (Exactly how to do this is illustrated in §198.) In any event the differential equation under consideration is then of the form

$$py" + qy' + ry = \begin{pmatrix}\text{polynomial}\\ \text{in } x\end{pmatrix}.e^{\text{power}}, \qquad \ldots (B)$$

where the power may be complex and the polynomial may be a constant.

__STEP 2.__ Put $y = ue^{\text{power}}$, where u is a function of x to be determined. This will involve calculating y' and y" in terms of u' and u" and setting them in equation (B).

__STEP 3.__ This gives a new differential equation of the form

$$\begin{pmatrix}\text{Left hand side in}\\ u", u' \text{ and } u\end{pmatrix} = \begin{pmatrix}\text{Another}\\ \text{polynomial in } x\end{pmatrix}. \quad \ldots (C)$$

__STEP 4.__ Find a particular integral for (C) using the methods from Chapter 5. This gives the function u.

STEP 5.   Substitute u back into the formula in Step 2. This gives a particular integral y for equation (B).

STEP 6.   If you did complexification in Step 1, you can now recover a particular integral of equation (A) by considering the real and/or imaginary parts of the particular integral of (B).   (§198 illustrates how.)

Notice: Complexification in Step 1 is only required when the function s(x) contains a factor involving sine or cosine.   So in a case like the equation in §197, where $s(x) = 8x^2e^{3x}$, the original equation is already equipped to play the role of (B) and only Steps 2 to 5 are needed.

197.   EXAMPLE.   Find the general solution of

$$y" - 10y + 25y = 8x^2e^{3x}.$$

Solution.   The complementary function is

$$C.F. = (Ax + B)e^{5x}.$$

For the P.I. put $y = ue^{3x}$, where u is a function of x to be determined.   So

$$y' = e^{3x}(u' + 3u)$$

and $y" = e^{3x}(u" + 6u' + 9u).$

Substituting these back into the original equation gives

$$e^{3x}(u" + 6u' + 9u - 10u' - 30u + 25u) = 8x^2e^{3x},$$

i.e. $u" - 4u' + 4u = 8x^2.$ ... (C)

Try for a particular solution of (C) of the form $u = Cx^2 + Dx + E$ as in §64.   This gives $u = 2x^2 + 4x + 3$. So, from above, the P.I. of the original equation is given by

$$y = (2x^2 + 4x + 3)e^{3x}.$$

Hence the general solution of the given equation is

$$y = (Ax + B)e^{5x} + (2x^2 + 4x + 3)e^{3x}.$$

Notice: (i) No complexification was required here and the original equation was ready to play (B) in §196.

(ii) The exponentials cancelled out to give the equation (C).   This is a feature of the method.

EXAMPLES TO DO: Page 192: Exs. 1, 2, 4, 5.

198.   **EXAMPLE.**   Find the general solution of

$$y'' + 16y = 64x \cos 4x.$$

<u>Solution.</u>   The complementary function is

$$C.F. = A \cos 4x + B \sin 4x.$$

To find the P.I. we choose (as explained in (iii) below) to look at the complexified equation

$$y'' + 16y = 64x(\cos 4x + i \sin 4x),$$

$$\text{i.e.} \quad y'' + 16y = 64xe^{4ix}. \qquad \ldots \text{(B)}$$

Now look for a P.I. of (B) of the form $y = ue^{4ix}$, where u is a function of x to be determined.   This means

$$y' = e^{4ix}(u' + 4iu),$$

$$\text{and} \quad y'' = e^{4ix}(u'' + 8iu' - 16u).$$

Putting these in (B) gives

$$e^{4ix}(u'' + 8iu' - 16u + 16u) = 64xe^{4ix},$$

$$\text{i.e.} \quad u'' + 8iu' = 64x. \qquad \ldots \text{(C)}$$

In (C) the LHS is degenerate in the sense of §64.   So we try $u = Cx^2 + Dx$ as a P.I. of (C).   This reduces to requiring that

$$16iCx + (2C + 8iD) = 64x.$$

So $16Ci = 64$ and $2C + 8iD = 0.$

So $C = -4i$ and $D = 1.$

So $u = (-4ix^2 + x).$

So this gives a P.I. of (B) as

$$y = (-4ix^2 + x)e^{4ix}.$$

Taking the real part of this gives a P.I. of the original equation, namely,

$$y = x \cos 4x + 4x^2 \sin 4x.$$

So the general solution of the original equation is

$$y = (A \cos 4x + B \sin 4x) + (x \cos 4x + 4x^2 \sin 4x).$$

Notice: (i) The labels (B) and (C) correspond to those in §196.

(ii) The exponentials again cancelled out to give equation (C).

(iii) To understand why we complexify the original equation suppose that $y = v(x) + i\,w(x)$, where $v(x)$ and $w(x)$ are real, is a solution of the equation (B), i.e. of

$$y" + 16y = 64xe^{4ix},$$

i.e. of $\quad y" + 16y = 64x\,(\cos 4x + i \sin 4x).$

Then

$$(v" + iw") + 16(v + iw) = 64x(\cos 4x + i \sin 4x),$$

i.e. $(v" + 16v) + i(w" + 16w) = 64x(\cos 4x + i \sin 4x).$

So equating real and imaginary parts gives

$$v" + 16v = 64x \cos 4x$$

and $\qquad w" + 16w = 64x \sin 4x.$

This tells us that the real part and imaginary part of the solution of (B) give solutions of

$$y" + 16y = 64x \cos 4x$$

and $\qquad y" + 16y = 64x \sin 4x.$

The advantage of introducing the complex exponential is that it can be made to cancel out to give equation (C) free from cosines and sines and with only a polynomial on the right hand side.

EXAMPLES TO DO: Page 192: Exs. 3, 6, 8.

199. EXAMPLE. Find the general solution of

$$y" + y = 25xe^x \sin x.$$

Solution. The complementary function is

$$\text{C.F.} = A \cos x + B \sin x.$$

Try for a P.I. of the complexified equation

$$Y" + y = 25xe^x e^{ix},$$

i.e. $\qquad y" + y = 25x\,e^{(1+i)x}. \qquad \ldots \text{(B)}$

Now put $y = ue^{(1+i)x}$, where u is a function of x to be determined.

So $\qquad y' = e^{(1+i)x}(u' + (1+i)u),$

and $\qquad y'' = e^{(1+i)x}(u'' + 2(1+i)u' + (1+i)^2u).$

Equation (B) then reduces to

$$u'' + 2(1+i)u' + (1+2i)u = 25x. \qquad \ldots \text{(C)}$$

Try $u = Cx + D$ as a P.I. of this equation, equating coefficients of powers of x. This gives

$$C = 5 - 10i \quad \text{and} \quad D = -2 + 14i.$$

This means $\qquad u = (5x - 2) - i(10x - 14).$

So a P.I. of equation (B) is given by

$$y = ((5x - 2) - i(10x - 14))e^x(\cos x + i \sin x).$$

Taking the imaginary part gives a P.I. of the original differential equation as

$$(5x - 2)e^x\sin x - (10x - 14)e^x\cos x.$$

So the general solution required is

$$y = (A \cos x + B \sin x) + e^x((5x-2)\sin x - (10x-14)\cos x).$$

Notice: The work involved here can be heavy.

EXAMPLES TO DO: Page 192: Exs. 7, 9, 10, 11.

EXAMPLES 13

Find the general solution of each of the following differential equations:

1. $\quad y'' - y' - 2y = xe^{3x}.$
2. $\quad y'' + 2y' + y = (9x^2 + 4)e^{-x}.$
3. $\quad y'' + y = x \cos 2x.$
4. $\quad y'' - 4y = x^2e^{2x}.$
5. $\quad y'' + 9y = 5xe^{-x} + 18 \sin 3x.$
6. $\quad y'' + 9y = 8x \cos 3x.$
7. $\quad y'' + 2y' + y = 6e^{-x}\sin x.$
8. $\quad y'' + y = 12x \sin x.$
9. $\quad y'' + 6y' + 10y = xe^{-3x}\sin x.$
10. $\quad y'' - 2y' + 5y = xe^x\cos 2x.$
11. $\quad y'' - 6y' + 10y = 50e^{3x}\sin x.$

XIV.   MATRICES: EIGENVALUES AND EIGENVECTORS

---

200.   In this chapter we take various basic ideas about matrices as known.   In particular, we take the ideas of addition and multiplication of matrices as familiar, together with the ideas of transpose, determinant and inverse.   There are two common methods for finding the inverse - one using the determinant together with the adjugate matrix, the other using elementary row operations.   At least one of these methods is assumed to be known.

201.   EXISTENCE OF THE INVERSE MATRIX

Recall that for a square matrix A, the inverse of A (if it exists) is denoted by A^{-1} and has the properties that

$$AA^{-1} = A^{-1}A = I.$$

Some square matrices have no inverse;   others do. Those with no inverse are called <u>singular</u>.   Those that have an inverse are called <u>non-singular</u> or <u>invertible</u>. The following result shows that calculating the determinant of a matrix settles whether it is invertible.

<u>RESULT</u>.   Let A be a square matrix.   Then A^{-1} exists if and only if det A ≠ 0.

<u>Proof.</u>   First suppose that A^{-1} exists.   Then

$$A^{-1}A = I.$$

So $(\det A^{-1}).(\det A) = 1.$

Since the product is 1, det A ≠ 0.   So if A^{-1} exists then det A ≠ 0.

Conversely, if det A ≠ 0 then the adjugate method for finding the inverse gives A^{-1} explicitly as

$$A^{-1} = \frac{1}{(\det A)} (\text{adj } A)^{T},$$

where T denotes the transpose.   So if det A ≠ 0 then A^{-1} exists.

<u>Notice:</u>   Let $A = \begin{bmatrix} 7 & 6 \\ 1 & 2 \end{bmatrix}$ and $B = \begin{bmatrix} 0 & 0 \\ 7 & 2 \end{bmatrix}$.   Here we have det A = 8 and det B = 0.   So the above result

tells us that A is invertible, while B is not.   So
on one hand, we have $A^{-1} = \frac{1}{8} \begin{bmatrix} 2 & -6 \\ -1 & 7 \end{bmatrix}$.   On the other
hand, searching for an inverse for B, i.e. searching
for a matrix C such that BC = I, leads only to
disappointment.

EXAMPLES TO DO: Pages 207 - 208: Exs. 1, 6.

202.   THE SYSTEM OF LINEAR EQUATIONS   AX = Y WHEN A IS INVERTIBLE

The set of equations

$$3x + 6y + 5z = 7,$$
$$x + y + z = 3,$$
$$2x + 6y + 4z = 4,$$

can be solved in elementary fashion by eliminating
variables.   A more sophisticated approach writes the
equations in matrix notation as

$$\begin{bmatrix} 3 & 6 & 5 \\ 1 & 1 & 1 \\ 2 & 6 & 4 \end{bmatrix} \begin{bmatrix} x \\ y \\ z \end{bmatrix} = \begin{bmatrix} 7 \\ 3 \\ 4 \end{bmatrix},$$

i.e. as   AX = Y,   ... (*)

where $A = \begin{bmatrix} 3 & 6 & 5 \\ 1 & 1 & 1 \\ 2 & 6 & 4 \end{bmatrix}$, $X = \begin{bmatrix} x \\ y \\ z \end{bmatrix}$ and $Y = \begin{bmatrix} 7 \\ 3 \\ 4 \end{bmatrix}$.

Provided that A is invertible we can write (*) as

$$A^{-1}AX = A^{-1}Y,$$

i.e. $IX = A^{-1}Y,$

i.e. $X = A^{-1}Y,$

which solves the given equations.   For the particular
set of equations above, A is indeed invertible and

$$A^{-1} = \frac{1}{2}\begin{bmatrix} -2 & 6 & 1 \\ -2 & 2 & 2 \\ 4 & -6 & -3 \end{bmatrix},$$

which gives

$$\begin{bmatrix} x \\ y \\ z \end{bmatrix} = \frac{1}{2}\begin{bmatrix} -2 & 6 & 1 \\ -2 & 2 & 2 \\ 4 & -6 & -3 \end{bmatrix}\begin{bmatrix} 7 \\ 3 \\ 4 \end{bmatrix} = \begin{bmatrix} 4 \\ 0 \\ -1 \end{bmatrix}.$$

So $x = 4$, $y = 0$, $z = -1$.

Notice: (i) The method is not confined to the 3 by 3 case: it applies to square matrices of any size.

(ii) For such a set of linear equations, if the matrix A is invertible, then the solution obtained (whether by the matrix method or by elimination) is unique.

(iii) For the matrix method shown above to succeed it is imperative that A be invertible. If A is not invertible (i.e. if det A = 0) then the drama unfolds differently as explained in §203.

203. THE SYSTEM OF LINEAR EQUATIONS AX = Y WHEN A IS NOT INVERTIBLE

§202 solves a system of n linear equations in n unknowns written as

$$AX = Y \qquad \ldots (*)$$

when A is invertible, i.e. when det A $\neq$ 0. If however A is not invertible (i.e. det A = 0) then there are two possibilities:

EITHER the given equations are inconsistent,

OR they are consistent but not independent.

The following cases of systems of equations (both with det A = 0) illustrate these two possibilities.

CASE 1. (INCONSISTENT) Take the three equations

$$x + y + z = 7,$$
$$2x + 2y + 2z = 30,$$
$$4x - 3y + z = 1.$$

Here dividing the second equation by 2 gives $x + y + z = 15$, which contradicts the first equation. Such a set of equations is called <u>inconsistent</u> and no solution exists.

<u>CASE 2</u>. (<u>CONSISTENT BUT NOT INDEPENDENT</u>) Take the three equations

$$x + y + z = 4,$$
$$2x - y - 2z = 1,$$
$$3x \qquad - z = 5.$$

If you try to solve these equations by hand you find that the third equation can be derived from the first two. So in effect there are really only two independent equations, namely

$$x + y + z = 4,$$
$$\text{and} \qquad 2x - y - 2z = 1.$$

Eliminating y gives $z = 3x - 5$ and so $y = 9 - 4x$. So in this case there is an <u>infinity of solutions</u> namely

$$x = t , \quad y = 9 - 4t , \quad z = 3t - 5 ,$$

where t can have any value whatsoever. This infinity of solutions reflects slackness in the original system of equations in the sense that there are really only <u>two</u> independent equations in the <u>three</u> unknowns.

204. THE SYSTEM OF LINEAR EQUATIONS AX = 0

The system of linear equations

$$a_{11}x_1 + a_{12}x_2 + \dots + a_{1n}x_n = 0,$$
$$a_{21}x_1 + a_{22}x_2 + \dots + a_{2n}x_n = 0,$$
$$\dots\dots\dots\dots\dots\dots\dots\dots\dots\dots\dots$$
$$a_{n1}x_1 + a_{n2}x_2 + \dots + a_{nn}x_n = 0,$$

$$\text{i.e.} \quad AX = 0,$$

is really just a special case of the equations in §202 – 203.

If A is <u>invertible</u>, (i.e. det $A \neq 0$), then §202 applies to give the <u>unique</u> solution $X = 0$, i.e.

$$x_1 = x_2 = \dots = x_n = 0,$$

and there is little more to be said.

Suppose now that A is not invertible, (i.e. that det A = 0).   Then §203 applies, or at least part of it does.   Notice that

$$x_1 = x_2 = \ldots = x_n = 0$$

(i.e. X = 0) automatically satisfies the equations in any case.   So the equations are certainly not inconsistent.   This rules out Case 1 and leaves only Case 2 in §203.   So if A is not invertible then the equations are consistent but not independent and there is an infinity of solutions, which incidentally includes the trivial solution X = 0.

These matters are important in the finding of eigenvectors in §206.

EXAMPLE.   Solve the set of linear equations

$$x + y - 2z = 0, \qquad \ldots (1)$$

$$5x - y - 6z = 0, \qquad \ldots (2)$$

$$-7x + 5y + 6z = 0. \qquad \ldots (3)$$

Solution. Eliminating z gives

$$2x - 4y = 0 \qquad \text{(from (1) and (2))}$$
$$\text{and} \quad -2x + 4y = 0 \qquad \text{(from (2) and (3))}.$$

So all the information is contained in the two equations

$$x - 2y = 0 \quad \text{and} \quad x + y - 2z = 0,$$

i.e. $\quad x = 2y \quad$ and $\quad 2z = 3y$,

i.e. $\quad x = 2y \quad$ and $\quad z = 3y/2.$

So putting y = 2t (for the convenience of avoiding fractions), we find

$$x = 4t, \quad y = 2t, \quad z = 3t$$

as the general solution, where t can have any value.   We can also write this as

$$\begin{bmatrix} x \\ y \\ z \end{bmatrix} = \begin{bmatrix} 4t \\ 2t \\ 3t \end{bmatrix} = t\begin{bmatrix} 4 \\ 2 \\ 3 \end{bmatrix}.$$

EXAMPLES TO DO: Page 207: Ex. 2.

205. EIGENVALUES AND EIGENVECTORS

In many machines raw material goes into the machine, is acted on by the machine and emerges as a finished product; the characteristics of the finished product generally depend on the characteristics of the raw material put in. You can regard a square matrix A as such a machine - a machine for multiplying vectors. A batch of raw material consists of a column vector X. The matrix acts on this column vector and gives back a new column vector AX as the finished product. In general the characteristics of the resulting vector AX depend on the original vector X.

For example, if

$$A = \begin{bmatrix} 2 & 5 & 2 \\ 6 & 2 & 1 \\ 3 & 4 & 2 \end{bmatrix} \quad \text{and} \quad X = \begin{bmatrix} 1 \\ 0 \\ 0 \end{bmatrix}$$

$$\text{then} \quad AX = \begin{bmatrix} 2 \\ 6 \\ 3 \end{bmatrix}.$$

Notice in this case that AX differs from X both in <u>direction</u> and in <u>length</u>: the direction is different because AX is not a multiple of X and the lengths of AX and X are respectively 7 and 1. This is very much the general pattern: for a randomly chosen vector Y, it seems likely that AY will differ from Y both in <u>direction</u> and in <u>length</u>.

What may be something of a surprise is that for <u>every</u> square matrix A, there exists at least one non-zero vector X such that AX is a multiple of the original vector X, i.e. AX has the same direction as X (for a positive multiple) <u>or</u> the opposite direction to X (for a negative multiple) <u>or</u> AX is the zero vector (for a zero multiple). Such vectors X are called <u>eigenvectors</u> (formal definition below).

For the particular case of the matrix A above the vector Z given by

$$Z = \begin{bmatrix} 1 \\ 1 \\ 1 \end{bmatrix}$$

is an eigenvector because

$$AZ = \begin{bmatrix} 2 & 5 & 2 \\ 6 & 2 & 1 \\ 3 & 4 & 2 \end{bmatrix} \begin{bmatrix} 1 \\ 1 \\ 1 \end{bmatrix} = \begin{bmatrix} 9 \\ 9 \\ 9 \end{bmatrix} = 9 \begin{bmatrix} 1 \\ 1 \\ 1 \end{bmatrix} = 9Z.$$

So in this case   AZ   lies in the same direction as   Z.
Admittedly the length of   AZ   is 9 times the length
of   Z   but the direction is unaltered.   The factor
9 is called the eigenvalue corresponding to the
eigenvector   Z.

Definition.   Let   A   be a square matrix.   Then if
there exists a non-zero column vector   X   such that

$$AX = \lambda X,$$

where λ is a scalar, then   X   is called an eigenvector
of   A   and the number λ is called the corresponding
eigenvalue.

Notice: (i)   Every square matrix has at least one
eigenvector.   This is not obvious and we cannot prove
it here.

  (ii)   The concepts of eigenvalue and eigenvector
apply only to square matrices.

206. FINDING EIGENVALUES AND EIGENVECTORS

The following result gives a method for finding
the eigenvalues of a given matrix.

RESULT.   Let   A   be a square matrix.   Then the
eigenvalues of   A   are the roots of the equation

$$\det(tI - A) = 0.$$

Proof.   Suppose that λ is an eigenvalue of   A   with
corresponding eigenvector   X.   Then

$$AX = \lambda X, \quad \text{where} \quad X \neq 0.$$

$$\text{So} \quad (\lambda I - A)X = 0, \quad \text{where} \quad X \neq 0.$$

Now suppose that $(\lambda I - A)$ has an inverse.   ... (*)

$$\text{So} \quad (\lambda I - A)^{-1}(\lambda I - A)X = 0,$$

$$\text{i.e.} \quad IX = 0, \quad \text{i.e.} \quad X = 0.$$

This contradicts the fact that by definition $X \neq 0$.
So the supposition (*) is false.   So $(\lambda I - A)$ is
not invertible, which means that $\det(\lambda I - A) = 0$,
i.e. λ is a root of the equation $\det(tI - A) = 0$
as required.   This has shown that every eigenvalue
of   A   is in fact a root of the equation $\det(tI - A) = 0$.

To complete the proof however we need to show that
every root of the equation $\det(tI - A) = 0$ is in fact
an eigenvalue of   A.   Proving this lies beyond the
scope of this book and we leave it.

Notice: Consider an n by n matrix A.   The equation
det(tI - A) = 0   (in the above result) is then a
polynomial equation of degree   n,   the eigenvalues being
the roots of this equation.   Accordingly there must be
n eigenvalues, some of which may be repeats.   Moreover,
if the original matrix   A   is real it is still possible
for some of the eigenvalues to be complex, such eigenvalues then occurring in complex conjugate pairs.

EXAMPLE.   Find the eigenvalues and corresponding
eigenvectors for the matrix

$$A = \begin{bmatrix} 3 & 1 & -1 \\ 2 & 7 & -8 \\ 1 & 4 & -5 \end{bmatrix}.$$

Solution.   We want   det(tI - A) = 0.

$$\text{So} \quad \det \begin{bmatrix} t-3 & -1 & 1 \\ -2 & t-7 & 8 \\ -1 & -4 & t+5 \end{bmatrix} = 0,$$

i.e. $(t-3)((t-7)(t+5) + 32) + (-2(t+5) + 8) + (8 + (t-7)) = 0,$

i.e. $(t-3)(t^2-2t-3) - 2(t+1) + (t+1) = 0,$

i.e. $(t-3)(t-3)(t+1) - (t+1) = 0,$ ... (*)

i.e. $(t+1)((t-3)^2 -1) = 0,$

i.e. $(t+1)(t-4)(t-2) = 0.$

So the eigenvalues of A are 4, 2 and -1.

To find the eigenvector corresponding to the
eigenvalue λ, we solve the equation $(\lambda I - A)X = 0$ as
follows:

$(\lambda = 4)$ We want $(4I - A)X = 0,$

$$\text{i.e.} \quad \begin{bmatrix} 1 & -1 & 1 \\ -2 & -3 & 8 \\ -1 & -4 & 9 \end{bmatrix} \begin{bmatrix} x \\ y \\ z \end{bmatrix} = \begin{bmatrix} 0 \\ 0 \\ 0 \end{bmatrix},$$

i.e.
$$x - y + z = 0, \qquad \dots (1)$$
$$-2x - 3y + 8z = 0, \qquad \dots (2)$$
$$-x - 4y + 9z = 0. \qquad \dots (3)$$

Eliminating x gives

$$5y - 10z = 0 \quad \text{(from (1) and (2))}$$

and $\qquad 5y - 10z = 0 \quad$ (from (1) and (3)).

So $\qquad y = 2z \quad \underline{\text{and}} \quad x - y + z = 0,$

$\qquad$ i.e. $\quad y = 2z \quad \underline{\text{and}} \quad x = z.$

So $\quad \begin{bmatrix} x \\ y \\ z \end{bmatrix} = \begin{bmatrix} z \\ 2z \\ z \end{bmatrix} = z \begin{bmatrix} 1 \\ 2 \\ 1 \end{bmatrix}.$

So $\begin{bmatrix} 1 \\ 2 \\ 1 \end{bmatrix}$ (or any non-zero multiple of it) is an

eigenvector for $\lambda = 4$.

($\underline{\lambda = 2}$ and $\underline{\lambda = -1}$) We solve similarly the sets of equations given by $(2I - A)X = 0$ and $(-I - A)X = 0$.

This gives $\begin{bmatrix} -1 \\ 2 \\ 1 \end{bmatrix}$ and $\begin{bmatrix} 0 \\ 1 \\ 1 \end{bmatrix}$ as eigenvectors for the

eigenvalues $\lambda = 2$ and $\lambda = -1$ respectively.

<u>Notice</u>: (i) In working out det(tI - A), you can adopt an unsophisticated approach and multiply out all the brackets and collect terms to produce the unfactorised cubic equation

$$t^3 - 5t^2 + 2t + 8 = 0.$$

You then have to find its roots with the Remainder Theorem or otherwise.

We avoided this in line (*) by carefully retaining factors to reveal the common factor (t + 1).   This deliberate hesitancy about multiplying out can sometimes pay dividends though in some examples you just have to multiply out and attempt to find factors for the cubic.

(ii) The polynomial det(tI - A) is called the <u>characteristic polynomial</u> of the matrix A.   The eigenvalues are the roots of this polynomial.

(iii) Any non-zero multiple of an eigenvector is also an eigenvector for the same eigenvalue.

<u>EXAMPLES TO DO</u>:   Pages 207 - 208: Exs. 3, 4.

207. DIAGONALISATION

A <u>diagonal</u> matrix is one of the form

$$D \;=\; \begin{bmatrix} \alpha_1 & 0 & \cdots & 0 \\ 0 & \alpha_2 & \cdots & 0 \\ \cdot & \cdot & \cdots & \cdot \\ 0 & 0 & \cdots & \alpha_n \end{bmatrix},$$

and can be written as $\mathrm{diag}(\alpha_1,\ \alpha_2,\ \ldots,\ \alpha_n)$.

The eigenvalues of a diagonal matrix are the entries on its main diagonal. For example, for

the diagonal matrix $\begin{bmatrix} 2 & 0 & 0 \\ 0 & 6 & 0 \\ 0 & 0 & 9 \end{bmatrix}$ the characteristic

polynomial is $(t-2)(t-6)(t-9)$, so that the eigenvalues are 2, 6 and 9.

In books on Linear Algebra there are many results which take a given matrix A and attempt to produce a matrix P such that

$$P^{-1}AP = D.$$

This process is called <u>diagonalisation</u> and it may or may not be possible for a given matrix A. If it is possible for a given matrix A then the diagonal entries $\alpha_1,\ \alpha_2,\ \ldots,\ \alpha_n$ <u>have to be</u> the eigenvalues of A. The following result proves this.

<u>RESULT</u>. Suppose that for a square matrix A there exists an invertible matrix P such that

$$P^{-1}AP = D = \mathrm{diag}(\alpha_1,\ \alpha_2,\ \ldots,\ \alpha_n).$$

Then $\alpha_1,\ \alpha_2,\ \ldots,\ \alpha_n$ are the eigenvalues of A.

<u>Proof</u>. The eigenvalues of the diagonal matrix $P^{-1}AP$ are $\alpha_1,\ \alpha_2,\ \ldots,\ \alpha_n$. So these are the roots of the equation $\det(tI - P^{-1}AP) = 0$. This equation can be

written as $\det(tP^{-1}P - P^{-1}AP) = 0$,

      i.e. $\det(P^{-1}(tI - A)P) = 0$,

      i.e. $\det P^{-1} . \det(tI - A) . \det P = 0$,

      i.e. $\det(tI - A) = 0$.

So $\alpha_1, \alpha_2, \ldots, \alpha_n$ are the eigenvalues of A.

Notice: (i) The order in which the eigenvalues appear on the diagonal can be altered by altering P as explained in §208.

    (ii) Diagonalisation is not always possible.   If the eigenvalues of the matrix A are all different, then diagonalisation is guaranteed: see §208.   If however A has a repeated eigenvalue, then diagonalisation may or may not be possible: see §209.

208. DIAGONALISATION OF A MATRIX WITH DISTINCT EIGENVALUES

RESULT.   Let A be a square matrix with distinct eigenvalues $\alpha_1, \alpha_2, \ldots, \alpha_n$.   Then there exists an invertible matrix P such that

$$P^{-1}AP = \text{diag}(\alpha_1, \alpha_2, \ldots, \alpha_n).$$

Proof.   For each eigenvalue α_i there exists a non-zero column vector X_i such that
$$AX_i = \alpha_i X_i.$$
Let $P = [X_1 \ X_2 \ \ldots \ X_n]$, i.e. the matrix of eigenvectors.

Then $AP = [AX_1 \ AX_2 \ \ldots \ AX_n]$

$$= [\alpha_1 X_1 \ \alpha_2 X_2 \ \ldots \ \alpha_n X_n]$$

$$= [X_1 \ X_2 \ \ldots \ X_n] \begin{bmatrix} \alpha_1 & 0 & \ldots & 0 \\ 0 & \alpha_2 & \ldots & 0 \\ \multicolumn{4}{c}{\ldots\ldots\ldots\ldots\ldots} \\ 0 & 0 & \ldots & \alpha_n \end{bmatrix},$$

    i.e. $AP = PD$.

It follows from results on eigenvectors beyond the scope of this book (but in books on Linear Algebra) that P is in fact invertible.   So we can premultiply the last equation to obtain

$$P^{-1}AP = P^{-1}PD = D, \quad \text{as required.}$$

Notice: (i) Permuting the order of the columns of P permutes the order of the diagonal entries in the diagonal matrix.

(ii) The fact that the n eigenvalues are distinct ensures that we are guaranteed a full set of n linearly independent eigenvectors, which provides a full set of n linearly independent columns for P.

(iii) In §209 we discuss briefly how things turn out for a matrix with a repeated eigenvalue or eigenvalues.

EXAMPLE. (Continuation of the example in §206) Let

$$A = \begin{bmatrix} 3 & 1 & -1 \\ 2 & 7 & -8 \\ 1 & 4 & -5 \end{bmatrix}.$$

Find an invertible matrix P such that

$$P^{-1}AP = D,$$

where D is a diagonal matrix.

Solution. As in §206, find the eigenvalues of A as 4, 2 and −1 with corresponding eigenvectors

$$\begin{bmatrix} 1 \\ 2 \\ 1 \end{bmatrix}, \quad \begin{bmatrix} -1 \\ 2 \\ 1 \end{bmatrix}, \quad \begin{bmatrix} 0 \\ 1 \\ 1 \end{bmatrix}.$$

Using the above result we now take

$$P = \begin{bmatrix} 1 & -1 & 0 \\ 2 & 2 & 1 \\ 1 & 1 & 1 \end{bmatrix},$$

which gives $P^{-1}AP = \text{diag}(4, 2, -1)$, as required.

Notice: You can check the details of the above example yourself. To help you note that

$$P^{-1} = \frac{1}{2} \begin{bmatrix} 1 & 1 & -1 \\ -1 & 1 & -1 \\ 0 & -2 & 4 \end{bmatrix}.$$

EXAMPLES TO DO: Page 208: Ex. 5.

209. MATRICES WITH A REPEATED EIGENVALUE: DIAGONALISATION MAY OR MAY NOT BE POSSIBLE

The following example illustrates that diagonalisation is not possible for some matrices.

<u>EXAMPLE</u>.   Show that the matrix

$$J = \begin{bmatrix} 0 & 0 \\ 1 & 0 \end{bmatrix}$$

<u>cannot</u> be diagonalised in the sense of §207.

<u>Solution</u>.   The eigenvalues of J are given by $\overline{\det}(tI - J) = 0$, i.e. the roots of the equation $t^2 = 0$, i.e. 0 and 0.   So J has the eigenvalues 0 and 0, i.e. a repeated eigenvalue 0.

Now suppose that J can be diagonalised.   ...(*)

So, recalling from §207 that the diagonal entries of the diagonal matrix will then have to be the eigenvalues of J, we conclude that there is an invertible matrix P   such that

$$P^{-1}JP = diag(0, 0),$$

i.e. $P^{-1}JP = 0.$

So $P(P^{-1}JP)P^{-1} = 0,$

i.e. $J = 0.$

This is a contradiction.   So the supposition (*) above is false.   So J cannot be diagonalised.

<u>Notice</u>:   (i) The above example shows that diagonalisation fails for the matrix J.   The root cause of the failure can be found if you try the method for diagonalisation illustrated in §208.   The matrix J has the two eigenvalues 0 and 0 but if you look for eigenvectors you find <u>only one</u> linearly independent eigenvector, namely the vector

$$\begin{bmatrix} 0 \\ 1 \end{bmatrix}$$ (or a non-zero multiple of it).

This means that we are unable to find two linearly independent columns to make up the matrix corresponding to P in §208.   (You cannot use the same column twice because P will then not be invertible.)

(ii) For some matrices with a repeated eigenvalue or eigenvalues (like J above) diagonalisation is impossible, but for others diagonalisation is still possible. The crux of the matter is the number of linearly independent eigenvectors that can be produced to make up the columns of the matrix   P   in §208: if you can make up the full number for the multiplicity of the eigenvalue then diagonalisation is ensured, but if you are short of the full number (as for   J   above) diagonalisation fails. This is fairly deep water and is rather beyond the scope of this book.

EXAMPLES TO DO: Page 208: Exs. 9, 10.

210. FURTHER PROPERTIES OF EIGENVALUES

RESULT 1.   Suppose that λ is an eigenvalue of the square matrix   A.   Then λ^2 is an eigenvalue of A^2.

Proof: We know that $AX = \lambda X$ for some $X \neq 0$.

So $A^2 X = A(AX) = A(\lambda X) = \lambda(AX) = \lambda^2 X$.

EXAMPLE.   (Extending Result 1)   Suppose that λ is an eigenvalue of square matrix   A.   Prove that λ^3 is an eigenvalue of A^3.   Show further that if $p(A)$ is a polynomial in   A   then $p(\lambda)$ is an eigenvalue of $p(A)$. Show also that if   A   is invertible then $1/\lambda$ is an eigenvalue of   the inverse of   A.

Definition.   For a square matrix   A,   the trace of   A is the sum of the entries on the leading diagonal, i.e. $\text{trace}(A) = a_{11} + a_{22} + \ldots + a_{nn}$.

Notice the following result, which we do not prove.

RESULT 2.   Let   A   be a square matrix.   Then

    (i)   trace(A) = the sum of the eigenvalues of   A;

    (ii)   det A = the product of the eigenvalues of   A.

Notice: (i) As evidence of Result 2 take the matrix   A in the example in §206: the eigenvalues are 4, 2 and -1, while   trace(A) = 5   and   det A = -8.

    (ii)   (A little German lesson)   The German word for eigenvalue is   Eigenwert,   made up of the adjective eigen   meaning proper,   own, characteristic,   together with the noun   Wert   meaning value.   In English, eigenvalues have over the years been called latent roots, characteristic roots   or   proper values   but it now seems that the appeal of the word eigenvalue has left these others washed up on the shore of time.

EXAMPLES TO DO: Page 208: Exs. 7, 8.

EXAMPLES 14

1. Find the inverses of

(a) $\begin{bmatrix} 5 & 3 \\ 2 & 7 \end{bmatrix}$, (b) $\begin{bmatrix} 1 & 1 & 2 \\ 3 & 1 & 1 \\ 2 & 0 & 1 \end{bmatrix}$, (c) $\begin{bmatrix} 4 & 5 & 0 \\ 2 & 3 & -1 \\ 2 & 0 & 4 \end{bmatrix}$.

2. Solve the following sets of linear equations:

(a) $2x + 2y + z = 0,$
     $x + 4y + z = 0,$
     $-7x + 2y - 2z = 0.$

(b) $2x - y - z = 0,$
     $3x - 3y + z = 0,$
     $x + y - 3z = 0.$

3. Find the eigenvalues of each of the following:

(a) $\begin{bmatrix} 6 & 1 \\ -3 & 2 \end{bmatrix}$, (b) $\begin{bmatrix} 3 & -2 \\ 2 & 3 \end{bmatrix}$,

(c) $\begin{bmatrix} 0 & 3 & 0 \\ 3 & 0 & 4 \\ 0 & 4 & 0 \end{bmatrix}$, (d) $\begin{bmatrix} 4 & -2 & 1 \\ 1 & 3 & -1 \\ 1 & 2 & 0 \end{bmatrix}$.

4. For each of the following matrices find the eigen-values and for each eigenvalue find a corresponding eigenvector:

(a) $\begin{bmatrix} 8 & 4 \\ -2 & 2 \end{bmatrix}$, (b) $\begin{bmatrix} 3 & 2 \\ 6 & 4 \end{bmatrix}$,

(c) $\begin{bmatrix} 5 & 1 & -1 \\ 0 & -1 & 2 \\ 0 & -1 & 2 \end{bmatrix}$, (d) $\begin{bmatrix} 1 & 2 & -2 \\ 6 & -7 & 12 \\ 4 & -8 & 13 \end{bmatrix}$, (e) $\begin{bmatrix} 0 & 1 & 0 \\ -2 & 3 & 0 \\ -2 & 7 & -4 \end{bmatrix}$,

(f) $\begin{bmatrix} 11 & -6 & 3 \\ 12 & -7 & 6 \\ 1 & -1 & 3 \end{bmatrix}$, (g) $\begin{bmatrix} 3 & -2 & 4 \\ 3 & -2 & 6 \\ -2 & 2 & 0 \end{bmatrix}$, (h) $\begin{bmatrix} 8 & -10 & 1 \\ 5 & -7 & 1 \\ 3 & -6 & 2 \end{bmatrix}$,

(i) $\begin{bmatrix} 2 & 0 & 1 & 0 \\ 0 & -1 & 0 & 3 \\ 2 & 0 & 3 & 0 \\ 0 & -1 & 0 & 3 \end{bmatrix}$, (j) $\begin{bmatrix} 5 & 0 & 0 & 4 \\ 0 & 9 & 3 & 0 \\ 0 & 3 & 9 & 0 \\ 4 & 0 & 0 & 5 \end{bmatrix}$.

5. Take each matrix in Ex. 4 in turn as the matrix A and find (using the eigenvalues and eigenvectors found in Ex. 4) an invertible matrix P such that $P^{-1}AP$ is a diagonal matrix.

6. Show that if A is a square matrix such that

$$5A^3 + 3A^2 + 3A + 2I = 0$$

then A is invertible and find A^{-1} as a polynomial in A.

7. Let $B = \begin{bmatrix} 1 & 1 & 1 & 1 \\ 1 & 1 & -1 & -1 \\ 1 & -1 & 1 & -1 \\ 1 & -1 & -1 & 1 \end{bmatrix}$ and $C = \begin{bmatrix} -11 & 6 & 4 \\ -12 & 7 & 4 \\ -12 & 6 & 5 \end{bmatrix}$.

Find B^2 and state the eigenvalues of B^2. By considering the trace of B, deduce the eigenvalues of B. Repeat the whole process for C.

8. A square matrix A is called _idempotent_ if $A^2 = A$. Prove that every eigenvalue of an idempotent matrix is either 0 or 1. Show that the matrices

$$B = \begin{bmatrix} -4 & -2 & 3 \\ -5 & -1 & 3 \\ -10 & -4 & 7 \end{bmatrix} \quad \text{and} \quad C = \begin{bmatrix} 1 & 0 \\ 0 & 0 \end{bmatrix}$$

are both idempotent. Without finding its characteristic polynomial find the eigenvalues of B.

9. Find the eigenvalues of the matrix

$$A = \begin{bmatrix} 5 & -3 \\ 3 & -1 \end{bmatrix}$$

and show that it cannot be diagonalised.

10. Show that the matrices A and B given by

$$A = \begin{bmatrix} 1 & 2 & 2 \\ 2 & 1 & -2 \\ 2 & -2 & 1 \end{bmatrix} \quad \text{and} \quad B = \begin{bmatrix} 11 & -40 & 20 \\ 2 & -7 & 5 \\ 0 & 0 & 3 \end{bmatrix}$$

both have a repeated eigenvalue. Find matrices P and Q such that $P^{-1}AP$ and $Q^{-1}BQ$ are diagonal.

XV. SYSTEMS OF LINEAR DIFFERENTIAL EQUATIONS

---

211. §71 deals with the solution of a system of simultaneous linear differential equations, where x and y are functions of an independent variable t. The method given there effectively involves eliminating variables.

In this chapter we look at matrix methods of tackling the same type of problem. §212 explains the basic idea, while §213 - §214 give examples.

212. THE BASIC IDEA

Consider the system of simultaneous linear differential equations

$$\dot{x}_1 = 2x_1 + 6x_2,$$

$$\dot{x}_2 = 3x_1 + 5x_2,$$

where x_1 and x_2 are functions of an independent variable t and $\dot{x}_1$ and $\dot{x}_2$ denote $\dfrac{dx_1}{dt}$ and $\dfrac{dx_2}{dt}$.

These equations can be written as

$$\dot{X} = AX, \qquad \dots (*)$$

$$\text{where} \quad X = \begin{bmatrix} x_1 \\ x_2 \end{bmatrix} \quad \text{and} \quad A = \begin{bmatrix} 2 & 6 \\ 3 & 5 \end{bmatrix}.$$

To solve such a system, we try to diagonalise A if possible. This means finding a matrix P such that

$$P^{-1}AP = \begin{bmatrix} \alpha_1 & 0 \\ 0 & \alpha_2 \end{bmatrix}$$

as in §208. We then set X = PY, where

$$Y = \begin{bmatrix} y_1 \\ y_2 \end{bmatrix}.$$

Then the equation (*) becomes

$$P\dot{Y} = APY,$$

$$\text{i.e.} \quad \dot{Y} = P^{-1}APY,$$

i.e.
$$\begin{bmatrix} \dot{y}_1 \\ \dot{y}_2 \end{bmatrix} = \begin{bmatrix} \alpha_1 & 0 \\ 0 & \alpha_2 \end{bmatrix} \begin{bmatrix} y_1 \\ y_2 \end{bmatrix},$$

i.e. $\dot{y}_1 = \alpha_1 y_1$,   ... (1)

$\dot{y}_2 = \alpha_2 y_2$.   ... (2)

The differential equations (1) and (2) are then linear and are easily solved as in §45 to give

$$\begin{bmatrix} y_1 \\ y_2 \end{bmatrix} = \begin{bmatrix} c_1 e^{\alpha_1 t} \\ c_2 e^{\alpha_2 t} \end{bmatrix} .$$

So
$$\begin{bmatrix} x_1 \\ x_2 \end{bmatrix} = P \begin{bmatrix} y_1 \\ y_2 \end{bmatrix} = P \begin{bmatrix} c_1 e^{\alpha_1 t} \\ c_2 e^{\alpha_2 t} \end{bmatrix} ,$$

where c_1 and c_2 are arbitrary constants. This is the required solution for x_1 and x_2. (§213 goes through the details of this example, while §214 - §215 show how to play variations on this theme.)

213.   EXAMPLE.   Solve the system of differential equations

$$\dot{x}_1 = 2x_1 + 6x_2,$$
$$\dot{x}_2 = 3x_1 + 5x_2,$$

where x_1 and x_2 are functions of an independent variable t.

Solution. This system can be written as $\dot{X} = AX$, where $X = \begin{bmatrix} x_1 \\ x_2 \end{bmatrix}$ and $A = \begin{bmatrix} 2 & 6 \\ 3 & 5 \end{bmatrix}$. Now,

$$\det(tI - A) = (t-2)(t-5) - 18$$
$$= (t-8)(t+1) .$$

So the eigenvalues of A are 8 and -1. As they are distinct we know from §208 that we can diagonalise A. So we set about finding the eigenvectors as in §206.

For $\lambda = 8$,

$$(8I - A)\begin{bmatrix} x \\ y \end{bmatrix} = \begin{bmatrix} 0 \\ 0 \end{bmatrix} \quad \text{is} \quad \begin{bmatrix} 6 & -6 \\ -3 & 3 \end{bmatrix}\begin{bmatrix} x \\ y \end{bmatrix} = \begin{bmatrix} 0 \\ 0 \end{bmatrix},$$

i.e. $x - y = 0$, i.e. $y = x$.

So an eigenvector is $\begin{bmatrix} x \\ x \end{bmatrix}$, i.e. $x\begin{bmatrix} 1 \\ 1 \end{bmatrix}$.

So $\begin{bmatrix} 1 \\ 1 \end{bmatrix}$ will do for $\lambda = 8$.

For $\lambda = -1$,

$$(-I - A)\begin{bmatrix} x \\ y \end{bmatrix} = \begin{bmatrix} 0 \\ 0 \end{bmatrix} \quad \text{is} \quad \begin{bmatrix} -3 & -6 \\ -3 & -6 \end{bmatrix}\begin{bmatrix} x \\ y \end{bmatrix} = \begin{bmatrix} 0 \\ 0 \end{bmatrix},$$

i.e. $x + 2y = 0$, i.e. $x = -2y$.

So an eigenvector is $\begin{bmatrix} -2y \\ y \end{bmatrix}$, i.e. $y\begin{bmatrix} -2 \\ 1 \end{bmatrix}$.

So $\begin{bmatrix} -2 \\ 1 \end{bmatrix}$ will do for $\lambda = -1$.

So take matrix P given by $P = \begin{bmatrix} 1 & -2 \\ 1 & 1 \end{bmatrix}$, and let

$X = PY$, where $Y = \begin{bmatrix} y_1 \\ y_2 \end{bmatrix}$. Substitute this in the

original matrix differential equation (*) to obtain

$$P\dot{Y} = APY,$$

i.e. $\dot{Y} = P^{-1}APY,$

i.e. $\begin{bmatrix} \dot{y}_1 \\ \dot{y}_2 \end{bmatrix} = \begin{bmatrix} 8 & 0 \\ 0 & -1 \end{bmatrix}\begin{bmatrix} y_1 \\ y_2 \end{bmatrix},$

because $P^{-1}AP = \text{diag}(8, -1)$, as explained in §208.

So $\dot{y}_1 = 8y_1$ and $\dot{y}_2 = -y_2$.

Solving these as linear equations as in §45 gives

$$y_1 = C_1 e^{8t} \quad \text{and} \quad y_2 = C_2 e^{-t}.$$

But then the relationship $X = PY$ lets us recover X.

So $X = PY$, i.e. $\begin{bmatrix} x_1 \\ x_2 \end{bmatrix} = \begin{bmatrix} 1 & -2 \\ 1 & 1 \end{bmatrix} \begin{bmatrix} c_1 e^{8t} \\ c_2 e^{-t} \end{bmatrix}$.

$$\begin{bmatrix} x_1 \\ x_2 \end{bmatrix} = \begin{bmatrix} c_1 e^{8t} - 2c_2 e^{-t} \\ c_1 e^{8t} + c_2 e^{-t} \end{bmatrix}.$$

This is the required solution for x_1 and x_2.

EXAMPLES TO DO: Page 214: Ex. 1, 3(a), 4 - 7, 8(a).

214.   EXAMPLE.   (Continuation of the example in §206
and §208)   Find the general solution of the
system of differential equations

$$\ddot{x}_1 = 3x_1 + x_2 - x_3,$$

$$\ddot{x}_2 = 2x_1 + 7x_2 - 8x_3,$$

$$\ddot{x}_3 = x_1 + 4x_2 - 5x_3,$$

where x_1, x_2, x_3 are functions of an independent
variable t and $\ddot{x}_1$ denotes $\frac{d^2 x_1}{dt^2}$ etc.

Solution.   Write the equations as $\ddot{X} = AX$, where

$$\begin{bmatrix} x_1 \\ x_2 \\ x_3 \end{bmatrix} \quad \text{and} \quad A = \begin{bmatrix} 3 & 1 & -1 \\ 2 & 7 & -8 \\ 1 & 4 & -5 \end{bmatrix}.$$

(Notice that A is the matrix diagonalised in §208.)
Finding the eigenvalues and corresponding eigenvectors
for A gives the matrix P found in §208 as

$$P = \begin{bmatrix} 1 & -1 & 0 \\ 2 & 2 & 1 \\ 1 & 1 & 1 \end{bmatrix}$$

with the property that

$$P^{-1}AP = D = \text{diag}(4, 2, -1).$$

Now set $X = PY$ (where Y is the column vector with
components y_1, y_2, y_3)   in the differential equation
in the first line of the solution.   This transforms
it into

$$P\ddot{Y} = APY,$$

i.e. $\quad \ddot{Y} = P^{-1}APY,$

i.e. $\quad \ddot{Y} = DY,$

which gives the three separate differential equations

$$\ddot{y}_1 = 4y_1, \quad \ddot{y}_2 = 2y_2, \quad \ddot{y}_3 = -y_3.$$

Solving these second order equations as in Chapter 5 gives

$$\begin{bmatrix} y_1 \\ y_2 \\ y_3 \end{bmatrix} = \begin{bmatrix} Ae^{2t} + Be^{-2t} \\ Qe^{\sqrt{2}t} + Re^{-\sqrt{2}t} \\ E\cos t + F\sin t \end{bmatrix}.$$

Then from $X = PY$, we find

$$\begin{bmatrix} x_1 \\ x_2 \\ x_3 \end{bmatrix} = \begin{bmatrix} 1 & -1 & 0 \\ 2 & 2 & 1 \\ 1 & 1 & 1 \end{bmatrix} \begin{bmatrix} Ae^{2t} + Be^{-2t} \\ Qe^{\sqrt{2}t} + Re^{-\sqrt{2}t} \\ E\cos t + F\sin t \end{bmatrix}.$$

Multiply out these matrices to find x_1, x_2, x_3.

EXAMPLES TO DO: Page 214: Exs. 2, 3(b), 8(b).

215. The method of §212 and the example of §213 show how to solve a system of equations

$$\dot{X} = AX$$

by diagonalising A, if that is possible.

The system of equations

$$B\dot{X} = AX$$

where B is invertible is easily reduced to the above case by premultiplying by B^{-1}, i.e. solve the system

$$\dot{X} = B^{-1}AX$$

by diagonalising $B^{-1}A$, if that is possible.

EXAMPLES TO DO: Page 214: Exs. 9, 10.

EXAMPLES 15

Solve the systems of linear differential equations in Examples 1 to 8.   In each part the functions x_1, x_2, x_3 are functions of the independent variable   t.

1. $\dot{x}_1 = 7x_1 - x_2$,

   $\dot{x}_2 = 8x_1 - 2x_2$.

2. $\ddot{x}_1 = -10x_1 + 3x_2$,

   $\ddot{x}_2 = -2x_1 - 3x_2$.

3. (a) $\dot{x}_1 = 5x_1 - 2x_2$,

   $\dot{x}_2 = x_1 + 2x_2$.

   (b) $\ddot{x}_1 = 5x_1 - 2x_2$,

   $\ddot{x}_2 = x_1 + 2x_2$.

4. $\dot{x}_1 = 3x_2$,

   $\dot{x}_2 = 3x_1 + 4x_3$,

   $\dot{x}_3 = 4x_2$.

   [See Ex.3(c) on p.207.]

5. $\dot{x}_1 = x_1 + 2x_2 - 2x_3$,

   $\dot{x}_2 = 6x_1 - 7x_2 + 12x_3$,

   $\dot{x}_3 = 4x_1 - 8x_2 + 13x_3$.

   [See Ex.4(d) on p.207.]

6. $\dot{x}_1 = x_2$,

   $\dot{x}_2 = -2x_1 + 3x_2$,

   $\dot{x}_3 = -2x_1 + 7x_2 - 4x_3$.

   [See Ex.4(e) on p.207.]

7. $\dot{x}_1 = 2x_1 + x_2 - x_3$,

   $\dot{x}_2 = -4x_2 + 2x_3$,

   $\dot{x}_3 = -x_2 - x_3$.

8.(a) $\dot{x}_1 = x_1 + x_2 - x_3$,

   $\dot{x}_2 = x_2 - 2x_3$,

   $\dot{x}_3 = x_2 - 2x_3$.

   (b) $\ddot{x}_1 = x_1 + x_2 - x_3$,

   $\ddot{x}_2 = x_2 - 2x_3$,

   $\ddot{x}_3 = x_2 - 2x_3$.

9. Using the matrix method outlined in §215, solve the sets of simultaneous linear differential equations in Ex. 5.12(a) and Ex. 5.12(b) on page 67.

10. Show that the matrix method of solution used in §212 and §213 fails for the set of simultaneous linear differential equations

$$\dot{x}_1 = 3x_1 + x_2, \quad \dot{x}_2 = -x_1 + x_2$$

and explain clearly the reason for the failure.   Solve these equations with the method illustrated in §71.

APPENDIX

216. QUADRATIC FORMS

We deal with quadratic forms $u^T H u$, where u is a real $n \times 1$ vector and H is a <u>real symmetric</u> $n \times n$ matrix. So, for example, for

$$u = \begin{bmatrix} x \\ y \\ z \end{bmatrix} \quad \text{and} \quad H = \begin{bmatrix} 5 & 3 & 2 \\ 3 & 10 & -4 \\ 2 & -4 & 17 \end{bmatrix},$$

we have the quadratic form

$$u^T H u = 5x^2 + 10y^2 + 17z^2 + 6xy + 4xz - 8yz. \quad \ldots (*)$$

Notice that the value of a quadratic form is a real number for each choice of the vector u.

Quadratic forms can be classified into types according to the type of real values the form can take as in the following definition.

<u>Definition</u>. The quadratic form $u^T H u$ and its corresponding matrix H are called

<u>positive definite</u> if $u^T H u > 0$ for all $u \neq 0$,

<u>negative definite</u> if $u^T H u < 0$ for all $u \neq 0$,

<u>indefinite</u> if $u^T H u$ can take both positive and negative values,

<u>positive semidefinite</u> if $u^T H u \geq 0$ for all u and there is at least one non-zero vector u with $u^T H u = 0$,

<u>negative semidefinite</u> if $u^T H u \leq 0$ for all u and there is at least one non-zero vector u with $u^T H u = 0$.

(<u>Note</u>: Every non-zero quadratic form is of one of these five types.)

As simple examples, we can take

$$\begin{bmatrix} 1 & 0 \\ 0 & 3 \end{bmatrix} \qquad \begin{bmatrix} -1 & 0 \\ 0 & -3 \end{bmatrix} \qquad \begin{bmatrix} 1 & 0 \\ 0 & -3 \end{bmatrix} \qquad \begin{bmatrix} 1 & 0 \\ 0 & 0 \end{bmatrix}$$

$$x^2 + 3y^2 \qquad\quad -x^2 - 3y^2 \qquad\quad x^2 - 3y^2 \qquad\quad x^2 + 0y^2$$

POSITIVE   NEGATIVE   INDEFINITE   POSITIVE
DEFINITE   DEFINITE   SEMIDEFINITE

In this book we are interested in how to decide whether a given matrix is positive definite, negative definite or indefinite. The following results can assist in this.

RESULT 1. A real symmetric matrix H is positive definite if and only if all its leading principal minors are positive, i.e.

$$\Delta_1 > 0, \quad \Delta_2 > 0, \quad \ldots \quad , \quad \Delta_n > 0 ,$$

where
$$\Delta_r = \det \begin{bmatrix} h_{11} & h_{12} & \cdots & h_{1r} \\ \ldots & \ldots & \ldots & \ldots \\ h_{r1} & h_{r2} & \cdots & h_{rr} \end{bmatrix} .$$

RESULT 2. A real symmetric matrix H is negative definite if and only if its leading principal minors are alternately negative and positive, starting with the 1×1 leading principal minor, i.e.

$$\Delta_1 < 0, \quad \Delta_2 > 0, \quad \Delta_3 < 0, \quad \Delta_4 > 0, \quad \ldots \quad .$$

So, for example,

$$\begin{bmatrix} 5 & 1 & 2 \\ 1 & 2 & -1 \\ 2 & -1 & 2 \end{bmatrix}$$
is positive definite because
$$\Delta_1 = 5, \quad \Delta_2 = 9, \quad \Delta_3 = 1,$$

while
$$\begin{bmatrix} -2 & 1 & -3 \\ 1 & -2 & 1 \\ -3 & 1 & -10 \end{bmatrix}$$
is negative definite because
$$\Delta_1 = -2, \quad \Delta_2 = 3, \quad \Delta_3 = -16.$$

If a quadratic form fails to meet the criteria of the Results 1 and 2 above then it may be indefinite, positive semidefinite or negative semidefinite. It is not possible however to give one simple criterion about the leading principal minors for recognising all indefinite forms. The following result does recognise some indefinite forms.

RESULT 3. If for a real symmetric $n \times n$ matrix H, we have that $\det H \neq 0$ and that the sign pattern of the leading principal minors is neither of those in the Results 1 and 2 above, then the matrix H is indefinite.

Notice: Result 3 gives no help with matrices H for which $\det H = 0$. In such cases other methods (e.g. writing the quadratic form as a sum of squares etc) are needed.

For a proof of the above results and other results about leading principal minors look at An Introduction to Linear Algebra by L. Mirsky, (Oxford University Press), 1963.

EXAMPLES 16 - EXTRA EXAMPLES ON SOLUTION OF PARTIAL DIFFERENTIAL EQUATIONS

1. Make the change of variables $u = x^2 y$, $v = x$ in the p.d.e.

$$x \frac{\partial f}{\partial x} - 2y \frac{\partial f}{\partial y} = 6x^5 y$$

and hence find its general solution. Find also the particular solution for which $f(x,y) = -3x^6$ on the line $y = x$.

2. Make the change of variables $u = y^2/x$, $v = x$ in the p.d.e.

$$2x \frac{\partial z}{\partial x} + y \frac{\partial z}{\partial y} = 4xy^2$$

and hence find its general solution. Find also the particular solution for which

$$z(x, 1) = x + \frac{2}{x} - \frac{3}{x^2}.$$

3. Make the change of variables $u = x^2 + y$, $v = x^2 - y$ in the p.d.e.

$$x \frac{\partial^2 z}{\partial x^2} - 4x^3 \frac{\partial^2 z}{\partial y^2} - \frac{\partial z}{\partial x} = 32x^3$$

and hence find its general solution.

4. Make the change of variables $u = x + \frac{1}{2}y^2$, $v = x$ in the p.d.e.

$$y^3 \frac{\partial^2 z}{\partial x^2} - 2y^2 \frac{\partial^2 z}{\partial x \partial y} + y \frac{\partial^2 z}{\partial y^2} = \frac{\partial z}{\partial y} + 24xy^3$$

and hence find its general solution. Find also the particular solution for which

$$z(x, 0) = 4x^3 + 4x^2 - 4x \quad \text{and} \quad z(0, y) = y^4.$$

5. Make the change of variables $u = xy$, $v = x$ in the p.d.e.

$$x^2 \frac{\partial^2 z}{\partial x^2} - 2xy \frac{\partial^2 z}{\partial x \partial y} + y^2 \frac{\partial^2 z}{\partial y^2} + 2y \frac{\partial z}{\partial y} = 6x^3$$

and hence find its general solution. Find also the particular solution for which

$$z(x, x) = 4x^4 + x^2 \quad \text{and} \quad z(1, y) = 4y^2 + 1.$$

HINTS AND ANSWERS TO THE EXAMPLES

[Note: References are to sections not to pages.]

EXAMPLES 1 (PAGES 17-21)

2. See §4. (a) x from 0 to 2, y from 0 to 3.   I = 26.
(b) x from 0 to 1, y from 0 to x.   I = 1/12.
(c) x from 0 to 2, y from 2x to 4. I = 8.

3. See §6. (a) y from 0 to 1, x from 0 to y.
I = (log 2)/6.   (b) y from 0 to 4, x from 0 to √y.
To integrate $y^2/\sqrt{(1+y^3)}$ put $u = 1+y^3$.   I = (√65 - 1)/6.
(c) y from 0 to 1, x from y^2 to y. I = (2 - √2)/6.
(d) y from 0 to 1, x from 1/y to ∞.   I = 1/(6e).
(e) x from 0 to 1, y from 0 to x.   To integrate
$x^3 e^{-x^2}$ put $u = x^2$ and integrate by parts. I = ½(1 - 2/e).
(f) y from 2 to 4, x from ½y to 2.   I = π/24.

4. (a) 1/3,   (b) 1/3,   (c) 6,   (d) ½(1 - 1/e²),
(e) 7/12,   (f) 9/200.   Note: Only (b) requires
to be split into two integrals as in §7.   In (a), (c),
(d), (e), (f) you can integrate first with respect to x.
In (d) the region is infinite.   You can of course split
these if you like and integrate w.r.t. y first.

5. Similar to §8.   Answer = 23/3.

6. See §11-12. (a) 341/5, (b) a,   (c) $a^4 \sqrt{3}/8$,
(d) π/(2e),   (e) 16/15,   (f) Similar to §12(b).   I = 9/16,
(g) $7\pi a^3/2$,   (h) the upper limit for r is the line x = 1,
i.e. r cos θ = 1, i.e. r = 1/cos θ.   I = π/12.

7. You can do it all analytically using polars.   For
the last part you can however see that ∬ x dxdy = 0
because x is positive in the first and fourth quadrants
and negative in the second and third.   The volume interpretation for a double integral then shows that the total
volume over all four quadrants is zero.

8. Similar to §13.   Use polars.   Volume in the first
octant = $\pi a^3/6$.   Multiply this by 8 for the total volume.

9. Similar to §13.   Volume = ∬(8 - ⅓x) dxdy over
the disc $x^2 + y^2 \le 9$.   From Ex.7 the second term gives
zero, while the first gives 8 times the area of the disc.
So the answer = 72π.

10. Similar to §13.   Use polars.   Answer = ½π.

11. For each part use the method of §14-15.
(a) Put u = xy, v = y/x².   I = 8 log 2.   (b) 1/3.
(c) 59/96.   (d) You need to express (y + 2x)² in terms
of (y - 2x) and xy.   In general, as here, it is often
better to bring the integrand and the Jacobian together
and simplify this before changing the result to the new
variables.   Answer = 115.

12. Use §9 together with the method of §14-15. The area = 1. Let $u = y - x$, $v = y + 3x$.

13. Similar to Ex.12 above.

14. By symmetry do only the first quadrant and multiply by 4. Put $x = au$, $y = bv$ as in §16. $I = \pi ab(a^4 + b^4)/8$.

15. Same integral as in Ex.9 above but over the ellipse $x^2 + 4y^2 \leq 16$. Make the change of variables $x = u$, $y = v/2$ to reduce the ellipse to a circle, etc. The answer = 64π.

16. See §17. (a) $a^2/4$, (b) $2/3$.

17. See §18. (a) $(\frac{1}{3}, \frac{1}{3})$. (b) Use polars. Centre of gravity is $(4\sqrt{2}a/(3\pi), 0)$.

18. See §19. Note that M.I. about the x-axis comes from $\Sigma y^2 \delta m$ <u>not</u> from $\Sigma x^2 \delta m$.

19. For the mass take $\iint k(x + 2y) \, dxdy$ over the square. For the other parts see §18-19. Mass = $3ka^3/2$. Centre of gravity is $(5a/9, 11a/18)$. M.I. about the x-axis is $2ka^5/3$.

20. See §17. (a) Take the disc as $x^2 + y^2 = a^2$ with the base at $(0,0)$. Average distance = $2a/3$. (b) Take the disc as $x^2 + y^2 = 2ax$ with the base at $(0,0)$. The average distance then is $32a/(9\pi)$.

21. The joint probability density function is $4e^{-(x + 4y)}$. Integrate this over the regions in the first quadrant with $x > y$ and with $x + y > 1$ for the two parts. Answers are (a) $4/5$, (b) $4/(3e) - 1/(3e^4)$. (Actually for (b) it may be easier to integrate the p.d.f. over the region with $x + y \leq 1$ and subtract the result from 1.)

EXAMPLES 2 (PAGES 30-32)

1. See §21. (a) x, y, z all from 0 to 1. $I = 1/6$. (b) x from 0 to 1, y from 0 to $1 - x$, z from 0 to $1 - x - y$. $I = 1/24$. (c) x and y from 0 to 1, z from 0 to $1 - y$. $I = 1/12$.

2. See §26: x from 0 to a, y from 0 to $b(1 - (x/a))$, z from 0 to $c(1 - (x/a) - (y/b))$.

3. See §22-24. <u>Remember the following two points:</u> (i) The result of §39 can help in evaluating trigonometric integrals from 0 to $\frac{1}{2}\pi$. Look also at §40. (ii) In using spherical polar coordinates the angle θ as defined in §22 <u>cannot</u> take negative values as explained in §23(ii). For $\overline{(a)}$ ϕ from 0 to $\frac{1}{2}\pi$, θ from 0 to $\frac{1}{2}\pi$, r from 0 to a giving $I = \pi a^5/30$. (b) $\pi a^4/8$.
(c) $\pi/2$. (d) For $\int r^3 e^{-r^2} dr$, put $u = r^2$. $I = 2\pi(1 - (2/e))$. (e) Similar to §24. $I = 16\pi/15$. (f) Find the upper limit for θ by looking at the geometry of where the plane $z = 1$ cuts the sphere. The lower

limit for r is given by the plane z = 1, i.e.
r cos θ = 1, i.e. r = 1/cos θ.   I = 2(13 − 6√2) π/15.
(g) Draw a good diagram.   This is really a three
dimensional version of the two dimensional region in
§12(b).   To find the upper limit for θ you must look
at the points where the spheres meet, i.e. $2az = a^2$, etc.
The limits for r also similar to §12(b).   Answer =
$13\pi a^4/10$.

   4.   The symmetry of the sphere and the interpretation
of §25 suggest that the integrals must be equal.
Alternatively you could check by integration of each.

   5.   Geometrically you can see that the integral is
zero because the integrand is positive for z > 0 and
correspondingly negative for z < 0, so that the contributions from the upper and lower halves of the sphere cancel
each other out.   Alternatively in spherical polars you see
it because $\int_0^\pi \cos^{2n-1}\theta \sin\theta \, d\theta = 0$.

   6.   You can use §26 but it really reduces to the type of
example in §13.   Answer = $\frac{4}{3}\pi(a^3 - (a^2 - b^2)^{3/2})$.

   7.   See §30.   Use spherical polars.

   8.   See §30.   Take B as (0,0,0) with the sphere as
$x^2 + y^2 + z^2 = 2az$, (a > 0) and K as (x,y,z) so that
|BK| = r.   Use spherical polars as in §24.

   9.   §138 shows a cone.   Use spherical polars.   Note
that θ cannot be negative as said in §23(ii).   So θ
runs from 0 to π/4.

   10.   See §24.   Note $x^2 + y^2 = r^2\sin^2\theta$.   Use the
result of §39 to evaluate the θ-integral.

   11.   See §25 for the formula for mass.   Mass = $\pi a^4/4$.

   12.   Use §26 and put x = au, y = bv, z = cw as in
§28.

   13.   Similar to §28.   I = $\pi abc^2/16$.

   14.   See §30 for the idea of mean value.   Ex.12 above
gives the volume of the ellipsoid, which is needed.   For
the integration convert the ellipsoid to a sphere by the
change of variables x = au, y = bv, z = cw as in §28.

   15.   The volume of the region is the difference between
two cones, i.e. $(\pi/3)(2^2.2 - 1^2.1) = 7\pi/3$.   Now integrate
z through the region with spherical polars: φ from 0 to
2π, θ from 0 to π/4 and the r-limits found from the
planes z = 1 and z = 2, i.e. r cos θ = 1, i.e.
r = 1/cos θ etc.   Mean value = 45/28.

   16.   Height of centre of gravity = 4/3.   Take the
density as k.   The mass of the mountain is then 8πk on
integrating in polars.   The height of the centre of
gravity is then $\frac{1}{8\pi k} \int\int\int zk \, dxdydz = \frac{4}{3}$.

   17.   Similar to Ex.16 above.   Take the hemisphere as

$x^2 + y^2 + z^2 \leq a^2$, $\quad z > 0$. $\quad$ Then $\bar{x} = \bar{y} = 0$, $\bar{z} = 3a/8$.

18. See §32 on moment of inertia. For (i) take the z-axis as axis of rotation and the cube with vertices at $(0,0,0)$, $(a,0,0)$, $(0,a,0)$, $(0,0,a)$, (a,a,a) etc. Use xyz-coordinates. For (ii) take the z-axis as axis of rotation and the cube with vertices at $(\pm\frac{1}{2}a, \pm\frac{1}{2}a, \pm\frac{1}{2}a)$. Again use xyz-coordinates.

19. Take the sphere as $x^2 + y^2 + z^2 \leq a^2$. Use §25 with spherical polars for the mass. Use §32 for the M.I. taking the z-axis as axis of rotation and using spherical polars.

20. Take the x-axis as axis of rotation. Then M.I. $= \iiint (y^2 + z^2)\rho\, dxdydz$ throughout the sphere. Use spherical polars. The result of §39 helps here.

21. $y^T P^T A P y = y^T \text{diag}(\alpha_1, \alpha_2, \alpha_3)y = \alpha_1 y_1^2 + \alpha_2 y_2^2 + \alpha_3 y_3^2$
$= 1$, i.e. $(y_1/a)^2 + (y_2/b)^2 + (y_3/c)^2 = 1$, where
$a = 1/\sqrt{\alpha_1}$, $b = 1/\sqrt{\alpha_2}$, $c = 1/\sqrt{\alpha_3}$. The volume of the ellipsoid $= \frac{4}{3}\pi abc$ (from Ex.12 above) $= 4\pi/(3\sqrt{(\alpha_1\alpha_2\alpha_3)})$.

However, since $\det P = \pm 1$, we have $\det A = \det(P^T A P) = \det(\text{diag}(\alpha_1, \alpha_2, \alpha_3)) = \alpha_1\alpha_2\alpha_3$. So the volume required is $4\pi/(3\sqrt{(\det A)})$.

EXAMPLES 3 (PAGES 37-39)

1. For the general ideas see §36-38 but the following individual substitutions are suggested.
(a) $u = 2x$. (b) $u = 2x$. (c) $u = ax$. (d) Double it from 0 to ∞. Put $u = \frac{1}{2}x^2$. (e) $u = ax^2$. (f) You want $4 - x$ to be $4 - 4u$. So take $x = 4u$. (g) It is already in the form (i) of §33. (h) $u = x^2$. (i) Similar to (f). (j) Put $u = x^2$. Write $\frac{\Gamma(\frac{3}{2})}{\Gamma(\frac{1}{4})}$ as $\frac{(\Gamma(\frac{3}{4}))^2}{\Gamma(\frac{1}{4}).\Gamma(\frac{3}{4})}$ and then use §34C to find the value of the denominator of this. (k) $16x^2 - x^6 = x^2(16 - x^4)$. You want $16 - x^4 = 16 - 16u$. (l) You want $4 - x^2 = 4 - 4u$. (m) $u = x^4$. Get rid of $\Gamma(\frac{3}{4})$ by a similar method to that used in (j) above. (n) $u = x^4$. It needs §34C. (o) $u = x^3$. It needs §34C. (p) $x^2 = 2u$. (q) $x^4 = u$. It needs §34C. (r) $u = 8x^3$. It needs §34C. (s) The areas between the graph and the x-axis for $x < 0$ and $x > 0$ cancel out to zero because one is below and one is above and they are of equal size.

2. For (a) - (e) use §39. Answers are (a) 2/15, (b) 1/40, (c) $\pi/32$, (d) 16/35, (e) $5\pi/32$, (f) $\pi\sqrt{2}/8$, on using §33(iii) with $2p - 1 = \frac{3}{2}$ and $2q - 1 = \frac{1}{2}$, and then §34C. (g) $\pi\sqrt{2}/2$ on writing $\tan x = \sin x/\cos x$ and using §33(iii).

3. (a) 16/15, (b) 0, (c) $5\pi/16$, (d) $5\pi/16$, (e) 0, (f) 4/15, (g) $3\pi/128$, (h) $3\pi/4$, (i) 0, (j) 0, (k) $5\pi/64$, (l) 0.

4. (a) Divide above and below by $\cos^2 x$, and put $u = 4\tan^2 x$. Answer $= \pi/4$. (b) First put $u = x + 2$. Then put $u = 4t$. Answer $= 2\pi$. (c) Put $u = \tan x$. Answer $= \frac{1}{2}\pi$. (d) Put $x = 1/y$. Answer $= \frac{1}{2}\pi$.

(e) Put $u = \log x$. Answer $= 6$.

5. Put $y = (1 - x)t$ in the inner integral. It then splits into two separate Beta functions. $I = 16/945$.

6. Put $x^2 = u$.

7. Express the volume as the triple integral of 1 with xyz-limits. Integrate w.r.t z and then put $y = (1 - x^3)^{1/3} t^{1/3}$ etc.

8. First put $y = (x - \mu)/\sigma$. Both then become integrals rather like Ex.1(d) above. The first one splits into two parts one of which is zero.

EXAMPLES 4   (PAGES 48-50)

Notice: Here your form of the general solution may differ from the answer given, as explained in §43(ii).

1. (a) $y = C(1 + x)^2$, (b) $Ce^{4x} = (1 + y)/(1 - y)$, (c) $\frac{1}{3}y^3 + y^2 + y = \tan x + C$, (d) $\frac{1}{2}e^{2y} = -(x + 2)e^{-x} + C$.

2. (a) $\frac{1}{2}y^2 + Cx^2 = x^2 \log x$, (b) $\sin(y/x) + C = \log x$, (c) $x = y(C + \log y)$, (d) $e^{-2y/x} = C - 6 \log x$.

3. Remember to reduce the coefficient of y' to 1 before finding the integrating factor. Remember also the comment in §45(iii). The individual equations give:

(a) I.F. is e^{3x}, G.S. is $y = e^{-3x}(x^2 + x + C)$,

(b) I.F. is $(x + 1)^2$, G.S. is $y(x + 1)^2 = xe^x + C$,

(c) I.F. is $1/\sqrt{x}$, G.S. is $y = -2 + \sqrt{x} \log x + C\sqrt{x}$.

4. (a) L, (b) H, (c) L, (d) L, (e) H, (f) L, (g) S, (h) H, (i) H, (j) L, (k) S, (l) L.

5. (a) $y = x^3(C + \sin x)$, (b) $x(y + 2x)^5 = C(y + 3x)^5$, (c) $y \cos x = \sin x + \frac{1}{4}\sin 2x + \frac{1}{2}x + C$, (d) $y = -\frac{1}{2}(x + 2)^2 + C(x + 2)^4$, (e) $2y^2(C + \log y) = x^2 + 6xy$, (f) $y = 6(x^2 + 4) + C\sqrt{(x^2 + 4)}$, (g) $2y^3 = C + 3x^2 + 6 \log x$, (h) $\tan^{-1}(y/x) = C + 2 \log(x^2 + y^2)$, (i) $\sin^{-1}(y/(2x)) = C + \log x$, (j) $y = (x^3 + x^2 + C)(x^2 + 1)$, (k) $(y - 1)e^y = C + \sin x$, (l) $yx^2(x + 1) = \frac{1}{2}x^2 + C$.

6. (a) $\frac{1}{2}y^2 + y - 6 = -2e^{-3x}$, (b) $(x^2 + 1)y = 2x^2 + x + 5$,

(c) $y = x^2 \log x - 2x + 3x^2$, (d) $y(t^2 + 2)^2 = 3t^4 + 12t^2 + 20$.

7. Use the method of §48. The general solutions are
(a) $(x + y - 3)^2 (y - x - 1) = C$, (b) $2 \tan^{-1}((y - 2)/(x - 4)) = \log(C((x - 4)^2 + (y - 2)^2))$, (c) $(y - 3x - 2) = C(x + y - 6)^2$.

8. Making the given substitution means $\frac{dz}{dx} = 3 - \frac{dy}{dx}$, giving a separable equation in $\frac{dz}{dx}$. The general solution is $2x - 2y - \log(6x - 2y + 5) = C$.

9. Use the method of §49 - i.e. reduction of order.
(a) $3y = x^3 + Cx^2 + D$, (b) $y = -x + Ce^x + D$,
(c) $y = 6 \log x - \frac{6}{x} + \frac{C}{x^2} + D$.

10. Use the method of §50. The general solutions are (a) $e^{-x^2}(1 - y^2) = Cy^2$, (b) $(x + 1)^3 = y^3(C - 3x - \frac{3}{2}x^2)$.

11. It is a separable differential equation with the initial condition $v = 0$ when $t = 0$ determining the arbitrary constant. For the terminal velocity notice that for the resistance to be meaningful we must have $k > 0$, so that $e^{-kt} \to 0$ as $t \to \infty$; so $v(t) \to g/k$ as $t \to \infty$.

12. The general solution of the differential equation is the same as in Ex.11 above. The initial conditions in this case are $v = U$ when $t = 0$. This gives $v(t) = \frac{g}{k}\left\{1 - \left(1 - \frac{kU}{g}\right)e^{-kt}\right\}$, from which the result.

13. The differential equation can be treated either as separable or linear and hence solved.

EXAMPLES 5 (PAGES 65-67)

1. The methods are illustrated in §53-55. The general solutions: (a) $y = Ae^{2x} + Be^{4x}$, (b) $y = Ae^{2x} + Be^{-3x}$, (c) $y = e^x(A \cos 5x + B \sin 5x)$, (d) $y = A \cos 2x + B \sin 2x$, (e) $y = (Ax + B)e^{-2x}$, (f) $y = Ae^{\frac{3}{2}x} + Be^{-2x}$, (g) $y = e^{2x}(A \cos 5x + B \sin 5x)$, (h) $y = A + Be^{3x}$, (i) $y = (Ax + B)e^{6x}$, (j) $y = A \cos ax + B \sin ax$.

2. The methods are illustated in §59-60. The general solutions: (a) $y = Ae^{4x} + Be^{-2x} - 2e^{-x}$, (b) $y = A \cos x + B \sin x + \frac{1}{2}e^{-3x}$, (c) $y = (Ax + B)e^{2x} + 4e^{3x}$, (d) $y = Ae^x + Be^{2x} + 8xe^{2x}$, (e) $y = e^{-x}(A \cos 4x +$

$B \sin 4x) + \frac{1}{2}e^{-x} + \frac{1}{2}e^{-3x}$, (f) $y = (Ax + B)e^{2x} + 3x^2e^{2x}$,
(g) $y = Ae^{\frac{1}{2}x} + Be^{7x} - (7/13)xe^{\frac{1}{2}x}$, (h) $y = (Ax + B)e^{-x} +$
$3x^2e^{-x}$, (i) $y = (Ax + B)e^{-2x} + 2e^x + 18e^{-x}$.

3. The method is given in §61. The solutions are:
(a) $y = \frac{1}{2}e^{4x} + \frac{1}{2}e^{-3x}$, (b) $y = -4e^x + 2e^{3x} + 4e^{-2x}$,
(c) $y = e^x(-4 \cos 3x + 2 \sin 3x) + 2e^{-x}$, (d) $y = 12 \cos 5t$,
(e) $y = (5t^2 + 2t)e^{-t}$.

4. For the method see §62-63. (a) $y = Ae^x + Be^{5x} +$
$3 \cos x + \sin x$, (b) $y = Ae^{-x} + Be^{2x} + 3 \cos 2x - 9 \sin 2x$,
(c) $y = A \cos x + B \sin x - 3x \cos x$, (d) $y = A \cos 3x +$
$B \sin 3x + x(\cos 3x - 4 \sin 3x)$.

5. For the method see §64. (a) $y = e^{-4x}(A \cos x +$
$B \sin x) + 3x + 2$, (b) $y = (Ax + B)e^{-4x} + x^2 - x + 2$,
(c) $y = A + Be^{-x} + 3x^2 - 6x$.

6. (a) $y = 3e^{4x} - e^{7x} + 3e^{2x}$, (b) $y = 2e^{3x} -$
$2 \cos x - \sin x$, (c) $y = (1 - \frac{1}{2}x)e^{-x}$,
(d) $y = 2e^{3x}\cos x + 25x^2 + 30x + 13$.

7. Use the method of §67. $y = (Cx^2 - x + D)e^x$.

8. Use the method of §67. (a) $y = x$ is a
solution. G.S. is $y = x(Ce^{-2x} + D)$. (b) $y = e^x$ is a
solution. G.S. is $y = e^x(\frac{1}{2}x^2 + x + C(x + 1)^{-1} + D)$.
(c) $y = x$ is a solution. G.S. is $y = x^2 + Cx(x - 1)^{-1} + Dx$.

9. $y = x + 4$ is a solution. G.S. is
$y = (x + 4)(\frac{1}{4}x^2 + 2x + C \log(x + 4) + D)$.

10. See §68-70. Methods 1 and 2 of §68 work in
both cases. The general solutions are: (a) $y = -2x +$
$C/x^2 + Dx^5$, (b) $y = -x - \frac{1}{2} + Cx^2 + D/x$.

11. Method 1 of §68 fails: you must therefore use
method 2 as illustrated in §70. The general solution is
$y = x(A \cos(\log x) + B \sin(\log x)) + (\log x)^2 + 2(\log x) + 2$.

12. See §71 for the method. The general solutions
are: (a) $x = -4Ae^{-3t} - 2Be^{-5t}$, $y = Ae^{-3t} + Be^{-5t}$,
(b) $x = Ae^{4t} + Be^{7t}$, $y = -5Ae^{4t} - 2Be^{7t}$, (c) $x = Ae^{-t} -$
$Be^{-3t} + 2t$, $y = 3Ae^{-t} + Be^{-3t} + t + 2$, (d) $x = Ae^t + Be^{-t} +$
$4 \cos t - 1$, $y = -Ae^t + 2Be^{-t} + 2 \sin t$.

13.   G.S. is $x = -4Ae^{2t} - Be^{-t} + 4t$, $y = Ae^{2t} + Be^{-t} + 1 - 2t$;   P.S. is $x = e^{-t} + 4t$, $y = -e^{-t} - 2t + 1$.

EXAMPLES 6   (PAGES 76-78)

1. (a) $3/(s^2 + 9)$,   (b) $6/s^4$,   (c) $(2/s^3) - (3/s^2) + (6/s)$,
(d) $\frac{1}{2}\sqrt{\pi}/s^{3/2}$,   (e) $1/(s - 4)$,   (f) $3/(s^2 + 2s + 10)$,
(g) $(s-4)/(s^2-8s+17)$, (h) $6/(s + 1)^4$,   (i) $(2/s^3) + (2/s^2) + (1/s)$,
(j) $(s-5)/(s^2-10s+50)$,   (k) $2/(s + 2)^3 + 4/(s + 2)^2$,
(1) $-\dfrac{d}{ds}\left(\dfrac{s}{s^2 + 4}\right) = \dfrac{s^2 - 4}{(s^2 + 4)^2}$,   (m) $(-1)^2 \dfrac{d^2}{ds^2}\left(\dfrac{4}{s^2 + 16}\right) =$
$8(3s^2 - 16)/(s^2 + 16)^3$.

2. (a) 1,   (b) $\frac{1}{2}x^2$,   (c) $1 + x^2$,   (d) e^{2x},   (e) xe^{2x},
(f) $2e^{2x} - xe^{2x}$,   on writing as $\dfrac{2}{s - 2} - \dfrac{1}{(s - 2)^2}$,   (g) $\cos x$,
(h) $\sin x$,   (i) $\frac{1}{2}\sin 2x$,   (j) $e^{-x}\cos 2x$,   on writing as
$\dfrac{(s + 1)}{(s + 1)^2 + 4}$,   (k) $\dfrac{2(s - 4)}{(s - 4)^2 + 1} + \dfrac{12}{(s - 4)^2 + 1}$ gives
$2e^{4x}\cos x + 12e^{4x}\sin x$,   (1) $\frac{1}{2}e^{5x} - \frac{1}{2}e^{3x}$,   (m) $2e^{2x} + \sin x$
from the partial fractions $\dfrac{2}{s - 2} + \dfrac{1}{s^2 + 1}$,   (n) $e^{-2x} -$
$e^{-x}\cos 7x$,   from $\dfrac{1}{s + 2} - \dfrac{s + 1}{s^2 + 2s + 50}$,   (o) $e^{2x} - \frac{5}{2}x^2e^{2x}$,
from $\dfrac{1}{s - 2} - \dfrac{5}{(s - 2)^3}$,   (p) $1 - x - e^{-2x}$,   from $\frac{1}{s} - \frac{1}{s^2} -$
$\dfrac{1}{s + 2}$,   (q) $2e^{-x} + e^{\frac{1}{2}x}\cos\left(\frac{x\sqrt{3}}{2}\right) + \sqrt{3}\,e^{\frac{1}{2}x}\sin\left(\frac{x\sqrt{3}}{2}\right)$ from
$\dfrac{2}{s + 1} + \dfrac{s + 1}{s^2 - s + 1}$.

3.   (a) $y(t) = 2 - 2e^{-3t}$,   from $\bar{y} = 6/(s(s + 3))$,
(b) $y(t) = t^3e^{-4t}$,   (c) $y(t) = 3e^{-2t}\sin t$,   from $\bar{y} =$
$\dfrac{3}{s^2 + 4s + 5}$,   (d) $y(t) = 2t^2 - 4t$,   (e) $-1 + e^{-t}\cos 3t$,
from $-\dfrac{1}{s} + \dfrac{s + 1}{s^2 + 2s + 10}$,   (f) $y(t) = 1 - 2t - e^{-2t}$,   from
$\bar{y} = \dfrac{1}{s} - \dfrac{2}{s^2} - \dfrac{1}{s + 2}$,   (g) $y(t) = 2t + e^{2t}\sin t$,   from
$\bar{y} = \dfrac{2}{s^2} + \dfrac{1}{s^2 - 4s + 5}$.

4.   (a) $x = 1 - t^2$, $y = 4t$ from $\bar{y} = 4/s^2$.
(b) $\bar{x} = \dfrac{6}{s(s - 1)(s + 2)} = \dfrac{-3}{s} + \dfrac{2}{s - 1} + \dfrac{1}{s + 2}$ which gives
$x = 2e^t + e^{-2t} - 3$ and $y = e^t - e^{-2t} - 3t$.

(c) $\bar{x} = \dfrac{1}{s(s+1)} = \dfrac{1}{s} - \dfrac{1}{s+1}$ which gives $x = 1 - e^{-t}$, and then on solving a linear differential equation, we obtain $y = -2e^{-t} + 2e^{3t}$. (d) $\bar{x} = \dfrac{-2}{s^2(s-1)(s+1)} = \dfrac{2}{s^2} - \dfrac{1}{s-1} +$

$\dfrac{1}{s+1}$ which gives $x = 2t - e^t + e^{-t}$, $y = 3e^t + e^{-t}$.

(e) $\bar{y} = \dfrac{s+1}{(s+1)^2 + 4}$ which gives $y = e^{-t}\cos 2t$ and $x = e^{-t}\sin 2t + 1$.

5. (a) §74(g) gives $-\dfrac{d}{ds}(s^2\bar{y} - 4) + 6\bar{y} - 9\left(-\dfrac{d\bar{y}}{ds}\right) = 0$, which gives the linear differential equation $(s+3)\dfrac{d\bar{y}}{ds} +$

$2y = 0$, giving $\bar{y} = \dfrac{C}{(s+3)^2}$, from which we obtain $y = 4xe^{-3x}$ on using $y'(0) = 4$.

(b) $-\dfrac{d}{ds}(s^2\bar{y} - y'(0)) - 2s\bar{y} - 4\bar{y} + \dfrac{d\bar{y}}{ds} = 0$, which reduces to $(s-1)\dfrac{d\bar{y}}{ds} + 4\bar{y} = 0$, giving $\bar{y} = C/(s-1)^4$ from which $y = 4x^3 e^x$ on using $y(1) = 4e$ to determine C.

6. Treat f''' as (f'')' and use §74(d). Then use §74(e). In the differential equation taking Laplace transforms gives $\bar{y} = 2/(s(s^2+1))$, from which $y = 2 - 2\cos x$.

7. The general method is illustrated in §83.
(a) $\bar{y} = -s/(s^2+1)$ gives $y(t) = -\cos t$.
(b) $\bar{y} = (20/s^2) + (12/s)$ gives $y(t) = 20t + 12$.
(c) $\bar{y} = (6/s^2) + (6/s^4)$ gives $y(t) = 6t + t^3$.
(d) $\bar{y} = \dfrac{(s-1)}{(s-2)(s-3)}$ gives $y(t) = -e^{2t} + 2e^{3t}$.
(e) $\bar{y} = (4/\sqrt{\pi})s^{-3/2}$ gives $y(t) = (8/\pi)\sqrt{t}$.

8. Transforms produce $\bar{y} \cdot \dfrac{\Gamma(1-k)}{s^{1-k}} = \dfrac{\Gamma(3-k)}{s^{3-k}}$ so that $\bar{y} = (2-k)(1-k)/s^2$ and $y(t) = (2-k)(1-k)t$.

EXAMPLES 7 (PAGES 98-101)

1. (a) $u_x = 2x$, $u_y = -2y$, $v_x = 2y$, $v_y = 2x$.
(b) $f_x = y^2\sin(y/x) - (y^3/x)\cos(y/x)$, $f_y = 2xy\sin(y/x) + y^2\cos(y/x)$.

2.   Similar to §87. $f_x = \frac{yz}{r^2} + xyz \cdot \left(\frac{-2}{r^3}\right) \frac{\partial r}{\partial x}$ etc.

Note $r^2 = x^2 + y^2 + z^2$,   so that $2r \frac{\partial r}{\partial x} = 2x$ and $\frac{\partial r}{\partial x} = \frac{x}{r}$.

3.   If you don't fully understand the meaning of $f(u)$,   look at §90(i).   For the method of finding $\partial\phi/\partial x$ look at §90(a)   and for $\partial^2\phi/\partial x^2$ look at §90(ii).   Then $\frac{\partial\phi}{\partial y} = 3x^2y^2 \, f'(u)$ and $\frac{\partial^2\phi}{\partial y^2} = 6x^2y \, f'(u) + 9x^4y^4 \, f''(u)$.

4. $\frac{\partial\phi}{\partial x} = f'(r) \frac{\partial r}{\partial x} = f'(r) \frac{x}{r}$.   Use Product Rule to

find $\frac{\partial^2\phi}{\partial x^2} = f''(r) \cdot \frac{x^2}{r^2} + f'(r) \left(1 \cdot \frac{1}{r} + x \cdot \frac{-1}{r^2} \frac{\partial r}{\partial x}\right)$ etc.   Then

$\partial^2\phi/\partial y^2$ can be read off $\partial^2\phi/\partial x^2$ by symmetry.

5.   Compare §89.   You find $n^2 = 4$,   but n is positive.   So $n = 2$.

6.   Compare §89. $n = \pm 3$.

7.   For the second part differentiate the first partial differential equation (p.d.e.) partially with respect to x.   Then differentiate the first p.d.e. partially with respect to y and multiply the result by 4.   Then add the two resulting equations, using the first p.d.e. to simplify the right hand side.

8.   For the second part differentiate the first p.d.e. partially with respect to x and multiply the result by x.   Repeat the process replacing x by y. Add the resulting equations.

9.   The first sentence is fairly easy, with

$\frac{\partial f}{\partial x} = 6x + \frac{2x}{r^2}$ and $\frac{\partial^2 f}{\partial x^2} = 6 + \frac{2}{r^2} - \frac{4x^2}{r^4}$.   Find $\frac{\partial f}{\partial y}$

by symmetry.   For the last part differentiate the first p.d.e. partially with respect to x twice,   then repeat the process with respect to y.   Add the results. [Actually Ex.4 above could be used for the first part.]

10.   (a) $f = \int 4xy \, dx = 2x^2y + \phi(y)$.   (Compare §95.)

(b) $f = \int (3x^2 + 3y^2) \, dy = 3x^2y + y^3 + \phi(x)$.

(c) $\frac{\partial f}{\partial y} = \int 0 \, dx = \phi(y)$.   So $f = \int \phi(y) \, dy = \psi(y) + \tau(x)$.

(d) $\frac{\partial f}{\partial x} = \int 0 \, dx = \phi(y)$.   So $f = \int \phi(y) \, dx = x\,\phi(y) + \tau(y)$.

(e) $\frac{\partial f}{\partial y} = \int 0 \, dy = \phi(x)$.   So $f = \int \phi(x) \, dy = y\,\phi(x) + \tau(x)$.

(f) $\frac{\partial f}{\partial x} = \int (6xy + 2) \, dx = 3x^2y + 2x + \phi(y)$.   So we have

$f = x^3 y + x^2 + x \, \phi(y) + \tau(y)$.

11.   The integrating factor is e^{-2x} so that $\frac{\partial}{\partial x}\left(e^{-2x} f\right) = 0$ giving $f = e^{2x} \phi(y)$.

12.   See §97 for the general method.

(a) $\frac{\partial f}{\partial v} = -2x$,   i.e. $\frac{\partial f}{\partial v} = -\frac{2u}{v^2}$.   So $f = \frac{2u}{v} + \phi(u)$,

i.e. $f(x,y) = 2xy + \phi(xy^2)$.

(b) $\frac{\partial f}{\partial u} = \frac{3y}{x}(y^2 - x^2)$,   i.e. $\frac{\partial f}{\partial u} = 3u^2 v^3 - 3u^2 v$.   So

$f = u^3 v^3 - u^3 v + \phi(v)$,   i.e. $f(x,y) = y^3 - x^2 y + \phi(y/x)$.

(c) $\frac{\partial f}{\partial v} - 2vf = 0$,   which has the I.F. e^{-v^2} similar to

Ex.11 above.   So $e^{-v^2} f = \phi(u)$.   So the solution is
$f(x,y) = \phi(x^2 - y^2) \, e^{y^2}$.

(d) $\frac{\partial z}{\partial v} + \tfrac{1}{2}\sec^2 v \; z = 0$.   I.F. $= e^{\frac{1}{2}\tan v}$.   So this gives

$z \, e^{\frac{1}{2}\tan v} = \phi(u)$.   So $z(x,y) = e^{-\frac{1}{2}\tan y} \phi(x^2 e^{\tan y})$.

13.   The example of §98 illustrates the method.   So

$\frac{\partial F}{\partial x} = 2x\frac{\partial f}{\partial u}$ and $\frac{\partial^2 F}{\partial x^2} = 2\frac{\partial f}{\partial u} + 4x^2 \frac{\partial^2 f}{\partial u^2}$.   If you have failed

to get the term $2\frac{\partial f}{\partial u}$ in $\frac{\partial^2 F}{\partial x^2}$ then you probably don't

understand remark (i) in §98.   Study it and try again.

Also $\frac{\partial F}{\partial y} = 2y\frac{\partial f}{\partial u} + \frac{\partial f}{\partial v}$ and $\frac{\partial^2 F}{\partial y^2} = 2\frac{\partial f}{\partial u} + 4y^2 \frac{\partial^2 f}{\partial u^2} + 4y\frac{\partial^2 f}{\partial u \partial v} + \frac{\partial^2 f}{\partial v^2}$.

14.   The example of §99 illustrates the method.   If you have trouble in (c), (d) or (e) read §100 carefully. You have little hope of success in (c), (d) or (e) if you cannot produce the correct second derivatives in Ex.13.

(a) It reduces to $\frac{\partial^2 f}{\partial u \partial v} = 0$,   which integrates as in Ex.10

to give $f(x,y) = \phi(x + 2y) + \psi(x - 2y)$.

(b) It reduces to $\frac{\partial^2 f}{\partial v^2} = 0$.   So $f(x,y) = y\,\phi(x + y) + \psi(x + y)$.

(c) It reduces to $\frac{\partial^2 f}{\partial u \partial v} = 0$.   So $f(x,y) = \phi(xy) + \psi(y)$.

If your equation does not reduce properly check that your $\partial^2 f / \partial x \partial y$ contains <u>three</u> terms and that one of them is $\partial f / \partial u$.   If it does not then read §100.

(d) It reduces to $\frac{\partial^2 f}{\partial v^2} = 0$.   So $f(x,y) = y\,\phi(x/y) + \psi(x/y)$.

(e) It reduces to $\frac{\partial^2 z}{\partial u \partial v} = 0$.   So $z(x,y) = \phi(3x + y^2) +$
$\psi(3x - y^2)$.   As a check notice that $\frac{\partial^2 z}{\partial y^2} = 2\frac{\partial z}{\partial u} - 2\frac{\partial z}{\partial v} +$
$4y^2 \frac{\partial^2 z}{\partial u^2} - 8y^2 \frac{\partial^2 z}{\partial u \partial v} + 4y^2 \frac{\partial^2 z}{\partial v^2}$.

15.   This is similar to §101.   The general solution
of the p.d.e is $f(x,y) = 3x + y\,\phi(x/y^2) + \psi(x/y^2)$.

16.   The most efficient method is to take Laplace's
equation in polar coordinates from near the top of page 95
and calculate $\partial^2 f/\partial r^2$, $\partial f/\partial r$ and $\partial^2 f/\partial \theta^2$ and put them
in this equation.   Alternatively you can take the given
function as $\frac{1}{2}A \log(x^2 + y^2) + B$,   calculate $\partial^2 f/\partial x^2$ and
$\partial^2 f/\partial y^2$ and use the form (*) at the foot of page 94.

17.   Here, as in the example in §103, it is not easy
to make a direct assault on $\partial f/\partial x$ and $\partial f/\partial y$.   (If you
don't understand the difficulty read the first paragraph
in the solution in §103.)   Here it is easier to calculate
$\partial g/\partial u$ and $\partial g/\partial v$ and solve the resulting equations for
$\partial f/\partial x$ and $\partial f/\partial y$.   These equations are in fact

$$\frac{\partial g}{\partial u} = \frac{\partial f}{\partial x} + v\frac{\partial f}{\partial y} \quad \text{and} \quad \frac{\partial g}{\partial v} = \frac{\partial f}{\partial x} + u\frac{\partial f}{\partial y}.$$

18. $\frac{\partial^2 f}{\partial x^2} = \left[\cos\theta\frac{\partial}{\partial r} - \frac{\sin\theta}{r}\frac{\partial}{\partial\theta}\right]\left[\cos\theta\frac{\partial g}{\partial r} - \frac{\sin\theta}{r}\frac{\partial g}{\partial\theta}\right].$

19.   The four values in order are $\cos\theta$, $1/\cos\theta$,
$1/\cos\theta$, $\cos\theta$.   The first and third come from the
equation $x = r\cos\theta$.   The second and fourth come from
the equation $x^2 + y^2 = r^2$.   The answers to the questions
are: NO.   NO.   The first and third must be reciprocals;
the second and fourth likewise.   (See §106 for clarific-
ation.)

20.   The method is similar to that in §105.   Take it
as $F(x, y, z(x,y)) = 0$ and differentiate it partially
w.r.t.   x   holding   y   constant.   This gives
$\frac{\partial F}{\partial x} + \frac{\partial F}{\partial z}\left(\frac{\partial z}{\partial x}\right)_y = 0$ so that $\left(\frac{\partial z}{\partial x}\right)_y = -F_x/F_z$.   Also take it
as $F(x(y,z), y, z) = 0$ and differentiate it partially
w.r.t.   z   holding   y   constant to find $\left(\frac{\partial x}{\partial z}\right)_y = -F_z/F_x$.

EXAMPLES 8   (PAGES 112-114)

1.   Similar to §113.   Answer = ±3%.

2.   Take logarithms first.   You need to introduce the percentage error for y by brute force as in §114. Answer = $(p - 2yq)$%.

3.   Take logarithms first.   Then take differentials and collect terms.

4.   Take logarithms.   Answer = $(p + 2q)$%.

5.   (a) Take $u = \sqrt{(x^2 + y^2 + z^2)}$ so that $du = (x\,dx + y\,dy + z\,dz)/\sqrt{(x^2 + y^2 + z^2)}$.   Then take $x = 8$, $y = 4$, $z = 1$, $dx = .03$, $dy = -.02$, $dz = .04$ etc. This gives an estimate 9.02222 against true value 9.02236.

In the second case the estimate is 8.99511 against the true value 8.99518.

(b) Estimate = 3.006, true value = 3.00604.

6.   Do not take logarithms.   Take differentials as it stands.   Answer = $(0.8p + 0.32q)$%.   (To achieve this you want +p% error in x and -q% error in y.)

7.   Take logarithms first.   Then take differentials and collect the dx terms over a common denominator etc. In each case then put in the values of x, y, z, i.e. 7, 1, 7 etc, and make suitable choices of sign in the ±1% errors to obtain the maximum possible positive percentage error.   The estimates are   (a) +2.8% ,   (b) +16%.
For the explicit values take   (a)   (6.93, 1.01, 7.07) which gives C = 3.5268 against a value of 3.43   for (7, 1, 7) [i.e. +2.82% difference], (b) (2.97, 1.01, 1.98) which gives C = 14.2012 against a value of 12 for (3, 1, 2) [i.e. +18.34% difference].

8.   For a similar example see §116, for the theory see §115.   In each case show that df is exact by showing that $\partial P/\partial y = \partial Q/\partial x$.   If you don't understand how to find f study §116 carefully.   Notice particularly as mentioned in §116 that you have two strategies to choose from and that in some cases one of them may be much easier to use than the other.   For the individual cases we may take: (a) $f(x,y) = 2x^2 - 7xy + 6y^2$.   (b) $f(x,y) = x^3 + 2x^2y + 4xy^2 - y^3$.   (c) $f(x,y) = x^2 + xy + 3y^2 + 4y^3$.   (d) Start from $\partial f/\partial y$ rather than $\partial f/\partial x$ as this is much easier.   This gives $f(x,y) = ye^x\sin x + 3xy^2$.   (e) Start from $\partial f/\partial y$. So $f(x,y) = x^2\log y - y^2 + x\log x$.   (f)   Start from $\partial f/\partial y$.   Then $f(x,y) = \log(x(x^2 + y^2))$.

9.   See §117 for the method for (a), (b), (c), (f). See §118 for the method for (d) and (e).   For the various parts we have:-

(a) I.F. = $1/x^4$. $f(x,y) = 3x^2 - (y^2/x^3)$.

(b) I.F. = y^2. $f(x,y) = y^4e^{2x} - (y^2 + 2y + 2)e^{-y}$.

(c) I.F. = y^2. $f(x,y) = xy^5 + y^3\sin x$.

(d) $\partial P/\partial y = \partial Q/\partial x$ gives the differential equation

$(y + 4)g'(y) - 2g(y) = 0$, so that I.F. $= (y + 4)^2$.
This gives $f(x,y) = (2x + 1)(y + 4)^3$.

10. (a) $xy^4 + y = C$. (b) $6x^2 + 8xy^2 + 3y^4 = C$.
(c) I.F. $= e^{2x}$; G.S. is $(xy^2 + 4)e^{2x} = C$. (d) From the
differential equation $(y+1)g'(y) + 3g(y) = 0$ find that
I.F. $= 1/(y+1)^3$. So G.S. is $x/(y+1) + 1/(y+1)^2 = C$.
(e) Denote xy^2 by u. The differential equation
$ug'(u) - 2g(u) = 0$ gives I.F. $= u^2 = x^2y^4$. The G.S.
is then $x^4y^5 + x^3y^7 = C$.

EXAMPLES 9 (PAGES 123-124)

1. grad $\phi = (2xyz^3, x^2z^3, 3x^2yz^2)$, div v $=$
$2xy + 2z + y$, curl v $= (z - 2y, -1, 1 - x^2)$, divgrad $\phi =$
$2yz^3 + 6x^2yz$.

2. Compare §126. $\partial\phi/\partial n = 4\sqrt{6}$.

3. At $(0,3,-2)$, grad $\phi = (3, -6, 9)$. This gives
(a) -5, (b) $6\sqrt{2}$, (c) 2. The maximum and minimum values
are $3\sqrt{14}$ and $-3\sqrt{14}$ obtained by taking n along $\pm$grad ϕ,
i.e. in the direction of the vectors $(3, -6, 9)$ and
$(-3, 6, -9)$. (For more explanation see Ex.11 below.)

4. Use §127(iii) with $\phi = r^n$ and v $=$ a. Note
that div a $= 0$ because a is constant, and grad(r^n)
can be found as in §128.

5. This is routine on using the product rule for
partial differentiation.

6. Take u $= (u_1, u_2, u_3)$ and v $= (v_1, v_2, v_3)$
and slog out both sides of the identity in terms of partial
derivatives: there are twelve terms on each side. For
the second part take u $= r$ and v $=$ grad ϕ, and use the
facts that curl(grad ϕ) $= 0$ and curl r $= 0$, from §127
and §128.

7. All these can be done by two methods –
either by writing out the components in terms of a_1, a_2, a_3
and x, y, z and then doing suitable partial differentiation, or by using the identities for div(ϕv) and
curl(ϕv) from §127. In some cases the use of identities
does shorten the work, but it is a great help to have
facts like div r $= 3$ and curl r $= 0$ (see §128) at your
fingertips. For (h), first make use of the identity

$d \times (e \times f) = (d.f)e - (d.e)f$ from elementary vector algebra.

10.   Find $\partial r/\partial x$ etc as in §128.

11.   At $(2,2,1)$,   grad $T = (1,3,16)$.   We are looking for two directions such that for unit vectors   n   along these directions $\partial T/\partial n$ has   its maximum and minimum possible values at $(2,2,1)$. Recall from §126 that $\dfrac{\partial T}{\partial n} = n.\,\text{grad}\,T$ so that $\dfrac{\partial T}{\partial n} =$

$1.|\text{grad}\,T|.\cos\theta$,   where θ is the angle   n   makes with grad T.   Since $-1 \leq \cos\theta \leq 1$,   the largest possible value comes when $\cos\theta = 1$ and the least when $\cos\theta = -1$, i.e.   choose   n   in the direction of $(1, 3, 16)$ for the fastest increase and in the direction of $(-1, -3, -16)$ for the fastest decrease.

12.   By checking whether   curl $F = 0$ we see that only   (a)   and   (c)   are irrotational.   The scalar function ϕ is determined by the method illustrated in §155.   (This method is really just the three dimensional version of the method for exact differentials illustrated in §116.)   The resulting functions ϕ are: (a) $x^2 + 8xy - xz + 2y^2 - 6yz + C$,   (c) $xy + 4yz^2 + C$.

EXAMPLES 10   (PAGES 146-151)

1.   Compare §132.   For (a) take $x = \cos t$, $y = \sin t$ for $0 \leq t \leq \frac{1}{2}\pi$.   Answer = $-\frac{1}{2}$.

2.   See §134-136.   Answer = $\pi a^4/4$.

3.   Do it by Green's theorem.   Answer = 2.

4.   Answer = 17/6.   In (b) the integrals along the sides in anticlockwise order (starting at the origin and moving along the x-axis) have the values   0, 53/6, -6, which add to give 17/6.

5.   Green's theorem gives $\int_1^2 dy \int_{1/y}^{\sqrt{y}} 8xy\, dx$, which gives the answer $\dfrac{28}{3} - 4 \log 2$.

6.   Green's theorem cannot be used because $\partial P/\partial y$ is not continuous throughout the enclosed region: in fact $\dfrac{\partial P}{\partial y} = \dfrac{2y}{x^2 + y^2}$ and this is not even defined at $(0,0)$, let alone being continuous.   So the conditions for Green's theorem in §134 are not satisfied.   To evaluate the integral proceed directly by setting $x = \cos t$, $y = \sin t$

for $0 \le t \le 2\pi$.   So $I = \int_0^{2\pi} (\log 2)(-\sin t)\, dt = 0$.

7.   See §137.   Use the method of §116 to find that the given form is df, where $f(x,y) = x^2 y^3 + 4xy^2$.   So, from §137(ii), the line integral I required depends only on the endpoints.   So $I =$ the difference of the values of $f(x,y)$ at $(1,2)$ and $(0,0)$, i.e. $I = 24$.

8.   Same method as Ex.7 above.   So we have

$$I = [x^2 + 3xy - 2y^2]\,{}^{(0,3)}_{(1,0)} = -18 - 1 = -19.$$

9.   Very similar to §142. $I = \sqrt{3}/6$.

10.   Similar to the first example in §143. $I = \pi a^3$.

11. $I = \pi a^5/2$.   On the whole sphere the answer is 0 (as in the last example in §143).

12.   See §144, §145.   Evaluation is similar to that in Ex.10 above.   Use polars.

13.   Similar to §145.   Draw a good diagram. Answer $= \sqrt{41}/4$.

14.   It becomes $\iint \sqrt{(1 + 4x^2 + 4y^2)}\, dx\, dy$ over the disc $x^2 + y^2 \le 6$.   Answer $= 62\pi/3$.

15.   Similar to Ex.12 above.

16.   Very similar to §145.   If $c = 0$ the cylinder will fail to cut an ellipse on the plane, for the reasons mentioned in the last paragraph of §141.

17.   Similar to §145.   Answer $= 2\pi\sqrt{35}$.   (Recall the area of an ellipse from §16(i).)

18.   By analogy with the definition in §17, the mean value here is $\left(\iint_S z\, dS\right)/(\text{surface area of the hemisphere})$. Answer $= a/2$.

19.   On simplification $\sqrt{(1 + p^2 + q^2)} = \tfrac{1}{2}\sqrt{6}$.   So $I = \iint \tfrac{1}{2}(x^2 + y^2).\tfrac{1}{2}\sqrt{6}\, dx\, dy$ for $2 \le x^2 + y^2 \le 18$. So $I = 40\pi\sqrt{6}$.

20.   By symmetry $I = \iint (az^2 + bz^2 + cz^2)\, dS = (a+b+c)\iint z^2\, dS = \pi(a+b+c)/6$.

21. $I = \iint_S (a^2 + b^2 + c^2)p^2\, dS$, where p is the length of the perpendicular mentioned in the hint.   The suggested rotation of axes gives $p = |Z|$, and transforms the sphere into $X^2 + Y^2 + Z^2 = 1$.   So, we then have

$I = (a^2 + b^2 + c^2) \iint_S z^2 \, dS$, where S denotes the surface of the sphere $X^2 + Y^2 + Z^2 = 1$. So $I = 4\pi(a^2 + b^2 + c^2)/3$.

22.　(a) $\pi k(145\sqrt{145} - 1)/6$, (b) $\pi k(145\sqrt{145} - 101\sqrt{101})/6$.

23.　(a) You can take $v = (axz^2, 0, 0)$ and $n = (x/a, y/a, z/a)$ in §146.　(Compare the examples in §147 and §148.)　So $I = \iiint az^2 \, dxdydz$ throughout the region $x^2 + y^2 + z^2 \le a^2$, by Gauss's Divergence Theorem. The answer is $4\pi a^6/15$.　[Alternatively you may take $v = (0, 0, ax^2 z)$ and $n = (x/a, y/a, z/a)$ to obtain $\iiint ax^2 \, dxdydz$ etc.]

(b) Treat it like the second example in §143.

24.　Use Gauss's Divergence Theorem.　Take $v = (ax, ay, az)$ and $n = (x/a, y/a, z/a)$.　Answer $= 4\pi a^4$. By symmetry the final integral $= 4\pi a^4/3$.

25.　For S_1, $n = (2x, 2y, 1)/\sqrt{(1 + 4x^2 + 4y^2)}$. Integral over $S_1 = 3\pi$.　For S_2, $n = (0, 0, -1)$. Integral over $S_2 = -\pi$.　So $\iint$ over $S = 2\pi$. In the Divergence Theorem we have $\text{div } v = 4$, which again gives the answer 2π.

26.　Compare §151.　C_1 is $(t, 0, 2)$ for $-1 \le t \le 1$. C is $(\cos t, \sin t, 2)$ for $0 \le t \le \pi$.　(a) I along the curve $C_1 = 4$.　I along the curve $C_2 = -4 + \frac{1}{2}\pi$.　So total integral $= \frac{1}{2}\pi$.　(b) $n = (0, 0, 1)$ and $\text{curl } v = (1, 3x^2, 1)$.　So integral $= \iint_S 1 \, dS = \frac{1}{2}\pi$.

27.　Compare §152.　Parameterise the sides of the triangle with $(1 - t, t, 0)$, $(0, 1 - t, t)$ and $(t, 0, 1 - t)$ for $0 \le t \le 1$.　The sum of the line integrals along these sides is $5/2$, i.e. the integral round the boundary curve.　For Stokes we have $n = (1, 1, 1)/\sqrt{3}$ and $\text{curl } v = (-1, 2, 4)$.　The surface integral then also gives the value $5/2$.

28.　Compare §153.　The curve is $(\cos t, \sin t, -2\cos t - \sin t)$ for $0 \le t \le 2\pi$.　The integral round this curve gives 2π.　For S take the part of the plane inside the cylinder.　Then $\text{curl } v = (2, 0, -2)$ and $n = (2, 1, 1)/\sqrt{6}$.　This again gives the answer 2π.

29.　Parametric representation of the curve gives $(\sqrt{2}\cos t, 2\sin t, \sqrt{2}\cos t)$ for $0 \le t \le 2\pi$.　(There is no direction specified round the curve in the question: we are effectively choosing a direction in the parametrisation.)　The line integral then has the value $-4\pi\sqrt{2}$. For Stokes we have $\text{curl } v = (0, 0, -2)$ and $n = (1, 0, 1)/\sqrt{2}$.　So $I = \iint -2/\sqrt{2} \, dS = -2 \iint 1 \, dxdy$ over the ellipse $2x^2 + y^2 = 4$, which gives the answer $-4\pi\sqrt{2}$. (See §16 for the area of an ellipse.)

30.　Here $n = (x, y, z)/5$.　Then $I =$

$\iint (0, 2, 1).(x, y, z)/5 \ dS$ (over the cap) $= \frac{1}{5} \iint 2y + z \ dS$
$\frac{1}{5} \iint z \ dS = 16\pi$.

31.   Use Gauss's Divergence Theorem.

32.   For (1) use Gauss's Divergence Theorem together
with §127(iii).   Then repeat with $\psi(\text{grad } \phi)$ instead of
$\phi(\text{grad } \psi)$ and subtract the result from (1) to obtain (2).
For the last part, notice that if ϕ and ψ are harmonic
in U, then the RHS of (2) is zero.

33.   For the first part use Gauss's Divergence
Theorem with the identity of §127(iii).   If then $\phi = 0$
on S the RHS is zero.   So the LHS is zero.   But then
v^2 is a continuous <u>non-negative</u> function whose triple
integral throughout R is zero.   It follows that $v^2 = 0$,
so that ϕ is constant throughout R.   Continuity at
the boundary surface forces ϕ to be zero throughout R.
    For the last paragraph, apply the previous part with
$\phi = \phi_1 - \phi_2$.

34.   See §155.   Here $\phi(x,y,z) = x^2 + 3xyz^2$.   The
integral $= -151$.

35.   Check that curl F $= 0$.   [See Ex.9.12 on page
124 if you don't know why you do this.]   The potential
function is $\phi(x,y,z) = x^3 + 2xy^2 + yz^2 - 2yz$.   As in §154,
the work done $= 23$.

36. $g(x,y,z) = 3y^2 + x^2 + h(z)$.   The particular g
is $g(x,y,z) = x^2 + 3y^2$.   Then $\phi(x,y,z) = x^2z + 3y^2z$.
The integral $= 147$.   The final answer $=$ YES.   [See §154
if you are unclear about this.]

EXAMPLES 11   (PAGES 167-170)

1.   The graphs are

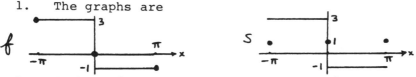

2.   Look at §162 for x and §163 for x^2.   You must
capitalise on the facts that x is an odd function and x^2
is an even function: this means (as explained in §161)
that half the coefficients in each case are automatically
zero.   So doing integration to find the coefficients a_n
in the case of x (or to find the coefficients b_n in the
case of x^2) is a sheer waste of time.

3.   §164 illustrates the general method.   The graph
of the sum function of the series is shown overleaf:

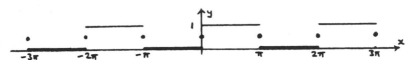

The values are   (a) $\pi/4$ (on setting $x = \tfrac{1}{2}\pi$), (b) $\pi\sqrt{3}/6$
(on setting $x = \pi/3$).

4.   §164 illustrates the method.   For the last part
set $x = 0$.   Note that the sum of the series for $x = 0$
is $\tfrac{1}{2}\pi$, (i.e. the average of   0   and π, by   1 in §160).

5.   Since the function is odd, all coefficients a_n
are zero (as explained in §161).   Use the identity
$2 \sin \tfrac{1}{2}x \sin nx = \cos(n - \tfrac{1}{2})x - \cos(n + \tfrac{1}{2})x$.   The F.S. is

$$\frac{8}{\pi}\left(\frac{\sin x}{1.3} - \frac{2 \sin 2x}{3.5} + \frac{3 \sin 3x}{5.7} - \ldots \right).$$

Put $x = \tfrac{1}{2}\pi$ for the last part.

6.   See §166-172 for results and examples on half
range series.   For (a) put $x = \tfrac{1}{2}\pi$.   For (b) put $x = \pi/4$.

7.   §171, §172 are similar.   The theory of how to
sketch the sum function is given in §170.   The sketch is:

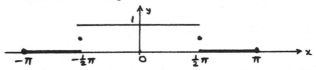

8.   In calculating the coefficients it may help to
consider the cases of $n = 4k$, $4k+1$, $4k+2$, $4k+3$ separately,
once you have done the integration.   Put $x = \tfrac{1}{2}\pi$ to find
the sum in (a) is $\pi/4$.   Put $x = \pi/4$ to find the sum in
(b) is $\pi\sqrt{2}/4$.   (Compare the sums in Ex.6 above.)

The sketch is:

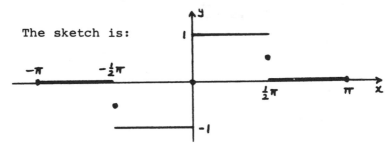

9.   Use the identity $2 \sin nx \cos x = \sin(n+1)x +$
$\sin(n-1)x$ in calculating the coefficients.   The sketch
(see §170) is:

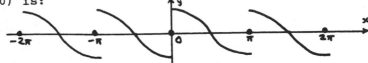

10.   The required series is given in §168.   As explained in §169 the required half range cosine series is the Fourier Series of $|x|$ on $[-\pi, \pi]$.   Put $x = 0$ to find the sum of the first series.   For Parseval and its use see §173.

11.   Before using Parseval you need to extend the function to $[-\pi, \pi]$, i.e. $f(x) = 1$ for $-\pi \leq x < \frac{1}{2}\pi$ and $f(x) = 2$ for $-\frac{1}{2}\pi \leq x \leq \frac{1}{2}\pi$.   Then proceed as in §173.

12.   Suppose that $-\pi < y < 0$.   Then $0 < -y < \pi$. So we can put $-y$ in the formulae in the last two lines in §165 to obtain

$$\cos(-y) + \frac{\cos(-3y)}{3^2} + \ldots = -\frac{\pi}{8}(-2y - \pi),$$

which gives $\cos y + \dfrac{\cos 3y}{3^2} + \ldots = \dfrac{\pi}{8}(2y + \pi).$ Similarly

$$\sin 2y + \frac{\sin 4y}{2} + \ldots = -\frac{1}{2}(2y + \pi).$$

13.   If you answered YES, notice that some of the work in the direct assault method can be saved if you realise that the F.S. of $x^2 + x$ is just the F.S. of x^2 (the cosine part) <u>plus</u> the F.S. of x (the sine part). So in calculating the coefficients you need only consider $\int x^2 \cos nx \, dx$ and $\int x \sin nx \, dx$ and <u>not</u> $\int (x^2 + x)\cos nx \, dx$ and $\int (x^2 + x)\sin nx \, \overline{dx}$.   The required F.S. is accordingly the sum of the series in §162 & §163.

14.   Similar to §165.   The sums are $\frac{1}{4}\pi(\frac{1}{2}\pi - x)$ and $\frac{1}{2}(\pi - x)$ respectively.   For the last part put $x = \pi/3$.

EXAMPLES 12   (PAGES 185-186)

1. (a) (3,5) saddle.   (b) (0,0) minimum.
(c) (1,0) maximum.   (d) (1,-1) saddle.   (e) (3,-2) and (3,2) both saddle.   (f) $(-\frac{2}{3}, 3)$ maximum, (2,3) saddle.
(g) (5,10) minimum, (h) (2,5) and (-2,7) both saddle.
(i) (1,1) and (-1,-1) both saddle.   (j) $(3, \frac{9}{2})$ minimum.
(k) (0,0) saddle, (1,2) and (-1,-2) both minimum.
(l) (0,2) and $(2,\frac{1}{2})$ both saddle.   (m) No stationary point.
(n) (1,1) and (-1,1) minima, (0,-1) maximum, (0,1), (1,-1) and (-1,-1) all saddle.   (o) (kπ,0) for k an integer gives a minimum, $(\frac{1}{2}k\pi, 0)$ for odd integers k gives a saddle.   (p) (0,0), (1,0), (-1,0) all saddle.   The Hessian method fails.   See §182-184.   For (0,0) look at $f(0,k) - f(0,0)$, for (1,0) look at $f(1,k) - f(1,0)$ etc rather as in §184.

2.   Use the Hessian method as in §187.   The Hessian is positive definite at (2,2,2), which therefore gives a local minimum.

3.   Minimise $(x-1)^2 + (y-2)^2$ subject to $x + 3y = 27$.
The required point is $(3,8)$.   [Clearly it can also be done by other methods.]

4.   The maximum value is $3\sqrt{3}a^4/16$ at $(a/2, a\sqrt{3}/2)$ and $(-a/2, -a\sqrt{3}/2)$.   The minimum value is $-3\sqrt{3}a^4/16$ at $(a/2, -a\sqrt{3}/2)$ and $(-a/2, a\sqrt{3}/2)$.

5.   The maximum value is   12   at $(2\sqrt{2}, 3\sqrt{2})$ and $(-2\sqrt{2}, -3\sqrt{2})$.   The rectangle with vertices at (x,y), $(-x,y)$, $(-x,-y)$, $(x,-y)$ has area $4xy$.   So the maximum area of the rectangle = 48 square units.

6.   You have to maximise $8xyz$ subject to the equation $\dfrac{x^2}{a^2} + \dfrac{y^2}{b^2} + \dfrac{z^2}{c^2} = 1$.   The vertices of the required box are $(\pm a/\sqrt{3}, \pm b/\sqrt{3}, \pm c/\sqrt{3})$ [all possible combinations of sign].   So the sides are of lengths $2a/\sqrt{3}$, $2b/\sqrt{3}$, $2c/\sqrt{3}$.

7.   Maximum value = 30 at $(\sqrt{6}, -2\sqrt{6})$ and $(-\sqrt{6}, 2\sqrt{6})$. Minimum value = 5 at $(2,1)$ and $(-2,-1)$.   For the geometrical interpretation first notice that $5x^2 + 4xy + 2y^2 = 30$ is an ellipse with its axes inclined at a non-zero angle to the   x- and y-axes.   Then $(x^2 + y^2)$ is the square of the distance of (x,y) from $(0,0)$.   So $\sqrt{30}$ is the greatest distance of any point on the ellipse from $(0,0)$ and $\sqrt{5}$ is the least distance of any point on the ellipse from $(0,0)$.   (Actually this also means that the lengths of the semi-axes of the ellipse are $\sqrt{30}$ and $\sqrt{5}$,   and moreover the points given above are the ends of the axes of the ellipse.)

8.   For the shape of the cylinder see §138.   The method of doing the example is similar to that in §192. The minimum value is   14   at $(6,2,8)$ and the maximum is 54   at $(-6,-2,60)$.

9.   Very similar to §192.   The minimum is   -13   at $(2,-6,-1)$ and the maximum is   14   at $(-1,6,2)$.

10.   Similar to §192.   The minimum is -1   at $(4,-4,-1)$ and the maximum is   4   at $(-1,1,4)$.

11.   Using the matrix approach in §192 gives $z(x - 3y) = 0$.   So either $z = 0$ or $x = 3y$.   If you suppose that $z = 0$ then $3x + y = 40$ and $x^2 + y^2 = 90$. Attempts to solve these equations lead to a quadratic with no real roots ($b^2 - 4ac < 0$).   So $z = 0$ is not possible and you are left with the possibility that $x = 3y$.   This leads to the required points, namely $(9,3,10)$ - [nearest to $(0,0,0)$]   and $(-9,-3,70)$-[furthest from $(0,0,0)$].

12.   See §193.   We require the point on the plane
$x + y + z = 180$ that is nearest to (a,b,c),   i.e. we wish
to minimise $(x - a)^2 + (y - b)^2 + (z - c)^2$ subject to the
condition $x + y + z = 180$.   The least squares estimates are
$(x,y,z) = ((180+2a-b-c)/3, (180-a+2b-c)/3, (180-a-b+2c)/3)$.
The particular solution is $(x,y,z) = (41,61,78)$.

13.   See §193.   The conditions on   x, y, z, t   are
$x + y + z + t = 360$ and $x + z = 180$.   You can use them as
they are or alternatively as $x + z = 180$ and $y + t = 180$.
The solution is $(x,y,z,t) = (\frac{1}{2}(180+a-c),\frac{1}{2}(180+b-d),$
$\frac{1}{2}(180-a+c),\frac{1}{2}(180-b+d))$.   The particular solution is
$(x,y,z,t) = (50,99.5,130,80.5)$.

14.   See §193.   Since it is a parallelogram there
are three conditions, namely $x = z$, $y = t$ and
$x + y + z + t = 360$.   Using the method of Lagrange Multipliers
we therefore minimise $(x - a)^2 + (y - b)^2 + (z - c)^2 + (t - d)^2$
subject to these three conditions.   This gives the
equation $x - y + z - t = a - b + c - d$,   which together with the
three conditions given leads to the required estimates,
namely $x = z = \frac{1}{4}(360+a-b+c-d)$, $y = t = \frac{1}{4}(360-a+b-c+d)$.

EXAMPLES 13   (PAGE 192)

1. $y = Ae^{2x} + Be^{-x} + e^{3x}\left(\frac{x}{4} - \frac{5}{16}\right)$.

2. $y = (Ax + B)e^{-x} + \left(\frac{3}{4}x^4 + 2x^2\right)e^{-x}$.

3. $y = (A\cos x + B\sin x) - \frac{x}{3}\cos 2x + \frac{4}{9}\sin 2x$.

4. $y = Ae^{2x} + Be^{-2x} + e^{2x}\left(\frac{x^3}{12} - \frac{x^2}{16} + \frac{x}{32}\right)$.

5. $y = A\cos 3x + B\sin 3x + \left(\frac{x}{2} + \frac{1}{10}\right)e^{-x} - 3x\cos 3x$.

6. $y = A\cos 3x + B\sin 3x + \frac{2}{9}x\cos 3x + \frac{2}{3}x^2\sin 3x$.

7. $y = (Ax + B)e^{-x} - 6e^{-x}\sin x$.

8. $y = A\cos x + B\sin x - 3x^2\cos x + 3x\sin x$.

9. $y = e^{-3x}(A\cos x + B\sin x) + \frac{1}{4}e^{-3x}(x\sin x - x^2\cos x)$.

10. $y = e^x(A\cos 2x + B\sin 2x) + \frac{1}{16}xe^x\cos 2x$
$+ \frac{1}{8}x^2 e^x\sin 2x$.

11. $y = e^{3x}(A\cos x + B\sin x) - 25xe^{3x}\cos x$.

EXAMPLES 14 (PAGES 207-208)

1. (a) $\dfrac{1}{29}\begin{bmatrix} 7 & -3 \\ -2 & 5 \end{bmatrix}$,   (b) $\dfrac{-1}{4}\begin{bmatrix} 1 & -1 & -1 \\ -1 & -3 & 5 \\ -2 & 2 & -2 \end{bmatrix}$,

   (c) $\dfrac{-1}{2}\begin{bmatrix} 12 & -20 & -5 \\ -10 & 16 & 4 \\ -6 & 10 & 2 \end{bmatrix}$.

2. (a) $(x, y, z) = (2t, t, -6t)$ (t   any real number).
   (b) $(x, y, z) = (4t, 5t, 3t)$ (t   any real number).

3. (a) 3, 5.   (b) $3 + 2i$, $3 - 2i$.   (c) 0, 5, -5.
   (d) 1, 3, 3.

4. (Here we give first the eigenvalues and then the eigenvectors in corresponding order. For convenience we give the eigenvectors as transposed rows.)

   (a) 6, 4; $[-2 \quad 1]^T$, $[1 \quad -1]^T$.

   (b) 7, 0; $[1 \quad 2]^T$, $[-2 \quad 3]^T$.

   (c) 5, 1, 0; $[1 \quad 0 \quad 0]^T$, $[0 \quad 1 \quad 1]^T$, $[1 \quad -10 \quad -5]^T$.

   (d) 5, 3, -1; $[0 \quad 1 \quad 1]^T$, $[1 \quad 3 \quad 2]^T$, $[1 \quad -3 \quad -2]^T$.

   (e) 2, 1, -4; $[1 \quad 2 \quad 2]^T$, $[1 \quad 1 \quad 1]^T$, $[0 \quad 0 \quad 1]^T$.

   (f) 5, 2, 0; $[1 \quad 1 \quad 0]^T$, $[1 \quad 2 \quad 1]^T$, $[3 \quad 6 \quad 1]^T$.

   (g) 2, 1, -2: $[2 \quad 3 \quad 1]^T$, $[1 \quad 1 \quad 0]^T$, $[-2 \quad -3 \quad 1]^T$.

   (h) 3, 1, -1; $[2 \quad 1 \quad 0]$, $[1 \quad 1 \quad 3]^T$, $[1 \quad 1 \quad 1]^T$.

   (i) 4, 2, 1, 0; $[1 \quad 0 \quad 2 \quad 0]^T$, $[0 \quad 1 \quad 0 \quad 1]^T$,
      $[1 \quad 0 \quad -1 \quad 0]^T$, $[0 \quad 3 \quad 0 \quad 1]^T$.

   (j) 12, 9, 6, 1: $[0 \quad 1 \quad 1 \quad 0]^T$, $[1 \quad 0 \quad 0 \quad 1]^T$,
      $[0 \quad 1 \quad -1 \quad 0]^T$, $[1 \quad 0 \quad 0 \quad -1]^T$.

5. The example of §208 shows how to make up P out of the eigenvectors in the solution to Ex. 4 above, i.e. P is the matrix whose columns are the eigenvectors. Notice however that P is not unique on two counts. Firstly any column of P can be multiplied by a non-zero scalar (because a non-zero multiple of an eigenvector is also an eigenvector): this does not affect the diagonal matrix. Secondly columns can be permuted within P: this alters the order of the entries in the diagonal matrix. So e.g. for

   (f) take P as $P = \begin{bmatrix} 1 & 1 & 3 \\ 1 & 2 & 6 \\ 0 & 1 & 1 \end{bmatrix}$.

6. This is a standard type. Write it as
    $-\frac{1}{2}(5A^2 + 3A + 3I)A = I$. So $A^{-1} = -\frac{1}{2}(5A^2 + 3A + 3I)$.

7. $B^2 = 4I$. So B^2 has eigenvalues 4, 4, 4, 4.
    So by Result 1 in §210, all eigenvalues of B are
    2 or -2. Now trace(B) = 4 and this is the sum of
    the eigenvalues (Result 2 in §210). So the eigen-
    values of B are 2, 2, 2, -2. For C a similar
    argument shows the eigenvalues are 1, 1, -1.

8. $AX = \lambda X$. So $A^2x = \lambda^2 X$, i.e. $AX = \lambda^2 X$. So
    $\lambda^2 X = \lambda X$. So $\lambda^2 = \lambda$ since $X \neq 0$. So $\lambda = 0$ or 1.
    Eigenvalues of B are 1, 1, 0 by considering its
    trace in the light of Result 2 in §210.

9. Eigenvalues are 2, 2. Go for a contradiction as
    in the example in §209.

10. Eigenvalues of A are 3, 3, -3. Corresponding to
    eigenvalue 3 you can find a pair of linearly
    independent eigenvectors like the vectors
    $[1 \quad 1 \quad 0]^T$ and $[1 \quad 0 \quad 1]^T$. For -3 you can take
    eigenvector $[1 \quad -1 \quad -1]^T$. This gives P as below.
    For B the eigenvalues are 3, 3, 1. Possibilities
    for P and Q are

$$P = \begin{bmatrix} 1 & 1 & 1 \\ 1 & 0 & -1 \\ 0 & 1 & -1 \end{bmatrix} \text{ and } Q = \begin{bmatrix} 5 & -5 & 4 \\ 1 & 0 & 1 \\ 0 & 2 & 0 \end{bmatrix}. \quad \text{[Note that}$$

    P and Q are not unique on the two counts mentioned
    in the solution to Ex.5 above and on the further
    count that the first two columns could be replaced
    by any two linearly independent columns spanning
    the same subspace as these first two columns.]

EXAMPLES 15   (PAGE 214)

    (In Exs. 1 to 8 the answer gives first the eigen-
values of the matrix corresponding to A in §213 and
§214.   Then the solution is given in the form X = PY,
where X, P, Y correspond to the matrices in §213 and
§214.)

1.   6, -1; $X = \begin{bmatrix} 1 & 1 \\ 1 & 8 \end{bmatrix} \begin{bmatrix} Ae^{6t} \\ Be^{-t} \end{bmatrix}$.

2.   -4, -9; $X = \begin{bmatrix} 1 & 3 \\ 2 & 1 \end{bmatrix} \begin{bmatrix} P \cos 2t + Q \sin 2t \\ R \cos 3t + S \sin 3t \end{bmatrix}$.

3.   (a) 4, 3; $X = \begin{bmatrix} 2 & 1 \\ 1 & 1 \end{bmatrix} \begin{bmatrix} Ae^{4t} \\ Be^{3t} \end{bmatrix}$.

(b)   4, 3 as in (a); $X = \begin{bmatrix} 2 & 1 \\ 1 & 1 \end{bmatrix} \begin{bmatrix} Ae^{2t} + Be^{-2t} \\ Ce^{t\sqrt{3}} + De^{-t\sqrt{3}} \end{bmatrix}$.

4.   5, 0, -5; $X = \begin{bmatrix} 3 & -4 & -3 \\ 5 & 0 & 5 \\ 4 & 3 & -4 \end{bmatrix} \begin{bmatrix} Ae^{5t} \\ B \\ Ce^{-5t} \end{bmatrix}$.

5.   5, 3, -1; $X = \begin{bmatrix} 0 & 1 & 1 \\ 1 & 3 & -3 \\ 1 & 2 & -2 \end{bmatrix} \begin{bmatrix} Ae^{5t} \\ Be^{3t} \\ Ce^{-t} \end{bmatrix}$.

6.   2, 1, -4; $X = \begin{bmatrix} 1 & 1 & 0 \\ 2 & 1 & 0 \\ 2 & 1 & 1 \end{bmatrix} \begin{bmatrix} Ae^{2t} \\ Be^{t} \\ Ce^{-4t} \end{bmatrix}$.

7.   2, -2, -3; $X = \begin{bmatrix} 1 & 0 & 1 \\ 0 & 1 & -10 \\ 0 & 1 & -5 \end{bmatrix} \begin{bmatrix} Ae^{2t} \\ Be^{-2t} \\ Ce^{-3t} \end{bmatrix}$.

8. (a) 1, 0, -1; $X = \begin{bmatrix} 1 & 1 & 0 \\ 0 & -2 & 1 \\ 0 & -1 & 1 \end{bmatrix} \begin{bmatrix} Ae^{t} \\ B \\ Ce^{-t} \end{bmatrix}$.

(b) 1, 0, -1 as (a); $X = \begin{bmatrix} 1 & 1 & 0 \\ 0 & -2 & 1 \\ 0 & -1 & 1 \end{bmatrix} \begin{bmatrix} Me^{t} + Ne^{-t} \\ Pt + Q \\ R\cos t + S\sin t \end{bmatrix}$.

9. (a)   It is $\begin{bmatrix} 1 & 1 \\ 0 & 1 \end{bmatrix} \begin{bmatrix} \dot{x} \\ \dot{y} \end{bmatrix} = \begin{bmatrix} -2 & 1 \\ -1 & -7 \end{bmatrix} \begin{bmatrix} x \\ y \end{bmatrix}$.   This gives

$\dot{X} = AX$, where $A = \begin{bmatrix} -1 & 8 \\ -1 & -7 \end{bmatrix}$, with eigenvalues -3

and -5, giving the solution as in Ex.5.12.

(b) As in (a) it reduces to $\dot{X} = AX$ with $A = \begin{bmatrix} 9 & 1 \\ -10 & 2 \end{bmatrix}$,

with eigenvalues 7 and 4.   Solution as in Ex.5.12.

10. The matrix $A = \begin{bmatrix} 3 & 1 \\ -1 & 1 \end{bmatrix}$ has eigenvalues 2, 2.

If it could be diagonalised, then we would have $P^{-1}AP = 2I$, i.e. $A = 2I$, which is a contradiction. So A cannot be diagonalised and the method of §212 fails. Using the method of §71 gives the solution $x_1 = (At + B)e^{2t}$, $x_2 = (A - B - At)e^{2t}$.

EXAMPLES 16 (PAGE 217)

1. G.S. is $f(x,y) = 2x^5y + \phi(x^2y)$. For the particular solution, putting $y = x$ gives $f(x,x) = 2x^6 + \phi(x^3) = -3x^6$, i.e. $\phi(x^3) = -5x^6$. Set $w = x^3$ in this, which gives $\phi(w) = -5w^2$. This has found the particular function ϕ required. So the particular solution is $f(x,y) = 2x^5y - 5x^4y^2$.

2. G.S. is $z(x,y) = xy^2 + \phi(y^2/x)$. For the particular solution, putting $y = 1$ gives $\phi(1/x) = (2/x) - (3/x^2)$. Set $w = 1/x$ in this to find ϕ. The particular solution is $z(x,y) = xy^2 + 2(y^2/x) - 3(y^4/x^2)$.

3. It reduces to $z_{uv} = 2$, which gives the G.S. as $z(x,y) = 2(x^4 - y^2) + \phi(x^2 + y) + \psi(x^2 - y)$.

4. It reduces to $z_{vv} = 24v$, from which we find the G.S. is $4x^3 + x\phi(x + \tfrac{1}{2}y^2) + \psi(x + \tfrac{1}{2}y^2)$. For the particular solution, first use $z(0,y) = y^4$ to give $\psi(\tfrac{1}{2}y^2) = y^4$. This gives $\psi(w) = 4w^2$. The other condition then gives $\phi(w) = -4$. So the required particular solution is $z(x,y) = 4x^3 - 4x + 4(x + \tfrac{1}{2}y^2)^2$.

5. It reduces to $z_{vv} = 6v$, from which we find the G.S. is $z(x,y) = x^3 + x\,\phi(xy) + \psi(xy)$. The particular solution is $z(x,y) = x^3 - x^2y + 4x^2y^2 + xy$.

SOME STANDARD INTEGRALS

function f	indefinite integral F
x^k $(k \neq -1)$	$\dfrac{x^{k+1}}{k+1}$
$1/x$	$\log |x|$
e^x	e^x
$\log x$	$x \log x - x$
$\sin x$	$-\cos x$
$\cos x$	$\sin x$
$\tan x$	$\log |\sec x|$
$\text{cosec } x$	$-\log |\text{cosec } x + \cot x|$
$\sec x$	$\log |\sec x + \tan x|$
$\cot x$	$\log |\sin x|$
$\dfrac{1}{x^2 + a^2}$	$\dfrac{1}{a} \tan^{-1} \dfrac{x}{a}$
$\dfrac{1}{\sqrt{(x^2 + a^2)}}$	$\log (x + \sqrt{(x^2 + a^2)})$
$\dfrac{1}{\sqrt{(x^2 - a^2)}}$	$\log |x + \sqrt{(x^2 - a^2)}|$
$\dfrac{1}{\sqrt{(a^2 - x^2)}}$	$\sin^{-1} \dfrac{x}{a}$

SOME LAPLACE TRANSFORMS

---

f(x)	Laplace transform L(f; s)
e^{kx}	$1/(s - k)$
1	$1/s$
x	$1/s^2$
x^2	$2/s^3$
x^n	$n!/s^{n+1}$ (for positive integer n)
x^k	$\Gamma(k + 1)/s^{k+1}$ (for any value of k > -1)
$\cos ax$	$\dfrac{s}{s^2 + a^2}$
$\sin ax$	$\dfrac{a}{s^2 + a^2}$
$e^{kx}f(x)$	$L(f; s - k)$
$x^n f(x)$	$(-1)^n \dfrac{d^n}{ds^n}\Big[L(f; s)\Big]$ (for positive integer n)
$f'(x)$	$s\bar{f} - f(0)$
$f''(x)$	$s^2\bar{f} - s f(0) - f'(0)$
$f^{(n)}(x)$	$s^n\bar{f} - s^{n-1}f(0) - s^{n-2}f'(0) - \ldots - f^{(n-1)}(0)$
$\int_0^x f(t) g(x - t)\,dt$	$L(f; s) L(g; s)$ [See §82.]

[N.B. For some of these formulae there are restrictions on the function f.   See §74 for some details of this.]

INDEX

(The numbers refer to sections not to pages.)